MYTH, HISTORY AND THE INDUSTRIAL REVOLUTION

MYTH, HISTORY AND THE INDUSTRIAL REVOLUTION

D.C. COLEMAN

THE HAMBLEDON PRESS

LONDON AND RIO GRANDE

Published by The Hambledon Press 1992
102 Gloucester Avenue, London NW1 8HX (U.K.)
P.O. Box 162, Rio Grande, Ohio 45672 (U.S.A.)

ISBN 1 85285 074 4

A description of this book is available from
The British Library and from the Library Congress.

Typeset by York House Typographic Ltd., London.
Printed on acid-free paper and bound in
Great Britain by Cambridge University Press.

Contents

Acknowledgements

The essays reprinted here first appeared in the following places and are reprinted by kind permission of the original publishers.

1   This chapter appears here for the first time; a much shorter version of it was given as the Creighton Trust Lecture for 1989 and was printed by the University of London (1989).

2   *Economica*, new series, xxiii (1956), pp. 1-22.

3   *Economic History Review*, 2nd series, vi (1953), pp. 134-55.

4   *Scandinavian Economic History Review*, x (1962), pp 115-27.

5   *Economic History Review*, 2nd series, xxxvi (1983), pp. 435-48.

6   *Economic History Review*, 2nd series, xxvi (1973), pp. 92-116.

7   *History of European Ideas*, 9 (1988), pp. 161-70.

8   *Enterprise and History: Essays in honour of Charles Wilson*, ed. by D.C. Coleman and Peter Mathias (Cambridge University Press, 1984), pp. 27-41.

9   *War and Economic Development: Essays in memory of David Goslin*, ed. J.M. Winter (Cambridge University Press, 1975), pp. 205-27.

10 *L.S.E. Quarterly*, 1 (1987), pp. 153-74. It also appeared in *Business History*, xxix (1987), pp. 141-56.

Mr. Foster. The manufacturing system is not yet purified from some evils which necessarily attend it, but which I conceive are greatly overbalanced by their concomitant advantages. Contemplate the vast sum of human industry to which this system so essentially contributes: . . . profound researches, scientific inventions, complicated mechanisms . . . employment and existence thus given to innumerable families, and the multiplied comforts and conveniences of life diffused over the whole community.

Mr. Escot. You present to me a complicated picture of artificial life and require me to admire it . . . Profound researches, scientific inventions: to what end? To contract the sum of human wants? . . . To disseminate independence, liberty and health? No; to multiply factitious desires . . . to invent unnatural wants . . . to accumulate expedients of selfish and ruinous profusion. Complicated machinery: behold its blessings . . . Wherever this boasted machinery is established, the children of the poor are death-doomed from their cradles. Look for one moment into a cotton-mill, amidst the smell of oil, the smoke of lamps, the rattling of wheels, the dizzy and complicated motions of diabolical mechanisms . . .

Thomas Love Peacock, *Headlong Hall* (1816)

Introduction

All the items in this collection of essays hinge upon one historical phenomenon: the Industrial Revolution in Britain, generally recognized as having happened some time between 1750 and 1850. In varying ways, directly or indirectly, they are concerned with attitudes and concepts and definitions; with industrial revolutions real and imaginary; with the history of the businessmen who carried through the process of change, their predecessors and their successors. None of the essays attempts to tell how or why it all happened. Nor do any seek to reconcile the conflicting viewpoints of the fictional guests of Squire Headlong in 1816. In common with their living contemporaries, Peacock's characters did not use the term 'industrial revolution' but they had no doubt that the advent of the 'manufacturing system' was a matter of great moment, for good or for bad.

The first essay, which also provides the title of the book, perhaps needs some words of explanation. It is an expansion of the Creighton Trust Lecture which I gave under the same title at London University in October 1989. Its specific concern is with the paths along which a term in the language of economic historians has come to be mythologized; with the folk meanings it has thus come to embody; and with the way it is currently regarded alike by the professional historian and the layman.

On the basis of this last concern it may be regarded as a special case of a much wider topic, to wit the gulf between professional and lay perceptions of the past. Since Lord Dacre elegantly elaborated upon that subject in his inaugural lecture over thirty years ago, that gulf has been widened and deepened.[1] The agents currently at work effecting the breach are various and well-attested. The topic has been aired in diverse professional journals and debated in the weekly heavies. A huge and fascinating spectrum of varying perceptions of the past has been laid out by David Lowenthal, who has also raised disturbing questions about the gap between the growth of nostalgic cults of a Romantic past and the current declining interest in academic history.[2] In Britain, the future of historical scholarship remains

---

[1] H.R. Trevor-Roper (Lord Dacre), *History Professional and Lay* (Oxford, 1957).
[2] *The Past is a Foreign Country* (Cambridge, 1985), p. 237 and *passim*.

unclear in the face of governments obsessed with the conviction that the market should be the dominant arbiter in the allocation of resources.

The large issues thus raised are not addressed here. But the fate of the Industrial Revolution concept suggests that the relationship between myth and history in modern societies deserves rather more attention than it is customarily given. It may well be true that the social function of the professional historian should be, as Geoffrey Elton has proposed, to act as 'mankind's intellectual conscience'.[3] The historian will not, however, be anyone's conscience if nobody reads or listens. Only if heeded can he or she even begin to help in trying to ensure that the gap between popular myth and historical learning is not too uncomfortably wide.

The remaining essays, chapters 2-10, have all appeared in print at various dates from 1953 to 1988. They are arranged, not in the order of their original publication, but in a sequence which seems more appropriate to their subject-matter. Each essay is prefaced by a short introduction in the form of an asterisked note. I have not attempted to bring the essays up to date nor to provide bibliographies of recent writings; and I have left unchanged expressions of opinion no longer held. The prefatory comments are limited to offering some contextual observations; correcting some known factual errors or omissions; or indicating something of more recent discussions of the subject.

In the course of writing the title essay I incurred various debts of gratitude: to the University of London and specifically to the Principal, Peter Holwell, for the invitation to give the Creighton Lecture; to the members of Charles Feinstein's seminar at All Souls College, Oxford, to which I read a slim edition of the lecture in November 1989, and in particular therein to Jonathan Clark and Raphael Samuel; and also to George Grün, Julian Hoppit, Gareth Stedman Jones, Christine Macleod and James Raven for help on assorted matters on various occasions. For the remaining essays acknowledgements are made at appropriate points in the footnotes. For his willingness to publish a mixture of reprinted essays and new material I am much indebted to Martin Sheppard who has also made numerous helpful suggestions and generally eased the path of publication. Finally, over the thirty-eight years during which these essays, and others, have been written my wife's help has been vital and incalculable.

Cavendish, 1991

[3]   G.R. Elton, 'The Historian's Social Function', *Transactions of the Royal Historical Society*, 5th series, 27 (1977), p. 210.

1

Myth, History, and the Industrial Revolution

The Industrial Revolution (complete with capital letters) has attained the status of popular myth in our national history. A well-known tourist venue in Shropshire today welcomes its clientele with the alluring claim: 'The Birthplace of the Industrial Revolution'. Further north, Lancashire is commonly hailed as containing 'cradles' of the same phenomenon. Note the anthropomorphic labels; not quite Bethlehem or Mecca, but certainly shrines to be visited. Powerful myths in the nation's history have usually been created from such subject-matter as Drake and the Spanish Armada, Robin Hood or, more distantly, the Arthurian legends. The austere terrain of economic history seems hardly propitious for the flowering of myth. But before asking how the British Industrial Revolution has achieved this status, the more general relationship of myth and history demands some brief attention.

Historians, in their professional search for evidence and relationships, have sometimes examined the intrusion of myth but for the most part it is a topic which has remained lodged in the domain of anthropology. It is thought of mainly as a phenomenon of pre-literate societies, bracketed with legend, symbol and folk-lore. Not surprisingly the world of the ancient Greeks, with its intertwining of gods and men, has provided the most fertile European soil for historians to become involved in myth or for anthropologists to become interested in history.[1] In English history, the troubles of the seventeenth century offer notable examples of nourishing myths of ancient freedoms. Pocock, for example, showed how potent were those which told of immemorial laws and ancient customs; and Hill has traced a different example in his account of the Norman Yoke.[2] Historians of social perception and popular culture have also, more recently, been grappling with the

---

[1] See, e.g. M.I. Finley, *The Uses and Abuses of History* (1975), pp. 11-59; G.S. Kirk, *Myth: Its Meaning and Function in Ancient and other Cultures* (Cambridge, 1970). The place of publication is London unless otherwise stated.

[2] J.G.A. Pocock, *The Ancient Constitution and the Feudal Law* (Cambridge, 1957); Christopher Hill, 'The Norman Yoke' in his *Puritanism and Revolution* (1958), pp. 50-122.

role of myth.[3] In fact, of course, myth is far from confined to pre-literate societies, though in literate communities it takes different forms and emerges by different routes. As has been observed, 'myth the characteristic form of belief of primitive and antique man, is sometimes a significant category for modern man'.[4]

An anthropologist writing about a primitive society provided, nearly half a century ago, some of the most pertinent comments on the function of myth in modern societies. 'Myth', wrote Bronislaw Malinowski, 'is . . . an indispensable ingredient of all cultures. It is . . . constantly regenerated; every historical change creates its mythology, which is, however, but indirectly related to historical fact. Myth is a constant by-product of living faith, which is in need of miracles; of sociological status which demands precedent; of moral rule, which requires sanction'.[5] Translated from the Trobriand islanders to the British islanders, Malinowski's dicta may need some marginal amendments (not *every* historical change perhaps) but the central interpretation remains intact. He defined myth in a primitive culture as fulfilling the crucial function of expressing, enhancing and codifying belief;[6] and that is surely what it does in cultures far less primitive than those of the Southern Pacific which he investigated.

History clearly contributes to the myth-making process. Perhaps indeed it is one of its chief social functions. But it is a particular sort of history that matters, viz. a people's concept of their history or of an historical episode rather than dull objective reality. As J.M. Roberts has put it: 'An effective myth is defined not by its correspondence with positive reality, but by its power to move men to action by giving them an interpretation of that reality'.[7] Particular myths obviously appeal to particular groups or classes; and some myths, like unwanted monarchs, are eventually dethroned. Historical myths do not have to involve the supernatural or Promethean heroes. They are sometimes derived from particular writings. Macaulay and Marx, for example, must rank high among historical myth-makers. Each of their differing versions of history acquired the power of myth by providing accounts of the past which seemed to carry a special relevance to the present – albeit to different groups in different places – by energizing, dramatizing, even sanctifying current attitudes and actions. That both legacies have lost some of their appeal merely testifies to the changing needs for particular myths experienced by societies over time. By different routes, for example, such historical episodes as the Battle of the Boyne have achieved mythic status for one highly vociferous group of Protestants, those in Northern

---

[3] Lowenthal, *The Past is a Foreign Country* and its extensive bibliography.
[4] B.Halpern, ' "Myth" and "Ideology" in Modern Usage', *History and Theory*, 1 (1961), p. 135.
[5] B. Malinowski, *Magic, Science and Religion and other Essays* (New York, 1958; London, 1974), p. 146.
[6] Ibid., p.101.
[7] J.M. Roberts, *The Mythology of the Secret Societies* (1972), p. 353.

Ireland; and in South Africa the Voortrekker monument outside Pretoria stands as a massive testimony to the potency of the myth of the Great Trek for another group of Calvinists, the Afrikaaner nationalists.

The route along which the British Industrial Revolution has travelled on its way to national mythic status has been far from straightforward. Influences bearing upon it on the way have included European romantic radicalism, Anglican Christian reformism, and native nostalgia for the supposed triumphs of Smithian economics. It is time to consider, first, how the concept originated and came into circulation.

The origins and dissemination of the term 'Industrial Revolution' have been the subject of learned enquiry. Received wisdom in Britain assigns responsibility for its adoption and extended usage to Arnold Toynbee (1852-83). His *Lectures on the Industrial Revolution of the Eighteenth Century in England*, posthumously published in 1884, seems to have been the first book to deploy the term in its title; and his immediate successors, among historians and economists, gave him the credit for originating the revolutionary label and for providing the first full account of the subject. In 1953 G.N. Clark examined, elaborated upon, and in effect confirmed that priority. More recently other historians have also accepted Toynbee as the first bringer of the term into the English language, and his interpretation as the begetter of modern discussions of the subject.[8]

Alas, it is not quite so simple. The first writer not only to use the term repeatedly but also to endow it 'with the full force of a revolutionary event' was Friedrich Engels.[9] He presented it, moreover, as a distinctive episode possessed of great historical significance for England. He did so first in an article, 'Die Lage Englands' ('The Condition of England') published in 1844 and then in 1845, at some length, in his celebrated book *Die Lage der Arbeitenden Klasse in England* (*The Condition of the Working Class in England*). Although this work remained untranslated into English for over forty years it is nevertheless with Engels that the idea of the Industrial Revolution began its first career as a crucial myth for the political Left.

Engels was, of course, by no means the earliest user of the term. Not surprisingly it was in France that the term seems first to have come into something approaching general parlance. The political revolutions of 1789 and 1830 invited the drawing of parallels with technical changes in manufacture and they were duly drawn in the 1820s and 1830s, if not earlier. Most of such usages were little more than literary similes, underlining the

[8] G.N. Clark, *The Idea of the Industrial Revolution* (Glasgow, 1953); David Cannadine, 'The Present and the Past in the English Industrial Revolution 1880-1980', *Past and Present*, 103 (1984), pp. 131-72; Alon Kadish, *Apostle Arnold: The Life and Death of Arnold Toynbee, 1852-1883* (Duke University Press, 1986), especially pp. 98-106.

[9] Gertrude Himmelfarb, *The Idea of Poverty* (New York and London, 1984), p. 282. It should be added that Kadish (pp. 103-4) also notes Engels' use of the term.

potency of, for example, the new cotton-spinning machinery or of steam engines, a 'révolution industrielle' being seen to happen in, for instance, the major textile manufacturing town of Rouen. An article of 1827 describing technical changes in various French industries appeared under the heading of 'Grande Révolution Industrielle'.[10] In 1837 the French economist Jerome Adolphe Blanqui (not to be confused with the radical Auguste Blanqui) briefly noted the wider social implications of the inventions at the end of the eighteenth century, and observed that 'la révolution industrielle se mit en possession de l'Angleterre'.[11] Two years later the Belgian writer Natalis Briavoinne made extensive use of the term in his two-volume work *De l'industrie en Belgique*. In a chapter entitled 'Révolution industrielle' he wrote discursively about the growth of population, trade and wealth in later eighteenth-century Europe, especially in England and France. France he saw as pre-eminent in scientific advances, England in industrial, starting around 1770-80 when 'la révolution industrielle avait pris en Angleterre un caractère déterminé', with consequences which were political, material and moral.[12] Other instances doubtless exist. It was presumably such usages that enabled Engels, in the opening sentences of *The Condition of the Working Class* to say that it was 'well-known' that the textile inventions together with the steam engine had given rise to 'an industrial revolution'.[13] Certainly he could not have derived the term from England because, despite much contemporary comment on economic change and its social consequences, the concept of an industrial revolution (even without its capital letters) seems at that time to have been virtually unknown in Britain, and the term itself hardly ever used, if at all.

The mere borrowing of the term from earlier continental European commentators, however, is of little moment. What matters is the new and enlarged significance which Engels gave to it. In what did that significance consist? And what influences bore upon its conception?

The most obvious feature of *The Condition of the Working Class* is the sustained description of the environment of urban workers in Manchester and, to a lesser extent, in other industrial towns and in London. This content and the vigorous, highly-charged and denunciatory prose in which it was presented have been seized upon by commentators, sympathetic or antagonistic, and given rise to much argument. The extent to which Engels

[10] Anne Bezanson, 'The Early Use of the Term Industrial Revolution', *Quarterly Journal of Economics*, 36 (1922), pp. 343-49.

[11] Adolphe Blanqui, *Histoire de l'économie politique en Europe* (2 vols., Paris, 1837), i, p. 209.

[12] Natalis Briavoinne, *De l'industrie en Belgique* (2 vols., Brussels, 1839), i, pp. 185-86, 191-98 and *passim*. A number of other uses in French can be found at about this time or a little later, e.g. Léon Faucher, *Etudes sur l'Angleterre* (2 vols., Paris, 1845), i, p. 307, ii, p. 135.

[13] Friedrich Engels, *The Condition of the Working Class in England* in Karl Marx and Friedrich Engels, *Collected Works* (1975), iv, p. 307.

exaggerated or distorted the lot of such workers in the 1840s is not my concern here. He was certainly not alone among foreign visitors in commenting upon some startlingly visible contrasts of wealth and poverty, be they in Manchester or in London. The 'condition-of-England' question had been raised; and the relevant social circumstances depicted not only by domestic observers of varying political hues but by visitors as diverse as Ledru Rollin, Karl Gustav Carus or Friedrich von Raumer.[14]

For its role in the myth-making process, however, its significance lies in Engels' vision of an historical sequence and causation. The technical inventions of the Industrial Revolution, he wrote, had created the proletariat; its factory hands were 'the eldest children of the Industrial Revolution', forming the nucleus of the workers' movement. Its machinery had turned men into machines, destroying thereby a feudal England in which rural workers had vegetated in an idyllic life. It had happened suddenly and rapidly in the late eighteenth century and had transformed civil society (bürgerliche Gesellschaft). This revolution had 'world-historical significance'; and England was the 'classic land' wherein to study this transformation. The historical dimension was widened and strengthened by a European comparison: the Industrial Revolution had been as important for England as the political revolution for France and the philosophical revolution for Germany. The gulf between the England of 1760 and that of 1844 was at least as great as that between France under the *ancien régime* and in 1830. To his historical vision Engels imparted a Messianic quality. He did so not simply by his presentation of what was happening in England as a classical example of a bigger historical development but by his stated conviction that England was therefore predestined to be the scene of a great social revolution. The workers would soon rise against the rich and the resulting revolution would make the French Revolution seem like child's play.[15]

---

[14] E.g. A. Ledru Rollin, *De la décadence de l'Angleterre* (2 vols., Paris, 1850), English translation, *The Decline of England* (2 vols., 1850); Karl Gustav Carus, *England und Schottland im Jahre 1844* (Berlin, 1845), transalted as *The King of Saxony's Journey through England and Scotland in the year 1844* (1846); Friedrich von Raumer, *England im Jahre 1835* (2 vols., Leipzig, 1836), English translation, *England in 1835* (3 vols., 1836). The introduction to the translation of Engels' *Condition of the Working Class* edited by W.O. Henderson and W.H. Chaloner (2nd. edn., Oxford, 1971) expresses an unsympathetic view of Engels as historian but has many useful editorial notes. The translation itself is not always very accurate although it reads better than that by Florence Wischnewetzky (New York, 1887, London 1892, see below p. 18) which is also used in the *Collected Works*.

[15] *Collected Works*, iv, pp. 307-24 (Henderson and Chaloner, eds., pp. 9-26). The translation in Henderson and Chaloner eds. (p. 9) of the crucial passage about England providing for Engels a classical example of what theory predicted is particularly inadequate. The original reads: 'England ist der klassiche Boden dieser Umwälzung, die um so gewaltiger war, je geräuschloser sie vor sich ging, und England ist darum auch das klassiche Land für die Entwicklung ihres hauptsächlisten Resultats, des Proletariats'; see *Marx-Engels Werke*, hereafter *M.E.W.*, (Berlin, 1962), ii, p.237. It should also be aded that although Engels did indeed use the

For the descriptive content Engels drew overwhelmingly upon English sources, and these are well-known. Among those 'English newspapers and books' upon which, he told Marx in November 1844, he was drawing for his work,[16] were official reports, for example, those of the Factories Enquiry Commission of 1833-34 and the Children's Employment Commission of 1841-43; such newspapers as the *Manchester Guardian* and the *Northern Star*; and contemporary books and pamphlets, notably those by J.P. Kay and Peter Gaskell.[17] From none of these, however, did he derive the term Industrial Revolution, least of all the meaning which he gave to it. He relied heavily on Gaskell's *Manufacturing Population of England* for his ideas on England's recent economic and social history. Gaskell had in some respects come nearest to expressing a view which was later to become familiar when he wrote that 'one of the most striking revolutions ever produced in the moral and social condition of a moiety of a great nation is that which has been consequent to the application of steam to machinery'.[18]But Gaskell no more identified the Industrial Revolution than did one of the French radicals whose work Engels evidently also knew. Eugène Buret's *De la misère des classes laborieuses en Angleterre* covers familiar ground and roundly condemns the history of the progress of the cotton industry as the history of the progress of misery. Although Buret was convinced that England was travelling along a blind alley and foresaw the possibility of 'la plus terrible des revolutions', in reality his historical argument and that of Engels had little in common.[19]

Among Engels' English language sources one provided a close link with the world of German Romanticism, itself a vital spring of Engels' historical argument. Thomas Carlyle was himself, of course, greatly influenced by Romanticism. He had already translated Goethe's *Wilhelm Meister* into English (in 1824) and, in the late 1820s and '30s, had already set off upon his crusade against 'the Machine Society' in *Signs of the Time* and in *Sartor Resartus* before his *Chartism* and *Past and Present* swam into Engels' ken in 1843. Just as one line of German Romanticism had provided a needed stimulus for a Scot disillusioned by eighteenth-century rationalism, so in turn Carlyle's thunderous rhetorical assault upon the 'condition of England'

term 'industrielle Revolution' frequently, that frequency was not so great as appears in the Henderson and Chaloner version, cf., for example, *M.E.W.* ii, pp. 243, 254, 306, 313 and Henderson and Chaloner eds., pp. 16, 28, 88, 95.

[16] Quoted Rosemary Ashton, *Little Germany: German Refugees in Victorian Britain* (Oxford, 1989), p. 251, n. 10.

[17] For notes on Engels' sources and contacts with Robert Owen and other English influences, see Henderson and Chaloner (eds.), pp. xviii-xxiv; W.O. Henderson, *The Life of Friedrich Engels* (2 vols., 1976), i, chap. 2; Ashton, *Little Germany*, pp. 56-61.

[18] P. Gaskell, *The Manufacturing Population of England* (1833), p. 52.

[19] Eugène Buret, *De la misère des classes laborieuses en Angleterre et en France* (2 vols., Brussels, 1842), ii, pp. 104. 326 and *passim*. On Engels' knowledge of Buret's work, see Henderson and Chaloner (eds.), p. xix, n. 2.

in *Past and Present* appealed to Engels' revolutionary sentiments as well as seeming to offer support for the evidence of his own eyes on his arrival in England in November 1842.

It appealed to him so much that he borrowed Carlyle's very phrase for the title of the long review article on *Past and Present* which contains much that was later to appear in *The Condition of the Working Class*. The article, 'Die Lage Englands', appeared in three parts. The first part was published in January 1844 in the *Deutsch-Französiche Jahrbücher*, a radical periodical edited from Paris by Karl Marx and Arnold Ruge. As this ceased publication the second and third parts of the article came out in another such periodical, *Vorwärts* between August and October 1844.[20] Part I contained translations into German of selective chunks of Carlyle's passionate attack upon industrial England in his *Past and Present*. Not surprisingly, however, it made no reference at all to Book II of *Past and Present* called 'The Ancient Monk' nor to Carlyle's particular brand of Romanticism in which a feudal world of medieval Christianity provides the path to a return to God, aided by heroic captains of industry.[21] This part of Engels' article, mainly descriptive in nature, does not use the term 'Industrial Revolution', any more than did Carlyle himself though he had got very near to it in earlier coining the word 'industrialism' in *Sartor Resartus*.[22] The second part of the article, however, appearing under the title, 'Die Lage Englands: die achtzehnten Jahrhundert' (The Condition of England: The Eighteenth Century) provides more anticipation of the crucial historical arguments of Engels' book, including the use of the term 'Industrial Revolution' as well as his statement of its meaning in English history: 'The most important effect of the eighteenth century for England was the creation of the proletariat by the Industrial Revolution'.[23]

This concept of the Industrial Revolution as a thing-in-itself – replete with significance in a transcendant historical process, to be set side by side with other sorts of revolutions in France and Germany, and carrying inevitable implications for the future – is clearly a child of Romanticism. More specifically, it is a child of the marriage of Romanticism and Revolution, a familiar union which, of course, flowered with especial luxuriance in continental Europe.

In shaping, creating and distorting popular images of the past, Romanticism has been a good servant to the generation of historical myths, be they of golden ages, of ancient equalities, or of general pre-lapsarian bliss. There are almost as many variants of Romanticism as there are books written about

---

[20] For the originals, see *M.E.W.*, i, pp. 525-49, 550-68 and 569-92. They are translated in *Collected Works*, iii, pp. 444-68, 469-88 and 489-513.

[21] *Past and Present* (1843, ed. A.M. Hughes, Oxford, 1918), especially pp. 35-121 and 242-48.

[22] Thomas Carlyle, *Sartor Resartus* (1833-34) in H. Sussman (ed.), *Sartor Resartus and Selected Prose* (New York, 1970), p.129.

[23] *Collected Works*, iii, p. 487.

it. If economics can be defined, with admitted circularity, as what economists practise, so Romanticism is similarly recognizable in terms of its characteristic products. In literature it means Wordsworth and Coleridge, Shelley and Byron or Herder and Novalis; in art it implies David and Friedrich, Turner and Martin, Géricault and Delacroix; in music it runs the gamut from Beethoven through Berlioz to Wagner and beyond. Numerous names could be added; and sundry sub-divisions set up (to be knocked down). Some small core of agreement might emerge: the flavour of rebellion against classical models and eighteenth century rationalism, a faith in the creative imagination, a whiff of the supernatural or fabulous, utopian visions of harmony and of liberty, equality and fraternity. Whatever elements preceded them, the ideals of 1789 cannot but loom large in those diverse strands of Romanticism which ran very roughly from Rousseau to Bakunin and nourished the hopes and creations of political radicals.[24] For Engels' concept of the Industrial Revolution what mattered was that more specific strand which contained Saint-Simon and Fourier, testifying to its French socialist pedigree; and, most important, Fichte, Hegel, Feuerbach and the reaction to Hegel typified by Moses Hess and the 'young Hegelians'.

In the three years before he sailed, aged twenty-two, for the Manchester branch office of his father's firm in November 1842, Engels had moved from being a clerk with literary aspirations to being an enthusiastic revolutionary.[25] The son of a prosperous cotton manufacturer in Barmen-Elberfeld, he reacted against the pious Protestantism of his father and the local Pietist community – a not unfamiliar happening. Attracted first by romantic poetry,[26] he soon moved on to find an outlet for his sentiments of revolt by publishing, in 1839, poems and satirical pieces attacking the religious and cultural milieu of the bourgeoisie from which he sprang. Other and more radical models influenced his reading. In 1841-42, when he went to do his military service in Berlin, he attended philosophy lectures at the university and rapidly came under the sway of those 'young Hegelians' who, though following Hegel in seeing the evolution of history as the

---

[24] Works on Romanticism abound. I have drawn mainly upon the following: Marilyn Butler, *Romantics, Rebels and Reactionaries*, (Oxford, 1981), which has a wide-ranging bibliography; and for political romantics and radicals, E.H. Carr, *The Romantic Exiles* (1933); G. Kitson Clark, 'The Romantic Element, 1830-50' in J.H. Plumb (ed.), *Studies in Social History* (1955); J.L. Talmon, *Political Messianism: The Romantic Phase* (1960); E.J. Hobsbawm, *The Age of Revolution* (1962) especially chaps. 12-14; and H.G. Schenk, *The Mind of the European Romantics* (1966).

[25] The brief account of Engels' early life which follows draws upon Henderson, *Life of Engels*, i, chap 1; P. Demetz, *Marx, Engels and the Poets* (Chicago, 1967), especially pp. 9-25, 34-35; and the somewhat idiosyncratic book by Steven Marcus, *Engels, Manchester and the Working Class* (1974).

[26] Notably by that of Ferdinand Freiligrath, an imitation of which by Engels was published in Bremen in 1838 (Demetz, p. 11). Freiligrath was later to become a fellow Communist exile in Britain and in time prompted Marx to some characteristically sour observations (Ashton, *Little Germany*, pp. 79-96).

embodiment of truth via the process of the dialectic, nevertheless totally rejected Hegel's conclusions about man, spirit and the state. They adopted instead materialist ideas firmly in opposition to religion, monarchy and state, not least the Prussian state. In the autumn of 1842, returning from Berlin, Engels had first meetings in Cologne with Moses Hess and with Karl Marx. The latter – already independently moving in the same revolutionary direction as both Engels and Hess but possessed of an immensely stronger intellectual equipment – was then editing the *Rheinische Zeitung*. Shortly afterwards he published therein Engels' first political article on England, dashed off soon after he arrived there and appearing with the date of November 1842. Hess played an important role in shaping Engels' views on the Industrial Revolution and its historical significance, so he demands some brief attention.[27]

Moses Hess (1812-75) provides an extreme example of the visionary Romanticism affecting the German intelligentsia of his day, of the 'political Messianism' which, in Talmon's words, found Hess 'deeply steeped in apocalyptic thinking'.[28] Just as Engels had reacted against the Pietism of a prosperous textile-manufacturing father, so Hess reacted against the strict Jewish tradition in which he was brought up by his father, a prosperous sugar refiner in Cologne. In 1837 he had expressed some of his visionary socialism in a chaotic book bearing the comprehensive title of *Die Heilige Geschichte der Menschheit* (The Sacred History of Humanity).[29] More immediately pertinent to the present topic, however, was his second book *Die Europäische Triarchie* (The European Triarchy) published anonymously in 1841.[30] Hess sought to transform Hegelian thought into revolutionary action, to shape the future by, so to speak, giving a helping hand to the Hegelian laws of history. Action would, as it were, permit man to collaborate with history. More specifically, he adumbrated the notion in the *Triarchie* that the three countries – England, France and Germany – were already working towards the emancipation of humanity. Europe had already experienced two revolutions: in Germany the Reformation had secured, though not completely, the liberty of religion from the state; and in France the French Revolution had gone far towards establishing political liberty. The future lay in England which was the home of freedom of expression; the practical English, moreover, provided a synthesis of the French and German spirits. The obstacle to the achievement of liberty and harmony was social and economic inequality. This obstacle would be swept away by a social revolution which would take place in England because only there was

---

[27] On Hess and the 'young Hegelians', see Edmund Silberner, *Moses Hess: Geschichte seines Lebens* (Leiden, 1966) and Auguste Cornu, *Moses Hess et la Gauche Hégélienne* (Paris, 1934); more generally and briefly, Isaiah Berlin, *The Life and Opinions of Moses Hess* (Cambridge, 1957).

[28] Talmon, *Political Messianism*, p. 211.

[29] *Die heilige Geschichte der Menschheit. Von einem Junger Spinozas* (Stuttgart, 1837).

[30] *Die Europäische Triarchie* (Leipzig, 1841).

to be found such an opposition between 'pauperism and the aristocracy of money' as to have reached the revolutionary level.[31]

The influence of Hess and his *Triarchie* is thus readily discernable as providing the basis for Engels' remarks about the English Industrial Revolution being as important as those other revolutions in France and Germany though in Engels' hands the German contribution becomes a philosophical revolution rather than one involving the Reformation and religion. Although Hess does not himself offer the concept of an English Industrial Revolution Engels clearly took over the Messianic vision of England as the scene of a great social revolution which was to be part of a major historical process. That vision is evident, moreover, in the apocalyptic language of the closing sentences of Engels' dedication (in English) of his book to the 'Working Class of Great Britain' urging them on as members of the 'One and Indivisible' family of Mankind.[32] Later, Hess's influence on Engels and Marx waned as he became more of a pacifist and idealist, and Marx came to pour scorn upon him. Before that development, however, Marx's faith in Communism as the purposeful fulfillment of history and Engels' particular concept of the Industrial Revolution in that process owed more than a little to Hess who had claimed, in a letter written in June 1843, that after their meeting of the previous autumn, Engels, already from the beginning a revolutionary, 'had left him an enthusiastic Communist'.[33]

Die Lage der arbeitenden Klasse in England came out in Leipzig in 1845 and was reprinted in 1848. The subject of some reviews in Germany, it was read both in radical and official circles, making a considerable impact.[34] In Britain, it made virtually none save amongst other émigré radicals, such as Georg Weerth. Although Weerth absorbed much of the Engels/Marx line on Chartism, his account of English industrial developments and his description of Bradford and other manufacturing towns echo Engels but do not include any use of the latter's concept of the Industrial Revolution.[35] The

[31] Hess, *Triarchie*, p. 173 ('Der Gegensatz von Pauperismus und Geldaristokratie wird nur in England die Revolutionshöhe erreichen'), also pp. 82, 84, 90, 131.

[32] *Collected Works*, iv, p. 298.

[33] Hess to Berthold Auerbach, 19 June 1843, quoted in E. Silberner (ed.), *Moses Hess: Briefwechsel* (The Hague, 1959), p. 103. Hess wrote of a young Hegelian then in England and writing 'ein grosses Werk über diese Angelegenheit', presumably referring to Engels and went on to say that in the previous year he had come to Cologne, they had talked on questions of the day and 'er, ein Anno I Revolutionär, schied von mir als allereifrigster Kommunist'. In the large literature analysing the origins and significance of Marxian political thought there are sundry comments on Hess. See, e.g. Richard N. Hunt, *The Political Ideas of Marx and Engels*, i (1975), pp. 105-6 and G. Claeys, 'The Political Ideas of the Young Engels, 1842-45', *History of Political Thought*, 6, (1985), pp. 455-77.

[34] Henderson, *Life of Engels*, i, pp. 61-65.

[35] Georg Weerth, *Sämtliche Werke* (ed. Bruno Kaiser, 5 vols., Berlin, 1957), especially iii, pp. 154-88 and *passim*; Ashton, *Little Germany*, pp. 71-79.

contacts between Engels and the Chartist leader G.J. Harney served simply to underline the gap between the theoretical structure of Marxism, with its foundations in a Messianic notion of history, and the empiricism of what was to emerge as Socialism in Britain.[36] There seems to be no indication that Engels' presentation of the Industrial Revolution as a crucial element in the social revolution of all working men had any influence on Harney or on most of his Chartist colleagues, let alone the rank and file of that movement. Only one of the Chartist leaders is likely to have known Engels' book: Ernest Jones. Born in Berlin in 1819 and educated in Germany until his family returned to England in 1838, Jones read and spoke German fluently. He exhibited familiar qualities in the romantic revolutionary: a literary bent, writing romantic verse in his youth and radical lyrics in later life; reaction against his parental background; and a sincere fervour in embracing revolutionary politics. He was seen by Marx and Engels as the most likely of the English radicals to be able to spread Communism though in the end he, like others, failed their hopes.[37]

Engels' concept of the Industrial Revolution was, of course, taken over by Marx in *Das Kapital*. In his massive extension of the historical and theoretical framework, merely sketched by Engels, Marx uses the term on a number of occasions, identifying its historical role in 'the capitalist mode of production' evolving in accordance with what he conceived to be its historical laws.[38] But, save for some scattered uses, the whole notion of the Industrial Revolution remained obstinately absent in the country which experienced this phenomenon until it was discovered, or rather rediscovered, in the 1880s. Foreign observers were certain that something called 'la révolution industrielle' or 'die industrielle Revolution' had happened in England starting in or around the 1780s. Yet it took a century before the natives began to decide that the Industrial Revolution was an identifiable happening in British history. It had been absent from the major sources which Engels had used; and it did not figure in the works of such popular British historians of the first half of the nineteenth century as Harriet Martineau let alone Macaulay. It does not appear in the social novels of Dickens or Disraeli or Mrs Gaskell. It seems unlikely to have resounded in the oratory of Chartism; if it did it has not been reported in excerpts from the pages of, for example, the *Northern Star*. If the literature of social protest had no use for it, its absence from that of economic approbation is scarcely surprising. The

[36] A.R.Schoyen, *The Chartist Chalenge* (1956), pp. 129-30, 143-44, 205, 214-17.

[37] John Saville, *Ernest Jones: Chartist* (1952); Ashton, *Little Germany*, pp. 78, 98, 103, 108-9, 240; and the valuable article by Kirk Willis, 'The Introduction and Critical Reception of Marxist Thought in Britain, 1850-1900', *Historical Journal*, 20 (1977), pp. 423-44.

[38] *Capital* (translated from the 3rd. German edn. by Samuel Moore and Edward Aveling; 3 vols., New York, 1967), i, pp. 372, 373, 376, 428, 472; *M.E.W.*, xxiii, pp. 392, 393, 396, 452, 498. The term was also used by Marx and Engels in their *Grundsätze des Kommunismus* (*M.E.W.*, iv, p. 363), a draft for the *Communist Manifesto* in the final form of which, however, it is not used.

interests of such writers as Charles Babbage and Andrew Ure, focused as
they were almost wholly on the economic virtues of machinery in bringing
new achievements in production and productivity, did not encompass
theories of social and industrial revolution.[39] Even by the mid century and
the succeeding decades, hardly anybody seems to have talked or written
about the country's history as having embraced something called the Industrial Revolution. The term does not appear, for example, in the second
edition of G.R. Porter's *Progress of the Nation* or later in the writings of Leone
Levi or Robert Giffen or in reports of official bodies.[40] It was used neither
by enthusiasts for entrepreneurial zeal, such as Samuel Smiles, nor by
satirists of the self-made such as Trollope in *The Way We Live Now* of 1875.

A few exceptions to prove the rule are provided by some economists,
perhaps familiar with French usage, for example John Stuart Mill and W.S.
Jevons. In the 1848 edition of his *Principles of Political Economy* Mill wrote of
the opening of foreign trade sometimes working 'a complete industrial
revolution'. But this is no more than a passing phrase in an abstract account
of the way in which new foreign trade can stimulate the use of previously
undeveloped resources. Moreover, the cautious Mill subsequently qualified
even this by changing it in later editions to 'a sort of industrial revolution'.[41]
Similarly, Jevons in *The Coal Question* of 1865 has merely one passing use of
the term which he seems to have derived from Briavoinne's work; and there
is no use of it in his collected papers and letters.[42]

Before examining how and why the concept came eventually to make so
triumphant and enduring an entry into the national consciousness, it is time
to consider the obvious but difficult question: Why not earlier? The early
absence of the concept from Britain may be variously viewed. It can be seen
as just one reflection of the different forms taken by Romanticism in this
country and elsewhere; as a minor tribute to some fundamental differences
in political history; as a by-product of a nearly total English ignorance at that
time of Hegelian philosophy; or as a consequence of an insularity which
sheltered empiricism and regarded anything foreign with suspicion and
distrust.

Certainly the marriage of Romanticism and Revolution proved far less

[39] See Charles Babbage, *On the Economy of Manufactures* (1832) and Andrew Ure, *Philosophy of Manufactures* (1835).

[40] G.R. Porter, *Progress of the Nation* (2nd edn., 1847); Leone Levi, *The History of British Commerce, 1760-1870* (2nd edn., 2 vols., 1880); Robert Giffen, *The Progress of the Working Classes* (1883).

[41] J.S. Mill, *Principles of Political Economy* (2 vols., 1848), ii, p. 19 and 7th edn. (1871), ii, p. 122.

[42] W.S. Jevons, *The Coal Question* (1865), p. 341. In referring elsewhere in the book to Briavoinne's work, Jevons uses the term 'commercial revolution' (p. 181) despite Briavoinne's own use of 'révolution industrielle', even when translating the very phrase quoted above (p. 4). There is no mention of industrial revolution in Jevons' papers and letters – see R.D. Collinson-Black and R. Könekamp (eds.), *Papers and Correspondence of William Stanley Jevons* (7 vols., 1972-81).

fruitful in England than in continental Europe. The retreat of Wordsworth, Coleridge and Southey to various shades of conservatism left Nature-worship to survive without revolutionary overtones; and neither Coleridge's political journalism nor his enthusiasm for things German ran to the full implications of Fichte and Hegel. Along with Blake and Byron, Shelley and Keats, the English Lake poets could all be heard at one time or another, in verse or in prose, declaiming against the new philosophy of individualism, the new political economy, the new urban squalor, the grim presence of the new factories, the insecurity brought by boom and slump, the plight of factory children, the corruption of the soul or the desecration of rural England. But despite sundry utopian visions, such as Coleridge's Pantisoc-racy or Robert Owen's New Harmony, despite Byron's posturings and his death at Missolonghi, Romanticism in England never issued in a faith rooted in a Messianic theory of history, let alone a commitment to action based upon it. It remained a literary and artistic phenomenon which sometimes carried reflections of the political and social scene. So rather than helping to give birth to the concept of an Industrial Revolution, English Romanticism left a rich legacy of poetry occasionally coloured with social protest; and a collection of canvases from Turner, Joseph Wright and others offering, as a comment on industrial change, sundry romantic vistas of furnaces, forges and mines, along with the illustrative fantasies of John Martin.[43]

When it did draw upon history, Romanticism in Britain nourished an obsession with a rosy myth of the Middle Ages. This offered up some multi-coloured dreams of order invoked by a supposedly stable and heroic medieval society. In its best-known literary manifestation, the novels of Walter Scott, paternalistic lords and well-fed peasants occupied a world of honour, valour and fidelity. The popular radicalism of Cobbett, champion of liberty and scourge of tax-eating governments, money-men, stock-job-bers and 'the Wen', carried its own brand of Romanticism which was deeply conservative in its invocation of a better world in the past. Convincing himself, against all the evidence, that in his day the population was falling, Cobbett saw medieval England as more prosperous and populous, full of a well-fed people, honest and God-fearing, living in contented agrarian order. His belief in a happy rural world of his own youth is nicely mirrored in Engels' picture of a pre-Industrial Revolution England peopled by farm workers vegetating in idyllic simplicity. Carlyle, of all the reformers the most explicitly influenced by the medieval myth, looked to a feudal past replete with Christian faith and heroic action. At its more colourful end romantic medievalism surfaced in Disraeli's social novels, especially *Coningsby*; and in an extreme form in Kenelm Digby's *Broad Stone of Honour* and the Young England movement. It achieved a rich dottiness in the Eglinton

---

[43] F.D. Klingender, *Art and the Industrial Revolution* (1947); on John Martin, see T. Balston *John Martin, 1789-1854: His Life and Works* (1947).

tournament of 1844; and was visibly perpetuated in numerous Pugin-inspired buildings in the Gothic style, those aspiring to the grand manner being peppered internally with suits of armour and antique weaponry.[44]

If in such an imaginative mental world 'revolution' was not a word to be lightly used, still less did it readily come to the lips in English political discourse save with one only too obvious a connotation. To early nineteenth-century insular Britons it carried a reminder of the 'excesses' of the French Revolution – and that was something which happened to foreigners. At home, as Macaulay observed in the 1840s, the revolution of 1688 was 'our last revolution'; and it was peculiarly different from those 'continental revolutions' which have 'during the last sixty years overthrown so many ancient governments'.[45] Here was myth of a different sort in the making: the Whig view of English history which was to dominate the native conception of the national past for the next hundred years or so. Confident in its assumption of political and economic superiority, it owed nothing to German historical philosophy. Nor, at those levels of political argument which were concerned with parliamentary reform, with voting and representation, did serious talk of revolution long survive, least of all considered as an inevitable product of industrialization and class warfare. Not even Tom Paine in his day could ignite the fires of revolution against a less than absolutist regime. And a few decades later, despite Marx's and Engels' faith in Chartism as a crucial manifestation of the struggle of the proletariat against the bourgeoisie – and hence a product of the Industrial Revolution which created that proletariat – Chartism proved to be nothing of the sort. Its objectives were essentially political; its concern was overwhelmingly with exclusion from political rights and representation. As a political movement it 'cannot satisfactorily be defined in terms of the anger and disgruntlement of disaffected social groups or even the consciousness of a particular class'.[46] Even after Chartism had patently failed Engels was still demonstrating his faith in an historical theory, in the face of unaccommodating reality, when he wrote to Marx in 1852 of 'the instinctive hatred of the workers for the industrial bourgeoisie' as providing the only basis for the reconstituting of 'the Chartist party'.[47] The evident absence of such instinctive hatred, as well as of any appropriately apocalyptic feeling about imminent social revolution, probably provided a further reason for the similar absence from Britain at that time of the concept of the Industrial Revolution.

The word 'revolution' by itself was of course diversely used, sometimes, as earlier in France, in relation to manufacturing processes. Edward Baines,

---

[44] In general, on these manifestations of medievalism, see Alice Chandler, *A Dream of Order: The Medieval Ideal in English Literature* (1971); and Mark Girouard, *The Return to Camelot* (1981).

[45] T.B. Macaulay, *The History of England* (5 vols., London, 1849-61), ii, pp. 661, 668.

[46] G. Stedman Jones, *Languages of Class* (Cambridge, 1983), p. 96.

[47] Engels to Marx, 18 March 1852, quoted Saville, *Ernest Jones*, p. 40.

for example in his *History of the Cotton Manufacture* wrote of the textile inventions effecting 'as great a revolution in manufactures as the art of printing effected in literature'.[48] Peter Gaskell, writing in a very different vein in 1833, had talked of a 'complete revolution' in the distribution of property arising from recent economic changes.[49] Carlyle, to judge from his extraordinary and bizarre prose, was obsessed by the violence of revolution. He talked of 'these revolutionary times' and in 1831, not long before he started work on *The French Revolution*, he wrote in his journal: 'all Europe is in a state of disturbance, of revolution'.[50] As the word took on the associations of 1789 and later of 1830 and 1848 it became all the more unlikely in English to have the word 'industrial' grafted on to it and for the result to be applied to a bunch of technical innovations in manufacturing. Despite reactions, horrified or admiring, such things did not represent opposition to the established government; nor were they in any sense uprisings visibly led by dangerous men needing to be suppressed by the authority of the state. Moreover, 'industry' was still normally used to mean work or industriousness: the opposite of idleness as typified in Hogarth's celebrated moral prints. 'There are some sorts of industry', Adam Smith had written in 1776, 'which can be carried on nowhere but in a great town. A porter, for example, can find employment and subsistence in no other place'. Comparing the manufacturer and the soldier, he observed that 'application and industry have been familiar to the one; idleness and dissipation to the other'.[51] Half a century later, commentators on the achievements of the day normally used, like Smith, 'manufacture' or 'trade' to designate what we have come to call industry. Likewise 'industrial' was little used save in the sense of 'the industrial classes'.[52] A characteristic example from the mid century is provided by this observer of the Great Exhibition of 1851: 'Let anyone who wishes to be instructed as to the character of the industrial classes of England and London especially go to the Exhibition and watch how well they behave themselves'.[53]

Arguing from negative evidence is notoriously hazardous but in these circumstances it is perhaps hardly surprising that for much of the nineteenth century, although Britons talked of mills (usually in relation to

---

[48] Edward Baines, *History of the Cotton Manufacture* (1835, ed. W.H. Chaloner, 1966), preface p.6. He also used much the same terminology in his *Account of the Woollen Manufacture in England* (originally presented as a paper to the British Association in 1858, printed in 1875, ed. K.G. Ponting, 1970), pp. 126-27. In neither does the term 'industrial revolution' appear.

[49] *Manufacturing Population of England*, pp. 33, 173-74.

[50] *Sartor Resartus* (ed. Sussman), p. 35; J.A. Froude, *Thomas Carlyle: A History of the First Forty Years of his Life, 1795-1835* (2 vols., 1882), ii, p. 95.

[51] Adam Smith, *The Wealth of Nations* (1776, ed. Cannan, Modern Library edn., 1937), pp. 17, 437.

[52] In general on these usages, see Raymond Williams, *Keywords* (2nd edn., 1983), pp. 165-68.

[53] Quoted in *The Great Exhibition of 1851: A Commemorative Album* (compiled by C.H.Gibbs-Smith for the Victoria and Albert Museum, 1950), p. 64.

textiles) or factories or of 'the manufacturing system', they did not normally talk of 'the Industrial Revolution'. Carlyle could fulminate against the 'millocrats' and 'Midas-eared Mammonism' and the Machine as 'one huge, dead immeasurable Steam-engine'; Cobbett could thunder against loan-jobbers, Scotch economists and boroughmongers; Harney could roast 'the vile shopocracy' and the 'nasty, filthy, crawling Aristocratic and Shopocratic bugs'; Martin could provide illustrations for an edition of *Paradise Lost* inspired by vistas of mines, tunnels and gas-light; and Blake could pen his celebrated image of 'dark Satanic mills'.[54] But only a romantic outsider, burning with a new philosophy, could conceive of England as undergoing that Industrial Revolution which was to be a necessary step to the great revolution of all working men.

The long delayed entry into English of the idea that Britain had experienced an historical happening called the Industrial Revolution was effected through a variety of channels.

Changes in the structure and growth of the economy secured some reflections, neither simple nor uniform, in the climate of thought and expression. The easy labels Victorian Boom and Great Depression attached by one generation of economic historians to the periods 1850-73 and 1873-96, respectively, have in recent years been largely discarded by successors in pursuit of statistical accuracy. Yet enough remains, not only from the diverse and long-used literary evidence but even from the new and better numbers, to suggest that contemporaries did indeed experience pervasive euphoria succeeded by widespread worry, social as well as economic, and that these sentiments sometimes had real justification. Of course, neither economic shifts nor expressions of social concern fit neatly into the periods nor were all sectors of groups similarly affected. The vocabulary of British comment on such matters did, however, begin to change from the 1860s and '70s onwards. It was not merely the spread and consolidation of factories and railways, the alleviation of some of the worst poverty and social hardship or the extinction of the older sorts of political radicalism which stimulated the change. It came from a growing awareness of new sorts of challenges; and they arose well before the 'condition-of-England question' resurfaced in the 1880s. The very name and location of the New York Industrial Exhibition of 1854 was no more than a symbol or portent; and it made no dent in the gigantic national self-esteem engendered by the Great Exhibition and all that it seemed to stand for. When, however, the Select Committee on Scientific Instruction reported worryingly in 1868 on 'the relation of industrial education to industrial progress', the new connotation of those words mirrored a new concern.[55] That concern was not lessened by adverse

---

[54] For Harney's blast, see Schoyen, *Chartist Challenge*, pp. 49, 96.
[55] *Select Committee on Scientific Instruction* (Parliamentary Papers 1867-68, xv), p. 20.

comments on native performance contained in the reports of sundry other committees and commissions, be they on overseas exhibitions or scientific education. A consciousness of living in 'the modern industrial system' or of being troubled in the 1870s by 'the great industrial questions of the day'[56] was unequivocally signalled in the title as well as the content of that massive enquiry of the 1880s, the Royal Commission on . . . the Depression of Trade and Industry.

Some groups – feeling the pinch of falling profits, of increased competition abroad, of markets more difficult to penetrate – came to question Free Trade and call for Protection. Others – distressingly aware of continuing poverty and sweated labour in London or the burgeoning industrial cities, of acute unemployment in the downswing of the trade cycle, of stirring unrest despite all the economic achievements – came to question the sanctity of laissez-faire. Such latter worries surfaced in a variety of predominantly middle-class movements which in one way or another looked to history, to idealism or to social statistics. In the process the concept of the Industrial Revolution was rediscovered.

Amongst the influences which may have aided this rediscovery some are necessarily shadowy. They include the upsurge of idealist philosophy and specifically a new enthusiasm for Hegel. The notable imprint it made at Oxford, especially at Balliol under Benjamin Jowett, carried through to Bradley, Bosanquet and especially to T.H. Green through whom it was transmitted to Arnold Toynbee. Looked at from a different angle, the interest in Hegel was but one illustration of a breaking down of English intellectual insularity. Although the great ferment of romantic idealism and revolutionary politics, seething in sundry European capitals in the 1830s and '40s and culminating in the debacle of 1848, had done little more for political England than encourage a flow of refugees and confirm a complacent individualism, by the 1870s the impact of continental events was evoking different sorts of responses. The unification of Italy, the Franco-Prussian war, the doings of Bismarck, the Paris Commune: to such matters English reactions were real though necessarily varied. On this tide of new interests there floated in Karl Marx and Socialism.

An English translation of the *Communist Manifesto* in 1850 passed virtually unnoticed; only slightly more attention was accorded to the first volume of *Das Kapital* published in Hamburg in 1867; a handful of English radicals had got to know Marx at or after the founding of the International in 1864. But when, in 1871, Marx published a pamphlet in English in praise of the Commune he and the International suddenly came to public notice in the guise of threats to civilized society.[57] When the tumult had died down, however, a growing though still very small number of reformers and

---

[56] *Royal Commission on Scientific Instruction* (Parliamentary Papers 1872, xxv), p. 623.
[57] Willis in *Historical Journal*, xx, pp. 425-26, 438-40; Ashton, *Little Germany*, p. 132.

socialists began to take heed of the doctrines expressed in *Das Kapital*; in the course of the '70s, for example, articles about it appeared in the *Fortnightly Review*.[58] Some, including George Bernard Shaw, William Morris and H.M. Hyndman, tackled the French translation.[59] Shaw, who worked at it in 1883, subsequently observed: 'Marx was a revelation . . . he opened my eyes to the facts of history and civilization'.[60] Some read it in German. Amongst them was a pioneer in the revival of socialism in England, dormant since the early days of Bray, Thompson and Hodgskin. E. Belfort Bax, who had studied in Germany and knew both Marx and Engels, wrote an article in 1881 on Marx's work in *Modern Thought*.[61] The more colourful but slightly absurd figure of Hyndman, who had read *Le Capital* in 1880, published in 1882 a little book called *England for All* setting out a popularized resumé of Marx's ideas though without the courtesy of mentioning the source by name. In 1883, however, a more substantial work by Hyndman, *The Historical Basis of Socialism in England*, acknowledged indebtedness to Marx and Engels and was clearly derived directly from their writings. Here was the English Industrial Revolution creating the proletariat; and likewise, in a modified version, Engels' comparison of the political, philosophical and industrial revolutions in France, Germany and England.[62]

This was probably the first published English version of Engels' concept of the Industrial Revolution. More bits of *Das Kapital* appeared in translation in a radical magazine *Today* in 1883; and in 1885, after *Today* had been bought by Hyndman it ran a serialized translation, probably made from the French edition, of the first ten chapters, thus again providing an exposition of the role of the Industrial Revolution.[63] Finally, in 1887, English translations of the first volume of *Das Kapital* and of *Die Lage der arbeitenden Klasse in England* were published in London and New York respectively; the London publication of the translated Engels work followed in 1892.[64]

In Marx's hands the concept of the Industrial Revolution lost some of the Romantic flavour originally imparted to it by Engels. This was no more than a particular case of the general way in which Marx – himself in his youth swept along by Romantic enthusiasms – sought to de-romanticize revolution. Priding himself on a contempt for Romanticism – well exhibited by his

[58] Willis in *Historical Journal*, xx, pp. 428-29.

[59] E.P. Thompson, *William Morris: Romantic to Revolutionary* (1955), pp. 308, 354, 889-90; H.M. Hyndman, *The Record of an Adventurous Life* (1911), p. 209. The first French translation of vol. I of *Das Kapital* came out in parts beteen 1872 and 1875. The translation, which did not meet with Marx's approval, was by Joseph Roy. See K. Marx, *Oeuvres* (Paris, 1963), i, pp. 538-41.

[60] Quoted in Michael Holroyd, *Bernard Shaw* (1988), i, p. 130.

[61] E. Belfort Bax, *Reminiscences and Reflections of a Mid- and Late-Victorian* (1918), p. 45; Willis in *Historical Journal*, xx, p. 438, n. 91.

[62] H.M. Hyndman, *The Historical Basis of Socialism in England* (1883), pp. viii, 138, 143.

[63] Willis in *Historical Journal*, xx, p. 420.

[64] See above, p. 5 n. 14.

scorn for such flamboyant but undisciplined revolutionaries as Bakunin and Lassalle – he offered instead a remarkable intellectual construct, 'an original amalgam of economic theory, history, sociology and propaganda'.[65] Dialectical materialism, Marxist economics, scientific socialism: these were the replacements for the idealistic yearnings of romantic revolutionaries. So he came to be seen by faithful adherents as, to use Bax's words, 'the great founder of the theoretic basis of modern scientific socialist economy'.[66] Conversely, economists nurtured in the tradition of classical political economy – tagged with the pejorative Marxist adjective, 'bourgeois' – came to criticize and reject his heterodox economics.[67] Between such extremes, however, stood the Hegel-derived signpost to history. Engels had defined the role of the Industrial Revolution in an historical process. Marx had incorporated it – along with Engels' descriptive material, greatly supplemented by his own researches – into a vast and elaborately articulated vision. Historians, and particularly the new breed of economic historians emerging in the last quarter of the nineteenth century, could not ignore it even though that vision repelled them intellectually, politically and morally. Nor could those middle-class liberal reformers, inspired by idealist philosophy, Christian ethics and social guilt.[68] They too looked to the past and, though disliking what they saw, equally disliked the Marxist remedy.

As both reformer and historian, Arnold Toynbee had a foot in each of these camps. Essentially a religious man and primarily a reformer, inspired by T.H. Green, influenced by Ruskin and encouraged by Jowett, he turned to political economy and the history of industry as paths towards such goals as 'the cure of social evils' and the fulfillment of his 'desire to raise the poor through themselves to a nobler life',[69] It seems impossible to discover precisely why he decided to use the term Industrial Revolution for the book which he was planning to write under that title while he was giving the lectures on that topic at Balliol between October 1881 and midsummer 1882. He had certainly read Mill and Jevons but he gave to the term a far greater significance than they had, one nearer to that of Engels. In his valuable recent biography, Alon Kadish suggests that Toynbee 'seems to have read at least part of Marx's *Das Kapital* in the French translation'.[70] This is certainly likely; and the *Lectures* contain a footnote reference to *Le*

---

[65] Isaiah Berlin, *Karl Marx* (3rd. edn., Oxford, 1963), p. 236.

[66] Bax, *Reminiscences*, p. 45.

[67] See Alon Kadish, *Historians, Economists and Economic History* (1989), pp. 118-19; Willis in *Historical Journal*, xx, p. 440f.

[68] Melvin Richter, *The Politics of Conscience* (1964); Peter Clarke, *Liberals and Social Democrats* (Cambridge, 1978), especially chaps. 1 and 2.

[69] F.C. Montague, *Arnold Toynbee* (Baltimore, 1889), p. 23; Evelyn Abbott and Lewis Campbell, *The Life and Letters of Benjamin Jowett* (2 vols., 1897), ii, p. 65.

[70] *Apostle Arnold*, p. 106.

Capital.[71] Just as English socialists made their first acquaintance with Marx in French, so might anti-socialists. Whether Toynbee read German, however, is not clear. When W.J. Ashley, who had attended Toynbee's lectures and was in part responsible for assembling them into the book, observed in 1900 that Toynbee was 'but scantily acquainted with German economic discussions' he was almost certainly referring to the German school of historical economists whom Ashley himself so admired.[72] However, as early as 1873 in a letter to his sister Mary, then in Germany, Toynbee had looked forward to her returning with 'a good deal of German' so that they could 'do some history together' and she would be able to help him 'in reading German books and learning the language'. Again, in 1877, writing to his younger brother Harry, he enquired how his German was progressing and advised him that 'German and French will be the most *useful* things you can know'.[73] His uncle George had earlier been at Bonn University; and in the cultivated middle-class ambience in which he had been brought up, a knowledge of German would not have been improbable.

So although there is no reference to Engels in the *Lectures* it is possible that Toynbee made his acquaintance with the idea of the Industrial Revolution, as something more than a mere metaphor, in Engels' work. He referred on a number of occasions to Marx's ideas and spoke of *Das Kapital*, along with Henry George's *Progress and Poverty*, as one of the 'great text-books of Socialism'.[74] The idea that his knowledge of the term came from Marx's writings perhaps acquired some credence from C.R. Fay's assertion (quoted by Kadish) in a 1940 textbook: 'Ask an Oxford student who is being viva'd in Modern Greats, "Who invented the term Industrial Revolution?", and he will reply smartly "Arnold Toynbee, who got it from Marx"'.[75] Perhaps such Oxford responses were indeed forthcoming, though it should perhaps be added that Fay was an exceedingly eccentric Cambridge historian.

Toynbee was at pains to distance himself from Marxian socialism; and to distinguish his brand of reformism from both the Marxist version and what he called 'Tory Socialism'.[76] Although at the end of the *Lectures on the Industrial Revolution* he offered a vision of progress, rather than of social revolution, the cataclysmic nature of industrial change set out in the *Lectures* carried strong echoes of Engels. As in the latter's work the Industrial Revolution was presented as having arrived suddenly at the end of the eighteenth century, replacing a rural, feudal, medieval England: 'the steam-

---

[71] Toynbee, *Lectures*, p. 61.

[72] W.J. Ashley, *Surveys Historic and Economic* (1900), p. 430.

[73] Gertrude Toynbee (ed.), *Reminiscences and Letters of Joseph and Arnold Toynbee* (n. d.), pp. 113-14, 116-17, 137.

[74] *Lectures*, p. 127.

[75] C.R. Fay, *English Economic History mainly since 1700* (Cambridge, 1940), p. 8; Kadish, *Apostle Arnold*, p. 106.

[76] *Lectures*, pp. 127, 130, 212; Richter, *Politics of Conscience*, pp. 287-90.

engine, the spinning-jenny, the power-loom, had torn up the population by the roots'. The essence of the Industrial Revolution was 'the substitution of competition for the medieval regulations'. The results were terrible, 'an enormous increase of pauperism . . . a rapid alienation of classes and . . . the degradation of a large body of producers'. Of course, aside from Engels, the echoes also evoke Peter Gaskell and Carlyle, from whose *Past and Present* Toynbee quoted, praising him as the greatest of those who 'assailed the new industrial world created by *The Wealth of Nations* and the steam-engine'.[77]

In thus fastening the name of Industrial Revolution to an historic thing-in-itself – supposedly caused by technical change and the free-market economics of Adam Smith and bringing catastrophic consequences – the impact of Toynbee in Britain was much greater than that of Engels and Marx. His book enjoyed a notable réclame; and in the dozen or so years after his death in 1883 the memory of his person was honoured and perpetuated in such ways as almost to create a minor myth in itself. The book – a miscellany of lecture notes on classical economics, the Industrial Revolution, working-class standards of life, and the future of industrial democracy – is unsatisfactory in both historical coverage and intellectual consistency. There seems little doubt, however, that Toynbee's personal impact, alike at Oxford and at sundry lectures up and down the country, was striking. On his death, at the age of only thirty, lavish tributes were paid by Jowett, Alfred (later Lord) Milner, F.C. Montague, W.J. (later Sir William) Ashley and others, presenting him as something between a crusader and a saint. Whatever working-class audiences made of him, his appeal to middle-class reformers, troubled by social guilt and concern at the manifestations of poverty both in London and in the industrial cities, was undoubtedly strong. That Canon Barnett's settlement amongst the poor of London's East End should be named after him, as Toynbee Hall, was wholly appropriate and can be seen as an act, albeit of relatively minor consequence, of historic myth-creation.[78]

Before looking at the further dissemination of the concept of the Industrial Revolution as social disaster, it is worth while pausing to consider briefly the characteristics, divergent or similar, of the two founding fathers – Engels and Toynbee – of an historical myth. The one, detesting the Pietism of his parents, saw the Christian church as an arm of the repressive state and regarded its Evangelical manifestations in England as the hypocritical outpouring of the 'parsonocracy'; the other, drawing upon an Evangelical background, was a deeply religious man in whom intellectual interests and

---

[77] *Lectures*, pp. 5, 84, 85, 193.

[78] Kadish, *Apostle Arnold*, pp. 218-23, 229-35, chap 5 *passim*. The theme of social guilt was made explicit in a much-quoted passage from a lecture given in London in January 1883. It is quoted in, for example, Beatrice Webb, *My Apprenticeship* (1926, edn. 1950), pp. 157-58; Richter, *Politics of Conscience*, p. 322; Cannadine in *Past and Prsent*, 103, p. 132; *Apostle Arnold*, p. 210.

Christian conviction were fused in the cause of social reform. The one thundered against classical political economy; the other, though influenced by Cliffe Leslie and other historicist critics, was rare in trying to combine its teachings, suitably humanized, with the study of history. The one sought the revolutionary overthrow of the state by the workers; the other urged the desirability of more intervention by the state on behalf of the workers. And, perhaps the most striking contrast in view of their having both sprung from comfortable circumstances in the bourgeoisie, the one preached hatred of the middle class as an essential ingredient of socialism; the other, suffused by a sense of sin, saw an awareness of middle-class social guilt as the pathway to reforms to be carried through by enlightened leaders of the middle class on behalf of the alienated workers.

Yet for all these divergencies, both drew upon romantic modes of thought: the one upon the political and revolutionary Romanticism of Hess and Hegel; the other upon Carlyle and the social idealism of Ruskin and Green. Both pointed to history as the vital ingredient in the understanding of the present and the fashioning of the future. Though the Messianic quality evident in Engels was absent in Toynbee both had romantic visions of a future society. Marx may have sought to de-romanticize the revolutionary vision and make Socialism scientific. Sidney Webb and the Fabians, having fallen out with the autocratic Hyndman and come to disagree with Marxian economics, may have tried to turn Socialism into statistics and administration. Toynbee may have helped to steer guilt-ridden middle-class liberals towards more state intervention. But what eventually emerged in Britain secured its support via ways of thinking which were romantic in the appeal to morals and emotions rather than to theory.[79] In that process, and later in the reactions thereto, the idea of the Industrial Revolution was to become one of the mythic phenomena of British history.

For the myth-making sequence the very real divergencies between Engels and Toynbee or amongst Marxists, Fabians and reforming Liberals, scarcely mattered. However diffused, the idea of the Industrial Revolution as social catastrophe gathered momentum for some sixty or seventy years, from roughly the 1880s to the 1950s.

In the early days it was bandied about in sundry reformist and socialist circles, whether it was drawn from Marx/Engels or from Toynbee. As early as December 1882 Milner used Toynbee's concept in a set of six lectures on socialism which he gave in the East End of London.[80] The so-called 'Hampstead Marx Circle' or 'Hampstead Historic Society', involving inter alia and at various times, Bernard Shaw, Belfort Bax, Graham Wallas and

[79] Stanley Pierson, *Marxism and the Origins of British Socialism* (Ithaca and London, 1973), p. 214.
[80] Kadish, *Apostle Arnold*, p. 213.

Sidney Webb, started meeting in 1885 to discuss the theory and history they found in *Le Capital*.[81] In Cambridge at the same time a group calling itself the Cambridge Economic Club was likewise using *Le Capital* to examine Marx's use of Blue Books.[82] In 1889 came the *Fabian Essays* in which, especially in Webb's contribution, there was much emphasis on history and 'the Industrial Revolution of the eighteenth century, which created the England of today', complete with references to both Engels' *Condition of the Working Class* and Toynbee's *Lectures*.[83] In 1891 Webb in the very first volume of the *Economic Journal* wrote of 'the subtle and pregnant analysis of the facts of the Industrial Revolution by Karl Marx'; and the bibliography of Sidney and Beatrice Webb's *History of Trade Unionism* of 1894 cited Engels' work in both the German and English-language editions as well as *Das Kapital* in both languages, though it did not include Toynbee's work.[84]

It was, however, through the newly emergent academic subject of economic history that the concept, and especially Toynbee's version of it, received its widest initial dissemination. The circumstances attendant upon the establishment of the subject in England have been well rehearsed: the influence of the German historicists notably Roscher and Schmoller; the native line of criticism of classical political economy stretching from Malthus to Cliffe Leslie; contemporary concern about a range of social and economic issues; and, in the immediate focus of individual effort, the work of Cunningham and Ashley.[85] To this evolving pattern Toynbee's *Lectures on the Industrial Revolution* gave a mighty boost. The book sounded the chord of reform; it popularized the term and put it into capital letters. And, willy-nilly, it confirmed, extended and made accessible an acceptable modified variant of Engels' original picture of the Industrial Revolution as catastrophe: 'a period', wrote Toynbee, 'as disastrous and as terrible as any through which a nation ever passed'.[86] By the time that the history of Toynbee Hall came to be written in 1935 it was certainly true to say that as an economic historian Toynbee was 'best known as the popularizer of the expression "the Industrial Revolution"'.[87]

[81] Pierson, *Marxism*, p. 119; Clarke, *Liberals*, pp. 30-31.

[82] Kadish, *Historians*, p. 118.

[83] Bernard Shaw, (and others), *Fabian Essays* (1889, ed. Asa Briggs, 1962), pp. 69-70, n. 2, 73n.2 and *passim*.

[84] S.Webb, 'The Difficulties of Individualism', *Economic Journal*, i, (1891), p. 360; S. and B. Webb, *The History of Trade Unionism* (1894), pp. 499-543. This bibliography, compiled by R.A. Peddie, does not appear in the 1920 edition. On the dissemination, in sundry guises and through various channels, of Marx's and Engels' ideas, including the role of the Industrial Revolution, see Brian Simon, *Education and the Labour Movement, 1870-1920* (1965).

[85] See in general N.B. Harte (ed.), *The Study of Economic History* (1971), pp. xi-xxx; Gerard M. Koot, *English Historical Economics, 1870-1926* (Cambridge, 1987); D.C.Coleman, *History and the Economic Past* (Oxford 1987); Kadish, *Historians*.

[86] *Lectures*, p. 84.

[87] J.A.R. Pimlott, *Toynbee Hall* (1935), p. 22.

The first edition of Toynbee's book in 1884 was soon sold out and by 1908 had gone through five editions; it was subsequently reprinted and did not go out of print until 1927; it was then reprinted again in 1969. As the teaching of economic history spread and as it found a place in the examinations of various professional bodies, so textbooks multiplied. Many, indeed most of them, presented the Industrial Revolution in what was rapidly to become its familiar guise of historic trauma, as 'nasty, mean, brutish and fast'.[88] H. de B. Gibbins' *The Industrial History of England* told its readers about the 'complete transformation' wrought suddenly and rapidly by the Industrial Revolution as well as the 'disastrous effects of the new industrial system' and provided a reference to Engels' *The Condition of the Working Class*.[89] Published in 1890, it subsequently ran to twenty-eight impressions. G. Townsend Warner's *Landmarks in English Industrial History* (1899) carried similar messages as did Charles Beard's *The Industrial Revolution* (1901). The latter, heavily derivative from Toynbee, provided a picture of contented rural workers in an eighteenth-century England which was virtually medieval, disturbed by the Industrial Revolution as by 'a thunderbolt from a clear sky'.[90] Townsend Warner's book sold very well as a school textbook for many years to come. Such works were followed by similar versions from other hands: in 1900 from L.L. Price who had earlier, in 1890, written about Toynbee and political economy; in 1908 from H.O. Meredith; and in 1914 from Ashley.[91] All helped to popularize the Toynbeean version, albeit modified as to periodization by Ashley. A more solid monograph came from France in the shape of Paul Mantoux's *La révolution industrielle au XVIIIe siècle*. Here a footnote observed that Toynbee was normally given credit for the term though noting Engels' use of it in 1845.[92]

By the time that the English translation of Mantoux had appeared in 1928, J.L. and Barbara Hammond had produced their well-known trilogy: *The Village Labourer* (1911); *The Town Labourer* (1917); and *The Skilled Labourer* (1919). Although they extended the chronology to 1760-1830 the import of their books, based on much research, was massively to confirm and disseminate the catastrophic version of the Industrial Revolution which they presented as a 'new civilization'. Their findings were synthesized and extended into textbook surveys, notably *The Rise of Modern Industry* (1925) and *The Bleak Age* (1947). Sales of these books in hardback or paperback

[88] Cannadine in *Past and Present*, 103, p. 138.

[89] H. de B. Gibbins, *The Industrial History of England* (1890), pp. 142, 156, 186, 193, etc.

[90] C.Beard, *The Industrial Revolution* (1901), p. 23.

[91] L.L. Price, *A Short History of English Commerce and Industry* (1900) and *A Short History of Political Economy in England from Adam Smith to Arnold Toynbee* (1890); H.O. Meredith, *Outlines of the Economic History of England* (1908); W.J. Ashley, *The Economic Organization of England* (1914).

[92] P. Mantoux, *La révolution industrielle au XVIIIe siècle* (Paris, 1906), p. 1 n. 1. The same note appears in the English translation, *The Industrial Revolution of the Eighteenth Century* (1928), p. 25 n. 1.

were very large, with numerous editions and reprintings.[93] Written with passion, vigour and evident sincerity, the Hammonds' books carried the catastrophic version beyond merely the readership of those absorbing the Industrial Revolution as part of the study of economic history.

Further diffusion through the channel of workers' educational movements got under way around the turn of the century. University extension lecturing, developed in the 1870s, had not been especially concerned with history or economics but by the 1890s industrial history was achieving a growing popularity. With the foundation of the Workers Educational Association in 1903 and the institution thereafter of the W.E.A. tutorial classes outside the limits of universities, rapid growth set in. By 1914 economic history and economics accounted for over half of all such classes.[94] It was reported in 1920 that working-class students usually requested 'facilities for the study of trade-union history, industrial history, problems of industrial control and economics.'[95] In 1928 H.L. Beales' essay *The Industrial Revolution, 1750-1850*, written specifically for the W.E.A., observed that after Toynbee had given it currency 'popular usage' had established the label Industrial Revolution. Though extending its historical duration and though discussing its shortcomings as a label, Beales, like the Hammonds, saw it as replacing 'one social system or one civilization by another'.[96]

The W.E.A. was not Marxist in orientation and many of its lecturers (including its most celebrated, R.H. Tawney) would have pursued a Toynbee/Hammond line on the Industrial Revolution. The Engels/Marx version of catastrophe and forthcoming revolution was disseminated through related but different channels. Hyndman, Morris and other Marxian socialists had stressed the need for workers to be better educated and thus better equipped for the forthcoming class-battle. Around the turn of the century in Glasgow, for example, the Industrial Revolution was being pursued in radical groups armed with de Gibbins and Marx.[97] The foundation of Ruskin College in 1899, of the Plebs League as a breakaway group in 1908, and of the Labour College in 1909 all furthered the dissemination of Marxist ideas on the Industrial Revolution and capitalism. The focus was

---

[93] By the 1950s *The Rise of Modern Industry* had run to eight reprints, *The Village Labourer* to ten and *The Town Labourer* to eleven. See R.M. Hartwell, introduction to the ninth edition of *The Rise of Modern Industry* (1966), pp. xv-xvi; and his *The Industrial Revolution and Economic Growth* (1971). pp. 377-78.

[94] Thomas Kelly, *A History of Adult Education in Great Britain* (2nd. edn., Liverpool, 1970), p. 254; Albert Mansbridge, *An Adventure in Working Class Education* (1920), pp. 10, 42, 66; W.H. Draper, *University Extension: A Survey of Fifty Years, 1873-1923* (Cambridge, 1923), pp. 71, 99-101; Mary Stocks, *The Workers Educational Association* (1953).

[95] Draper, *University Extension*, p. 100.

[96] Beales, *Industrial Revolution* (1928, edn. 1958), pp. 27-30.

[97] Simon, *Education*, pp. 298-301.

made explicit in a report of 1918, just prior to the formation in 1921 of the National Council of Labour Colleges:

> The Labour College teaches the workmen to look for the causes of social evils and the problems arising therefrom in the material foundations of society; that these causes are in the last analysis economic; that their elimination involves in the first place economic changes of such a character as to lead to the eradication of the capitalist economy.[98]

The divergence between Engels and Toynbee was thus reflected in the context of adult education. For the gradual consolidation of the role of the Industrial Revolution as myth the gap did little more than help to impart a more political flavour. In 1924 Raymond Postgate, then a functionary of the Plebs League, attacked the W.E.A. approach announcing that it, and indeed 'all education that is not based on the central fact of the class struggle', was 'false history and false economics'.[99] It is one of the nicer ironies of the class struggle that Postgate should later have founded *The Good Food Guide* and thereby contributed substantially to the improvement in the gastronomic standards of the British bourgeoisie.

The notion of the Industrial Revolution as social catastrophe was thus moving from economic and social history as an academic subject into the wider world of politics and popular usage. Along diverse paths it reached the adherents of the New Liberalism and the New Socialism. At Harrow in the 1900s, via Townsend Warner's textbook, it reached the future Whig historian G.M. Trevelyan;[100] in Liverpool in the 1920s, via Karl Marx, it reached the future trade union leader Jack Jones. As the latter recalled, he attended the local Labour College and 'even had a go at Marx's *Capital* . . . the first part made a big impression on me . . . the enclosures and the revelations about factory conditions'. He admitted that it was hard going but 'found it was an exposure of capitalism. It helped me a great deal'.[101] For trade unionists such economic history offerings had an obvious appeal. They seemed so much more pertinent to their past and expressive of their hopes than conventional historical learning. Indeed, the trade union movement as a whole, growing in strength and confidence, increasingly drew upon its own history as myth. Its early struggles were readily identified with the trauma of the Industrial Revolution as catastrophe, complete with heroes, banners and martyrs. Of these the Tolpuddle farm labourers, celebrated in a centenary volume published by the Trade Union Congress in 1934, are the best known. This collective folk-lore provides a pertinent

---

[98] *Final Report of the Adult Education Committee* (1918), quoted Simon, p. 330. See also Kelly, *Adult Education*, p. 258.

[99] Quoted Stocks, *Workers Educational Association*, p. 88.

[100] G.M. Trevelyan, *An Autobiography and Other Essays* (1949), pp. 11-12.

[101] Jack Jones, 'A Liverpool Socialist Education', *History Workshop*, 18 (1984), p. 95.

example of myth, enhancing and dramatizing belief.[102] Appeals to history have long remained an important ingredient of reformist as well as revolutionary political thinking. So between the poles of Marxian socialism and middle-class guilt-inspired reformism, the emergent Labour Party and the trade unions created yet another focus upon the concept of the Industrial Revolution.

The term soon began to appear in sundry sorts of popular books, thus implanting it in ever-widening circles of public consciousness. It appeared in best-selling histories by authors as divergent in the political spectrum as H.G. Wells and Arthur Bryant. In Wells' *Outline of History* first published in 1920 and then selling widely in popular editions during the inter-war years, the 'great change in human affairs known as the Industrial Revolution' brought a 'new barbarism'.[103] Bryant's *English Saga, 1840-1940* is a good example of history as myth, complete with patriotic sentiments, a golden age, and a hideous dragon in the shape of industrial capitalism. Although certainly no Marxist, Bryant had evidently swallowed Engels' *The Condition of the Working Class* more or less whole and quoted him on the Industrial Revolution.[104] From the 1930s onwards various well-known writers on philosophy, politics and literature took it up, underlining both the romantic and the catastrophic associations of the term. Stephen Spender's Left Book Club volume *Forward from Liberalism* and Raymond Williams' *Culture and Society* were likely enough repositories of such sentiments.[105] Bertrand Russell produced this remarkable variant of the catastrophic vision:

> The industrial revolution caused unspeakable misery both in England and America. I do not think any student of economic history can doubt that the average happiness in England in the early nineteenth century was lower than it had been a hundred years earlier; and this was due almost entirely to scientific techniques.[106]

To have packed so many false, unverified and indeed unverifiable contentions into so short a space needed unusual intellectual ingenuity. That was in 1952. Perhaps it was inevitable that in 1968 he should have offered this still more startling belief: 'the industrial revolution has destroyed the home, and the discovery of contraception is destroying the family'.[107]

The concept was paraded in all sorts of publications in the literary field.

---

[102] See especially H. Phelps Brown, *The Origins of Trade Union Power* (p/b edn., Oxford, 1986), p. 215; Alan Fox, *History and Heritage: The Social Origins of the British Industrial Relations System* (1985), p. 91.

[103] H.G. Wells, *Outline of History* (1920, popular edn. 1930), pp. 856-57.

[104] Bryant, *English Saga, 1840-1940* (1940), p. 48.

[105] Spender, *Forward from Liberalism*, (1937), pp. 35, 87; Raymond Williams, *Culture and Society, 1780-1950* (1958), pp. xiii-xiv, 30-31, 56-57.

[106] Bertrand Russell, *The Impact of Science on Society* (1952), p. 31.

[107] *Autobiography* (1968; p/b. edn., 1971), ii, p. 203.

The introduction to a 1969 paperback edition of Dickens' *Hard Times*, for example, spoke of 'the first maniac onset of the Industrial Revolution' and assured its readers that Britain had changed from a rural to an urban civilization inside two generations.[108] Across the Atlantic, American contributors to literary and political history likewise continued the catastrophic emphasis. In 1957, for instance, Richard Altick, quoting Engels on the Industrial Revolution, went on to present it as encompassing an era when 'the English masses approached a state of downright bestiality'.[109] And even as late as the 1980s, the theme of rapid and total transformation could still be heard there, enunciated by various reputable writers. Igor Webb, for example, arguing that any novel written between roughly 1780 and 1850 was necessarily a response to the Industrial Revolution, spoke of it as having 'transformed every aspect of English life'.[110] In art and architecture too historical enquiries latched on to it as a great transforming agent. F.D. Klingender's *Art and the Industrial Revolution* stressed its formative impact on romantic painting and poetry; and J.M. Richards recorded and depicted its role in furthering the construction of mills, docks and warehouses in his *The Functional Tradition*.[111] In a popular television series of 1969, *Civilization*, Kenneth Clark illuminated the familiar catastrophic vision and categorized the Industrial Revolution as 'part of the Romantic movement'.[112]

While this wider diffusion of the concept was spreading, the scholarly attack upon the vision of social catastrophe was growing in strength. The attack certainly did not impede the gradual build-up of the Industrial Revolution's status as historic myth; indeed it may well have assisted that process. The attack began on a very small scale with a review by J.H. Clapham in 1912 of the Hammonds' *Village Labourer*.[113] It was consolidated in the three volumes of his *Economic History of Modern Britain* which came out between 1926 and 1938. By the use of statistics – many of them available to, but not used by, the Hammonds – Clapham poured some quantitative cold water on, as he put it, 'the legend that everything was getting worse for the working man, down to some unspecified date between the drafting of the People's Charter and the Great Exhibition'.[114] He was very sparing in his use of the term Industrial Revolution. His three massive volumes did not reach the interested general reader as did the Hammonds' works but his

[108] Dickens, *Hard Times* (ed. David Craig, Harmondsworth, 1969), p. 16.
[109] Richard D. Altick, *The English Common Reader* (Chicago, 1957), pp. 94-96.
[110] Igor Webb, *From Custom to Capital: The English Novel and the Industrial Revolution* (New York, 1981), pp. 9, 162. See also Isaac Kramnick, 'Children's Literature and Bourgeois Ideology: Observations on Culture and Industrial Capitalism' in P.Zagorin (ed.), *Culture and Politics from Puritanism to the Enlightenment* (Berkeley, 1980), pp. 204-5.
[111] J.M. Richards, *The Functional Tradition in Early Industrial Buildings* (1958).
[112] Kenneth Clark, *Civilization* (1969; p/b. edn., 1971), p. 324ff.
[113] *Economic Journal*, xxii, (1912), pp. 248-55.
[114] *The Economic History of Modern Britain* (1939 edn.), i, p. vi.

views kindled the fires of an academic controversy in the 1930s which was to burst into flames in the 1950s. The proximate cause of the conflagration was the work of T.S. Ashton. His compact and lucid survey *The Industrial Revolution* of 1948 was probably responsible more than any other single book for shifting the emphasis of interpretation from catastrophe to achievement. The time was propitious, for in the ensuing decades the boom in the popularity of economic history over an expanded university population ensured that the Industrial Revolution dominated syllabuses and loomed ominously large in examination papers. Ashton's reinterpretation was built partly upon an extension of Clapham's use of statistics of prices and wages and cyclical fluctuations therein; and partly upon an economist's approach to the counterfactual proposition that the pressure of population growth *c.* 1760-1830 was such that if the Industrial Revolution had not happened, then the standard of living would have worsened. He supported his general survey with detailed statistical analyses; and his approach was supported in turn by R.M. Hartwell in a number of related articles.[115] Further reinforcement came, in more overtly political terms, by F.A. Hayek in his *Capitalism and the Historians* (1954) and by W.W. Rostow who, seeking to fit the Industrial Revolution into a model of economic growth, gave the explicit sub-title of *A Non-Communist Manifesto* to his *Stages of Economic Growth* (1960).

This anti-romantic economists' onslaught upon the vision of catastrophe provoked counter-blasts. The post-war upsurge in the numbers of those studying economic history brought much reprinting of earlier books. The biggest reprints of the Hammonds' volumes came after the war. They were joined by such similarly anti-capitalists text as *The Common People, 1746-1938* by G.D.H. Cole and Raymond Postgate. First published in 1938, an enlarged and up-dated edition appeared in 1946 and was reprinted in 1956 and 1961. Fiercely denunciatory of capitalism, it sustained the idea of the Industrial Revolution as a disaster for the working class, even though it took on board some of Clapham's criticisms. Meanwhile the Hammonds' *Rise of Modern Industry*, which reached its ninth reprint in 1966, was still assuring its readers that even when 'the fullest account has been taken of all the qualifications that the case demands, it remains true that what happened at the Industrial Revolution could not justly be described by any phrase with less of catastrophe in its sense and sound'.[116] A new generation of more sophisticated Marxist historians, notably E.J. Hobsbawm and E.P. Thompson, rapidly joined the fray. The resulting controversy about the immediate social effects of the Industrial Revolution, between 'optimists' and 'pessimists' largely took place in learned journals and was thus in the main limited to embattled

---

[115] Reprinted in Hartwell's *Industrial Revolution and Econommic Growth* which also provides a useful guide to Ashton's articles.

[116] *Rise of Modern Industry* (ed. Hartwell, 1966), p. 241.

intellectuals. But both Hobsbawm and Thompson published widely read books. The former, like Engels, stressed the primacy of the cotton industry in the revolutionary events creating the proletariat; the latter, in a popular study of the English working class, was still in the 1960s emphasizing the 'truly catastrophic nature of the Industrial Revolution'.[117] More and more of the general public caught a whiff of the smoke of battle. It spilt over first into new textbooks, some offering more balanced pictures, then into popularization on radio, television and in the press as a growing general interest in the country's social and economic past made itself felt.

This learned debate on interpretation shifted the balance away from catastrophe towards achievement even though in popular usage the old vision still remained powerful. From the 1960s and '70s onwards, however, new influences outside learned controversy were coming to bear upon the idea of the Industrial Revolution. As they did so the popular image was increasingly shifted towards an heroic myth of historical achievement. In the process the myth itself became, at least in part, a totem for the political Right rather than for the political Left.

The central pillar of this edifice of historical achievement was, of course, technology. Technical advances, especially in power-driven machinery, had figured as the crucial elements in the writings of contemporary enthusiasts; without them the analytical encomia of Ure, Babbage or Baines, let alone Smiles' romantic biographies of industrial heroes, could not have existed. Moreover, although Engels' powers of descriptive writing soon took over from his initial awareness of the role of technical innovation, Marx's superior analytical mind soon seized upon technical change as a vital part of his concept of historical economic development. The same was true of non-Marxist interpretations of the Industrial Revolution. Despite the continuing power of the catastrophic vision, analyses of technical advances figured, until very recently, at least, as central features in virtually all such texts.[118]

It was by this criterion of technical achievement that the term, gaining in popularity the while, was increasingly applied to periods and places other than that of the original usage. National economies or parts of them, were said to have experienced, or failed to do so, something imprecisely called an 'industrial revolution' (without the capitals, in honour perhaps of the prime British exemplar). Even Clapham, so sparing in his employment of the term, committed himself to the supposition that despite the remodelling of most French industries in the course of the nineteenth century, 'it might be

[117] 'Whoever says Industrial Revolution says cotton' – E.J.Hobsbawm, *Industry and Empire* (1968), p. 56; E.P.Thompson, *The Making of the English Working Class* (1965), p. 198.
[118] See, for example, P. Mathias, *The First Industrial Revolution* (1969, 2nd. edn. 1983).

said that France never went through an industrial revolution'.[119] More
positively, industrial revolutions were discovered to have happened in the
U.S.A., Germany and Japan at various dates in the later nineteenth and
early twentieth centuries. Joseph Schumpeter lent his authority to the idea
that each of the long waves of economic activity detected by the Russian
statistician N.D. Kondratieff, consisted of 'an "industrial revolution" and
the absorption of its effects'.[120] So the contention that a 'second industrial
revolution', based on a new wave of technical changes had happened in
Britain in the later nineteenth and twentieth centuries, began to appear in
the language of economic historians. Not content with this relatively conservative application to industrialized societies, some scholars were adventurous enough the discover industrial revolutions, again allegedly
consequential upon some technical advance, in less probable eras ranging
from the Bronze Age to the seventeenth century.[121]

Such notions testified to a certain lack of definitional clarity on the part of
economic historians. Nevertheless, they all helped the diffusion of the idea
of the Industrial Revolution as technical achievement. It was not perhaps
accidental that the extension of this usage coincided with the proliferation
of sundry innovations affecting everyday life. By the 1950s this multiplicity
of industrial revolutions was moving out of learned works into more
popular media. There was much talk of a second industrial revolution going
on or just about to happen – usually from authors unlikely to have heard of
the alleged existence of several already. Various writers on science and
industry presented it as a creature of factory automation, opened up by the
development of electronic devices. It was to be a portent of social change for
the better – an ironic contrast to the old catastrophic vision. Technology and
its history was very much in the air, as witness the publication in 1954-58 of
the massive five-volume Oxford *History of Technology*. It was a hopeful boom-
world, after the constraints of the war and its immediate aftermath, and in
that world the temples of technology seemed to be rising all round. The
Industrial Revolution, in its guise of heroic technical achievement, was now
being presented as a great historical curtain-raiser, the 'take-off' to sustained
economic growth to be followed by the 'drive to maturity' and the age of
'high mass consumption'. The very wording of this metaphor, invented and
popularized by Rostow in his *Stages of Economic Growth*, nicely reflected the
current technological and economic optimism.

Politicians took up the theme and in the 1960s the 'white heat' of yet
another technologically-based industrial revolution was being promised in
Britain, even by Left-wing enthusiasts who seemed to have entirely mislaid

---

[119] *The Economic Development of France and Germany, 1815-1914* (Cambridge, 1921; 4th edn.
1945), p. 53.
[120] J.A. Schumpeter, *Capitalism, Socialism and Democracy* (1943; 4th p/b. edn., 1966) pp. 67-68.
[121] See my 'Industrial Growth and Industrial Revolutions', below, pp. 43-65.

their copies not just of Engels but perhaps of the Hammonds too. By this time the term was really entering into common parlance. Knowing men, in buses or in bars, talked confidently about the Industrial Revolution, less as catastrophe and more as achievement. If its precise meaning was becoming more and more obscure, cloaked in a comfortable fog of vagueness, that, after all, was the normal fate of any truly worthwhile historical myth.

What, however, was finally to establish it in the great mythic pantheon of British history was not any new industrial revolution but rather the shrink- age or collapse of just those industries upon which the original Industrial Revolution had been founded. This had the effect of ensuring that, perhaps for the first time in history, an economic and technical phenomenon was wrapped around with nostalgia, its monuments preserved as relics of a glorious past. It was not, of course, the personal nostalgia of long ago and far away, of half-remembered things and events, but the collective, orga- nized, commercialized nostalgia for the imagined past, for a history of sorts preserved in museums, old houses and national monuments.

The gigantic boom in mass tourism, under way since the 1950s, nourished by rising incomes, paid holidays, increased air travel and the ubiquitous motor car, had already ensured that in Britain visitors and natives alike were spending millions of tourist-hours peering bemusedly at the past. By the '70s, as the country's decline in manufacturing competitiveness accelerated so hundreds of old industrial plants came to a stop. The one-time glory of Lancashire's cotton industry finally departed; textile mills closed by the dozen. In iron and steel, blast furnaces fell derelict and rolling mills were abandoned. Ancient shipyards and engineering works, venerable docks and rural railways: all and more went the same way. Nostalgia took them, or at any rate some of them, into her welcoming arms. The relics of Britain's industrial past were transformed into tourist shrines. Thus did *the* Indus- trial Revolution and its heroic achievements enter Valhalla. Pioneered by the British but acquiring a name from the vocabulary of European political Romanticism, it secured immortality, appropriate or inappropriate, at last. Attended at its obsequies by cohorts of steam-railway buffs, canal restorers, cotton-mill conservers, industrial archaeologists and tourists galore, it suf- fered the ultimate humiliating takeover: it passed into the hands of the heritage business.[122]

In the 1970s some two hundred industrial sites of Britain's former glory were being restored. Laudatory testimonials rang out from celebrants: 'the Industrial Revolution was Great Britain's greatest single contribution to world civilization. The monument to its early stages are as unique to Great Britain as those of classical antiquity to Greece or the Renaissance to the

---

[122] See Robert Hewison, *The Heritage Industry* (1987), especially chap.4.

cities of northern Italy'.[123] Long-obsolete machinery has been lovingly restored and put to work in museums. By the mid-80s no less than 464 museums, many of them founded only since 1970, possessed collections of industrial material.[124] For enthusiasts, industrial archaeology sprouted as a new subject with academic pretensions. For the tourist, the heritage purveyors and the press offered the appropriate guidance. 'Save Britain's Heritage' and take the 'Pennine Mill Trail' to see where 'Yorkshire and Lancashire were transformed by the Industrial Revolution'.[125] Travel the towns of Lancashire and see that 'everywhere in the area is evidence of its past glory as the birthplace of the Industrial Revolution'. Tramp the Calder Valley on foot 'to explore . . . one of the cradles of the Industrial Revolution'.[126] Even those steam enthusiasts who operate ancient locomotives in their spare time attribute their passion to the same old cause: 'I think it's because the British were at the forefront of the Industrial Revolution that we have a fascination for machinery'.[127] And so on. As Robert Hewison observed, 'the heritage industry has become a vital part of the economic underpinning of the country'.[128] It creates jobs; it encourages tourists. And in the process of all this, the Industrial Revolution, complete with much dubious history, has at last become a myth to be venerated; a new tradition has been invented.[129]

Engels and Toynbee may well be turning in their graves. What has happened to the vision of social catastrophe? The saga of achievement has not totally displaced it, but it has shrunk with the shrinkage of the old-style Labour party and the near-disappearance, in Britain at least, of old-style Marxism. It survives as an evocation more of muted disapproval than of catastrophe. Kenneth Harris's observation in his biography of C.R. Attlee, published in the 1980s, sounds the characteristic note: 'The Industrial Revolution . . . had released forces of greed, cruelty and selfishness which had rendered society ugly in aspect and materialistic in outlook'.[130] Carlyle, Ruskin and Morris – the prime influences on Attlee himself – lie readily detectable behind the judgment. But by this time, as de-industrialization

---

[123] B. Trinder, 'Industrial Conservation and Industrial History', *History Workshop*, 2 (1976), p. 172.

[124] Hewison, *Heritage Industry*, p. 91.

[125] SAVE, *Pennine Mill Trail* (n.d.).

[126] For these examples of media exhortation, see the *Independent*, 13 July, 5 September and 22 October 1988 and the *National Trust Magazine*, Summer 1991, advertisement by the Wrekin Council. The brochure of the Ironbridge Gorge Museum in Coalbrookdale explicitly states that it is 'The Birthplace of the Industrial Revolution'.

[127] *The Times*, 18 March 1991, in a feature on 'The Bluebell Line', appealing for £1m. from 'lovers of steam'.

[128] Hewison, *Heritage Industry*, p. 102.

[129] To join those set out in E.J. Hobsbawm and T. Ranger (eds.), *The Invention of Tradition* (Cambridge, 1984).

[130] Kenneth Harris, *Attlee*, (1982; p/b edn., 1984). p. 23.

proceeded, popular sentiment had for the most part plumped instead for the nostalgia of past technological glory. Both the process and the sentiment were assisted by political and economic policy and supported by a version of history much publicized by ideologues of the radical Right.

When the 'condition-of-England' question had surfaced and resurfaced in the nineteenth century the issue on both occasions was essentially the paradox of poverty amidst wealth. The fact of wealth was not in contention; the concern was for its distribution. In the new version of the 1970s and '80s however, the paradox was reversed: much redistribution had been carried out but the wealth which had facilitated it was seen to be slipping away as the industrial base decayed. The policy response, sanctioned by the return to power at three successive elections of the Thatcher governments, has been unique in British history in seeking to promote wealth creation by a return to what are today *believed* to have been the attitudes and beliefs attendant upon the Industrial Revolution.

The version of intellectual history pressed into service runs, in a simplified (though publicized) form, on these lines: John Locke's individualism plus Adam Smith's free-enterprise economics had as their fruits the Industrial Revolution and the political revolutions which brought democracy to Britain, France and America; thereby was liberal capitalism established. From this it is said to follow that because the British economy enjoyed its finest hour in the nineteenth century, as a consequence of that Industrial Revolution, therefore the values of the time and especially its entrepreneurship should be re-born and cherished. The name of Adam Smith has been frequently invoked by influential bodies concerned to promote the maximum of competition and the minimum of government intervention; an 'enterprise culture' has been lauded and contrasted with a 'dependency culture', alleged to have sapped entrepreneurial vitality.[131]

In thus enlisting Smith to a cause, some central elements of his body of thought have been ignored or side-tracked. His concept of natural justice and his ideas upon ethics as set out in his *Theory of Moral Sentiments* have virtually disappeared under the swell of admiration for the invisible hand and the benefits of the market as set out in the *Wealth of Nations*. Little heed is paid to his frequently expressed hostility to businessmen, not simply to their 'impertinent jealousy' and their 'sneaking arts' but to his views of their inappropriateness to influence political affairs: 'the mean rapacity, the monopolizing spirit of merchants and manufacturers, who neither are nor ought to be, the rulers of mankind'.[132] This last expression of Smith's disapprobation presumably weighed little in the collective Cabinet mind as,

---

[131] An excellent survey of such pronouncements will be found in James Raven, 'British History and the Enterprise Culture', *Past and Present*, 123, (1989), pp. 178-204.

[132] On these and other observations by Smith on this topic, see my 'Adam Smith, Businessmen and the Mercantile System', below pp. 153-63.

in the 1980s, businessmen were appointed to sundry positions of power, be they running departments of state or funding universities. Although much is heard of Smith's approbation of other matters little is heard of his scepticism, his moderation, his qualifications upon the role of the market or his concern with the 'science of a statesman or legislator'.[133]

That this should be so is not inherently surprising. Sustaining myths and finding historical support for political programmes have in common a distaste for the tiresome qualifications and subtleties of scholarship. The history of political and economic ideas has, indeed, not been the only area of intellectual enquiry that has seen some vulgarized variants put to the service of political programmes. The decline of the British economy has stimulated a variety of publications – some scholarly, some very far from it. Both categories have included accounts in which the Industrial Revolution has figured as a high point, the subsequent decline from which has been attributed to a wide variety of cultural-cum-economic causes. All sorts of candidates, from imaginable runners to improbable outsiders, have been marshalled to the starting gate: the public schools, the Christian religion, the civil service, Marxism, socialism, liberalism, the Empire, the welfare state, the class system, the 'decline of the industrial spirit', the English vision of rural bliss, too much overseas investment, too little scientific management, not to speak of over-mighty trade unions and too many cloistered academics in too many universities nurturing anti-industrial attitudes. Some cases have been carefully argued, with respectable if not always convincing, supporting evidence. One such, Martin J. Wiener's *English Culture and the Decline of the Industrial Spirit, 1850-1980*, has become a cult-book appealing at once to the doctrinaire Right and the anti-capitalist Left. Others have simply asserted, with little argument and less evidence. The latter category has included some attacks on universities and historians penned by journalists with a combination of malevolence and ignorance.[134] Some, on the other hand, have come from those who should have known better.

Whatever the source, bold and simple colours have been used to advocate free-market policies as supposedly adumbrated by Adam Smith and ushered in with the Industrial Revolution. Any suggested modification or restraint upon such policies has been attacked as subversive. Ministerial authority has blessed such enterprises in appropriate ways. A new edition in

---

[133] For some newspaper expressions on the debate, cf. *Independent*, 29 June 1990 and the article (by Donald Winch) in *Guardian*, 16 July 1990, both in celebration of the bi-centenary of Smith's death.

[134] Two examples. For spite, it would be hard to beat Paul Johnson, *Daily Telegraph*, 7 January 1987 in which it was announced that 'the spirit at our universities is one of whining mendicancy and malevolent parasitism', (quoted Raven in *Past and Present*, 123, p. 202). And, for ignorance and arrogance from a distinguished source, see the articles by William (Lord) Rees Mogg in the *Independent* 19 and 26 February 1990, together with the accompanying correspondence in the issues of 22 February, 1 and 5 March.

1986 of Samuel Smiles' *Self Help*, complete with the imprimatur of an introduction by Sir Keith (now Lord) Joseph, then Secretary of State for Education and Science, sanctified 'Victorian values'. Readers were told that 'of all economic histories ever written, it is Smiles' *Self Help* that most explicitly and vividly portrays, celebrates and – above all *understands* – the entrepreneur'.[135] One cannot but wonder how many of 'all the economic histories ever written', Sir Keith had in fact read. Historians not normally associated with enquiries into Britain's economic past testified to the value of free enterprise in bringing about the Industrial Revolution. In 1978, for example, Hugh Thomas (now Lord Thomas) provided just such an offering. It was duly published complete with a foreword by Margaret Thatcher in which she deplored that 'the blackest picture of precisely those periods of our history when the greatest progress was achieved . . . and when Britain was furthest in advance of other nations' had been drawn by 'our Socialist academics'.[136] The new entrepreneurial version of the great Industrial Revolution myth was thus consecrated by the leader of the Conservative Party, shortly before her election as Prime Minister. The trophy had been captured by the radicals of the Right; the trade unionists had lost a banner; Toynbeean liberals and democrats had been pushed out into a wet wilderness; and the Marxists had been alienated (a process seemingly completed by later events in eastern Europe and Russia).

What meanwhile have economic historians been doing about that one item of the British economic past which the public has taken to heart? Here there is a rich irony. For just when popular culture and political rhapsody have been combining to celebrate the Industrial Revolution as a symbol of national historical glory, by contrast the latest fashion amongst the professionals has been so to cut the Industrial Revolution down to size as almost to make it disappear. Disapproval of the term has long been familiar in learned debate, evident of course more among 'optimists' than 'pessimists'. Reservations are regularly aired in articles or in the introductory pages of textbooks. Various justifications have been offered for abandoning the term as inappropriate or confusing. It has even been suggested that the Industrial Revolution is a myth in the vulgar usage of that word, that is that it simply did not exist.[137] Limited definitions are periodically provided and

[135] Samuel Smiles, *Self-Help* (1859; ed. with introduction by Sir Keith Joseph, Harmondsworth, 1986), p. 16.

[136] Margaret Thatcher, foreword to Hugh Thomas, *History, Capitalism and Freedom* (1978). This pamphlet originated as a lecture given under the auspices of the Centre for Policy Studies at the Conservative Party conference in 1978.

[137] The contention that it simply did not happen can be found in M. Fores, 'The Myth of a British Industrial Revolution', *History*, 66 (1981), pp. 181-98; and a stout rebuttal in A.E. Musson, 'The British Industrial Revolution', *History*, 67 (1982), pp. 252-58. For a recent view of its capacity to mislead, see Rondo Cameron, 'A New View of European Industrialization',

revised. It remains in the professional vocabulary if only for the practical reason that Ashton gave, viz. that it had been used 'by a long line of historians and had become so firmly embedded in common speech that it would be pedantic to offer a substitute'.[138]

In common speech, yes; but in specialist speech, no. The most recent trend in interpretation has virtually deprived the term of meaning. According to David Cannnadine this interpretation – which he calls the 'limits to growth' phase – was the fourth in a series starting with Toynbee's 'social consequences' interpretation. He sees them as paradigms related to changing perceptions of the present.[139] Maybe, though the conjuring trick of making the Industrial Revolution nearly disappear seems to have been less of a reflection of the present economic conjuncture than the result of work by econometrically-minded historians using the familiar statistical tool of the growth rate. Half a century ago it was fashionable to write about the shape of industrial growth curves and their long-term steadiness was noted. In 1951, for example, Simon Kuznets observed of W.G. Hoffman's index of British industrial production that 'the Industrial Revolution does not appear as a truly revolutionary upheaval'.[140]

Today the current interpretation, using more sophisticated methods and improved estimates, has effectively reduced the experience of the Industrial Revolution years to an assemblage of decadal growth rates, sectoral and aggregate, covering such variables as real output in industry, commerce and agriculture, gross national product, capital formation, productivity, value added, population change, and more besides.[141] A prime result has been to squash the revolution into evolution; its origins are to be found earlier, its effects evident only later. It has been 'almost written out of modern British history'.[142] If the evidence, largely in the form of contemporary statistics or ingenious modern reconstructions, is approximately correct – and not

Economic History Review 2nd. ser, xxxviii (1985), pp. 1-23. A rather different sort of attack on the concept, particularly on the catastrophic version, can be found in J.C.D. Clark, *English Society, 1688-1832* (Cambridge, 1985), pp. 64-93 and in his *Revolution and Rebellion* (Cmbridge, 1986), pp. 37-39 wherein it is suggested that it should be added to the 'list of spurious revolutions' (p. 38).

[138] T.S. Ashton, *The Industrial Revolution* (Oxford, 1948), p. 2.

[139] Cannadine in *Past and Present*, 103, p. 170.

[140] Below, p. 54, n. 25.

[141] N.R. Crafts, *British Economic Growth during the Industrial Revolution* (Oxford, 1985) offers the clearest embodiment of this approach. See also R. Floud and D. McCloskey (eds.), *The Economic History of Britain since 1700* (2 vols., Cambridge, 1971), especially vol. I; and C.H. Lee, *The British Economy since 1700* (Cambridge, 1986).

[142] David Cannadine, 'British History: Past, Present – and Future', *Past and Present*, 116 (1987), p. 183. It should perhaps also be noted at this point that some economic historians have written it out by a different technique, viz. by constructing meta-histories of world economic development from prehistoric times onwards. This ensures that the actions and reactions of men and women in *any* one country in *any* relatively brief period of history are so dwarfed as to be imperceptible.

everybody believes that it is[143] – then it would seem that before 1830 economic growth was slow, with neither output not incomes per head showing much increase; and notable change, economic and technical, was severely limited. Only after the mid century did the economy show much significant difference and even then it was more a matter of structural change, from agriculture towards industry, than the attainment of higher productivity. In short, continuity has been stressed and the discontinuity implied by the idea of a revolution downgraded or even dismissed.

The contrast between these econometric findings and those of the romantic versions, be they catastrophic or entrepreneurial, could hardly be greater. In the one, just a little happened. In the other, individual endeavour was crowned by transformation, wonders proliferated, suffering and exploitation were endured, the Age of Machinery ground all before it, multiplying wealth and poverty alike. In the one, virtually the only contemporary evidence used is that which can be made to yield statistics. In the other, mighty volumes of committee reports and evidence, literary outpourings, travellers' commentaries, moralists' reflections and political thunderings are all pressed into service. The latter sort of evidence is deemed as biased – as it undoubtedly is; the former sort of evidence is seen as embodying logic and, via the precision of numbers, attaining a closer approximation to economic reality – which may or may not be true. A musical analogy may help to illuminate the contrast. Wagner's *Ring* cycle can be seen as enshrining the romantic, revolutionary myth. (The *Ring* itself has of course been variously interpreted as myth; and it is no coincidence that in one well-known production, symbols of the Industrial Revolution have figured on stage, with Wotan cast as a Victorian entrepreneur.) Conversely, the current enthusiasm for mathematically constructed musical minimalism provides an evident parallel to the econometric version of history – both providing repetitive sequences with minimal marginal variations.

'Historians of all persuasions', it has been observed by Joel Mokyr, have come to the conclusion 'that the Industrial Revolution in Britain constituted a new point of departure in human history, an event of such moment to daily life that it compares to the advent of monotheism or the development of language'; and, more recently, in a work on the history of technology, he has called 1750-1830 'The Years of Miracles'.[144] Such labelling well fits the romantic vision but it is certainly *not* how it appears in recent influential studies. Historians tackling any 'new point of departure in human history' might reasonably be expected to take heed of contemporary reactions. In practice, however, the perceptions of those experiencing that new

---

[143] Julian Hoppit, 'Counting the Industrial Revolution', *Econ. Hist. Rev.* 2nd. ser. xliii (1990), pp. 173-93.

[144] J. Mokyr (ed.), *The Economics of the Industrial Revolution* (1985), p. 1; and his *The Lever of Riches* (New York, 1990), p. 81.

departure in human history, whether they rejoiced in it or loathed it, are almost totally ignored by our quantitative minimalists. The bibliographies they provide for the guidance of students are largely devoid of contemporary writings. To deplore this is not in the least to imply that such quantitative analysis is either unimportant or irrelevant. Within the limits imposed by the reliability of its sources, it advances our knowledge of the nature and extent of economic change. But its calculations, necessarily made from the retrospective vantage point of today, tell us nothing, nor indeed do they seek to tell us anything, of either the motives or the responses of those participating in or affected by that change. Views of the past consisting simply of measurable economic movements or of judgments based upon assumptions of rational self-interest bear only a partial resemblance to history. Yet to salute them as saviours come to demonstrate the falsity of a Marxist myth is as misleading as to hail them as scientific truths hitherto hidden from those blinkered by old-fashioned techniques of enquiry.[145]

What contemporaries thought themselves to be doing or believed they were witnessing, feeling, enjoying or suffering is surely an essential component of any sort of history. And it is doubly so when the object of historical study is something which has acquired the quality of myth. Subsequent actions and convictions rest upon the potency of that myth. The entrepreneurial vision of the Industrial Revolution is as much a half-truth as the catastrophic. Both, however, are reflections of the past which elude those who confine their attention to the measureable but which continue to dazzle the impressionable. Like the romantic vision of Irish history wrapped in a cloudy Gaelic mist or an American past cocooned in the hazy history of the Frontier or the Founding Fathers, the Industrial Revolution now looms in English history as a potent myth. Historians must therefore take due cognizance of it. The anthropologist's advice of Malinowski is once again pertinent:

> The historical consideration of myth . . . shows that myth, taken as a whole, cannot be sober, dispassionate history, since it is always made *ad hoc* to fulfill a certain sociological function, to glorify a certain group, or to justify an anomalous status.[146]

The fulfilment of sociological function, the glorification of a group, the justification of an anomalous status: these have been seen and noted. But what of 'sober dispassionate history'? The writing of this is the role of the professional. How does he (or she) go about it? What is the moral of this tale for the historian whose topic, in this case the Industrial Revolution, has been swept up into the mythic category? Is there any scope for demythologizing?

---

[145] The former salutation will be found in Clark, *Revolution and Rebellion*, p. 39; the latter greeting has long been favoured by the more dogmatic cliometricians.

[146] *Magic, Science and Religion*, p.125.

Truth is what historians seek; myth is what societies need. The duality can be stated simply but requires elaboration. No professional historian of today – be he or she political, economic, social or of whatever variety – would suppose that there is some objective truth out there in the past, waiting to be secured from the documents and given to the waiting present. Certainly we interpret the past in our own image; even the barest of chronicles can hardly avoid that. Nevertheless, the nature and extent of that subjectivity varies greatly, as it should. To be recognized today as professional it must be contained within the bounds of an accepted scholarly discipline controlling accuracy and consistency, the critical use of records and the presentation of results. If it is not so contained then it is no different from fiction, from historical novels or from those 'drama-documentaries' beloved of television producers. It is indeed from such providers that have emanated in recent times powerful reinforcements for those myths needed by literate societies as by their pre-literate forerunners.

Oral tradition, so long the channel through which flowed tales of golden ages, legendary creatures, wonder-working gods or even, more prosaically, of bad employers and heroic inventors has been supplemented or replaced by sundry sorts of fictional history, romantic fantasies and nostalgic arte-facts. They combine to offer a past more satisfying and accessible than that provided by the professionals, thereby shoring up specific myths.[147] Governments have long demonstrated their awareness of the social potency of what they regard as the right sort of past by including historical myths in their arsenals of coercion and control. Theocracies have burned books and people alike in the name of religious myths; secular tyrannies, of more than one political hue, have at best deprived people of various freedoms and at worst exterminated whole groups in the name of myths of colour, race or class. States mercifully free from such odious habits have been content gently to burnish suitable historical myths, blessing and encouraging them as part of the country's cultural inheritance and as part-time aids to their own retention of power. In Britain today a rosily entrepreneurial version of the Industrial Revolution as myth, sanitized for tourists and theme parks,[148] is being dutifully burnished and helped on its way just as in the past the catastrophic version was officially sanctified as an aid to the justification of a different set of social and economic policies.

In these circumstances, what lines should historians follow? Obviously,

---

[147] Lowenthal, *The Past is a Foreign Country*, especially pp. 224-50. Note his comment on the small screen: 'the adaptation of history to television exacerbates tendencies to accept versions of the past as gospel' (p. 230).

[148] Here is an example of the procedure apropos the former Quarry Bank textile mill. The Apprentice House there is 'reinstated as a visitor attraction of historical significance and value . . . visitors are guided around the house by costumed staff who bring to life the working and living routines of the mill children in the Industrial Revolution' (*National Trust Magazine*, Spring 1989, p. 41).

truth should be pursued along whatever paths seem appropriate to the researcher. Obviously, the pretentious should be debunked or absurdities exposed, no doubt generating the while the same sort of indignation as that which recently greeted scholars who deflated the great Spanish Armada myth. To 'Disgusted, Plymouth Hoe' may well be added 'Outraged, Coalbrookdale'. Beyond such evidently desirable procedures, however, there looms the far more important goal of incorporating contemporary perceptions into the framework of retrospective analysis. Contemporaries necessarily knew only the partial truths of their own limited vision, filtered and distorted through the glass of irrationality and prejudice, ignorance and conviction. An understanding of the economics of the Industrial Revolution needs to be complemented by an understanding of the political and social structure in which it took place or the variant brands of Christianity which inspired so much of the contemporary response.

The mythological status which it has acquired may perhaps be eroded over a long period but is unlikely to be removed by professional sapping in the foreseeable future. Because it is now enjoying a new incarnation as a symbol for entrepreneurial enthusiasm, it is especially necessary that the historian should seek to present it in the round if only to rescue it from the hands of the nostalgia-merchants and the tub-thumpers. The serious historian of the Industrial Revolution is indeed in a difficult but challenging position. A *trahison des clercs* would be disgraceful; a return to the romantic version of social catastrophe is clearly untenable; and a continued devotion to econometric minimalism, however seductive to the cognoscenti, looks like a pathway to neglect by the laity. Even though contemporaries did not use the term 'Industrial Revolution' many saw themselves as passing through a profoundly strange and, in some senses, traumatic experience, wonderful to some, appalling to others. So let it be seen warts and all: successes and failures, the howls of indignation and the cheers of approval. Continuity and change need to be variously balanced: speed and intensity in the celebrated regions of concentrated impact and impressions both faint and slow in the by-passed areas. The fame of triumphant innovators must not obscure the numerous failures of those who lost in the race, any more than should the measurable be accorded supremacy over the immeasurable or the records of brutality conceal those of enlightenment.

Such desiderata probably imply an end to the Industrial Revolution being the peculiar preserve of the economic historian. However well-equipped for the technical analysis of such phenomena, his preoccupations seem increasingly remote from the task of placing them in the context of contemporary consciousness or of assessing their role in national history. However unfashionably insular it may seem, there is a need for the Industrial Revolution to be placed in the continuum of British history. Most authorities on it do little more than glance at the world of Tudor and Stuart England. The country's economic and social history has been chopped up, for examination purposes, into what are thought to be manageable teaching chunks; as a result students rarely study such periods as, say, 1600-1950 or 1450-1850. Because of the extreme specialization of historical studies, both chronologically and by subject-matter, and because of the Whiggishness of economic history, the Industrial Revolution is commonly treated as a necessary gateway to the future, as a launching pad to the industrialized world of today. Removed from its immediate historical context, analysed as a specimen of measurable economic development or slotted into a spectrum of global change since Neolithic times, it loses the human dimensions without which our reconstructions of the past become arid and unappealing. Too much of the currently modish treatments are limited in range and ahistorical in approach, the price unfortunately of the real gains in analysis which have been made.

The concept of the Industrial Revolution is ultimately a metaphor for a complexity not otherwise describable. The metaphor has become myth – emotive, politically useful, detachable from reality. Spawned by Romanticism and its meaning variously distorted, it will not readily be demythologized. Whatever its position in a wider analysis of economic growth, the British Industrial Revolution cannot but remain a central topic in the country's history. Unless, however, it is addressed by historians in more comprehensive terms than are currently fashionable, then that gap between the truth which the historian seeks and the myth which societies need will not be narrowed and may even widen.

2

Industrial Growth and Industrial Revolutions[*]

The idea of the Industrial Revolution is one of the few items in the private language of economic historians which has passed into common parlance.[1] By now *the* Industrial Revolution has surely earned its right, along with ancient Greeks and early economists, to be called 'classical'. But as Sir

[*] This essay was a by-product of research into the economic history of the British paper industry which I started in the early 1950s. As a topic of study it had the advantage of being open to some quantitative investigation from the sixteenth to the nineteenth centuries: trade statistics were available from the sixteenth century and excise duties, on the basis of which production estimates could be calculated, from the beginning of the eighteenth. It was therefore possible, unusually, to investigate the growth of an industry before, during and after the Industrial Revolution. To traverse periods of history which are conventionally treated in separate compartments seems in itself a desirable goal. The immediate occasion of the essay, however, was mounting disbelief in what seemed to me to be a current over-abundance of 'industrial revolutions' detected by various historians.

One of these alleged revolutions – that invented by J.U. Nef and located in the period 1540-1640 – supposedly involved Tudor and Stuart paper mills. On the criteria apparently being adopted by Nef and other discoverers of industrial revolutions, papermaking (and, indeed, other industries) could be presented as having undergone two or three such revolutions at various dates in history. Such a profusion of 'revolutions' seemed more than usually muddling.

Processing production data and presenting them as growth curves over long periods, from 1710 to 1950, provided an opportunity to develop definitions which I hoped might clarify some of the confusions surrounding the too enthusiastic use of the term. Today it seems rather less fashionable to discover numerous industrial revolutions though 'the Second Industrial Revolution' *c.* 1850-1914, has its adherents. The growth curves also demonstrated their own inadequacy if attempts were made to use them as 'pieces of economic history'. An industrial revolution or even the Industrial Revolution could be made almost to disappear. In comparison with more sophisticated modern usages of similar statistics, these curves may well seem crude, not to say jejeune. But the message may still have some relevance as the Industrial Revolution continues to be ground down into a compound of growth rates.

Studies of the history of the paper industry which have appeared since this essay was originally published include my own *The British Paper Industry 1495-1860* (Oxford 1958); A.H. Shorter, *Paper Making in the British Isles* (Newton Abbot, 1971); and A.G. Thomson, *The Paper Industry in Scotland, 1590-1861*, (Edinburgh, 1974). Amongst numerous books on the Industrial Revolution, and in addition to those mentioned above, Maxine Berg, *The Machinery Question and the Making of Political Economy, 1815-1848* (Cambridge, 1980) and E.A. Wrigley, *Continuity and Change: The Character of the Industrial Revolution in England* (Cambridge, 1988) examine significant aspects of the concept.

[1] True in 1956 when this was written and even more so now – see above, Chap. 1.

George Clark pointed out some years ago,[2] other industrial revolutions are amongst us. In the writings of economic historians, revolutions abound. Leaving aside more than one commercial and agrarian 'revolution', the student of our subject is confronted with a succession of industrial revolutions. The late Bronze Age, the thirteenth century, the fifteenth century, the century from 1540 to 1640, the later seventeenth century and, passing over the classical industrial revolution, the late nineteenth and the early twentieth centuries – in all these periods it seems there may be observed industrial revolutions in the economic development of England alone. Other countries have their claimants, for example, Germany and Japan in the late nineteenth century.[3] At the present time, the possibilities of 'automatic factories' opened up by the development of electronic devices and their use in industrial control, has stimulated talk of an imminent 'second industrial revolution'.[4] This is largely an offspring of the writings of engineers, mathematicians and others normally unacquainted with the works of economic historians. Were they familiar with these they would find, for example, in the writings of the late Professor Schumpeter, that the notion of a 'second industrial revolution' had long made its appearance. This variety of uses of the term 'industrial revolution' can scarcely fail to be confusing. May it not be that the term has achieved its wide application at the expense of losing its true significance?

In the writing of economic history, three main forms of economic or technical 'revolutions' may be noted:

1. The application to a particular industry. This frequently occurs in accounts of the growth of individual industries during the classical industrial revolution and is normally used to describe the introduction of a particular machine or technique which the writer regards as 'revolutionising' the productive process in question and carrying with it comparably striking consequences, irrespective of what may or may not be happening in unrelated industries. Professor Carus-Wilson's 'Industrial Revolution' of the thirteenth century,[5] resting as it does on the mechanisation of the process of fulling, comes within this category.

2. One stage more extensive than this use is the application of the term to

---

[2]   *The Idea of the Industrial Revolution*, David Murray Foundation Lecture, University of Glasgow (October 1952). Glasgow University Publication xcv, 1953.

[3]   Reference to the sources for most of these will be found in Clark, op. cit., pp. 12-13. J.A. Schumpeter, *Business Cycles*, (2 vols., New York, 1939), contains various references to industrial revolutions in the late nineteenth and early twentieth centuries, e.g. pp. 397 and 753.

[4]   See: Norbert Wiener, *Cybernetics* (New York, 1949), and *The Human Use of Human Beings*, (1950); 'Towards the Automatic Factory', in *Planning* (P.E.P.), xxi, 30, June 1955; also corresponence in *The Times*, 8 and 11 November, 1954; articles (by R.H. Macmillan) in the *Listener*, 24 and 31 March, 7 April, 1955; *Manchester Guardian*, 17 June, 1955, etc.

[5]   E.M. Carus-Wilson, 'An Industrial Revolution of the Thirteenth Century', in *Econ. Hist. Rev.*, xi, 1941; also reprinted in *Essays in Economic History* (ed. E.M. Carus-Wilson) (1954), and in E.M. Carus-Wilson, *Medieval Merchant Venturers*, (1954).

particular branches of the economic activities of a society – industrial, commercial, agrarian and so forth. Thus the term 'industrial revolution' here means something which happens to industry as a whole, though not necessarily to other branches of the economy. It is implied in the *O.E.D.* definition: 'the rapid development *in industry* owing to the employment of machinery, which took place in England in the late eighteenth and early nineteenth centuries'.[6] (My italics).

3. The widest application is that to a national economy. Here the emphasis is not simply on the effect felt by an industry or by industry as a whole, but upon the consequences to the economy of a variety of changes in the sense that it moves rapidly into some new shape, normally that of the modern industrialized society. The classical English industrial revolution, as usually interpreted nowadays, is the prime example of this but the usage is increasingly extended to cover the same process experienced subsequently by other countries such as the U.S.A., Germany and Japan.

Variations have been played on these themes. One such variation is the building up of (3) out of material used for (2). Professor Nef's 'industrial revolution'[7] of the hundred years from 1540 to 1640 falls within this category. To some extent this implies an equating of the terms 'industrial revolution' and 'industrialisation'.

The appearance in the subject of so many and such a variety of industrial revolutions raises the question of their identification. How are they to be recognised? Are they all of the same nature? The increasing use of quantitative methods in economic history presents us with industrial revolutions in statistical clothes. Is the concept something which can be measured, or at any rate detected, in appropriate statistical series? What is the relation of the concept, as used and developed by historians, to the studies by economists or statisticians of long-period industrial growth?

The aims of this essay are as follows: to examine some of the implications of the use, by certain economic historians, of the term 'industrial revolution'; to relate these implications to the use of industrial growth curves; to examine the claim that the automatic factory is precipitating a second 'industrial revolution'; and finally in an attempt to give some recognisable meaning to the term 'industrial revolution', to suggest certain very rough criteria for the continued employment of this overburdened phrase. In order to illustrate some of the problems involved in the relation between growth curves and industrial revolutions, it is proposed to examine one industry in some detail and to suggest the possible applicability of the argument to other fields.

The one industry which it is proposed to examine in some detail is the

[6] Quoted Clark, op. cit., p. 11.
[7] J.U. Nef: *The Rise of the British Coal Industry*, (1932) i p. 165; 'The Progress of Technology and the Growth of Large-scale Industry in Great Britain, 1540-1640', in *Econ. Hist. Rev.* v, 1934 (reprinted in *Essays in Economic History*); and *War and Human Progress* (Cambridge, MA, 1950).

English paper industry. A number of reasons combine to make this suitable for the purpose. It has a long history, spanning several centuries; it is an industry which peculiarly mirrors the growth of our industrial civilisation, for its products find their way into extremely diverse and characteristic uses. Furthermore, it is especially useful for the purpose of examining the 'industrial revolution' in one industry and seeing it in quantitative terms, for it is possible to construct tolerably reliable series to cover the period from the early eighteenth century to the present day. And finally, its technical and economic history follows a course similar to that of other and better known industries.

Before examining the quantitative evidence of industrial growth which it offers, it is necessary to make a brief digression into some of the details of its technical and economic development.[8]

The techniques of paper making can be readily divided into a number of processes, just as can, for example, the techniques of the cloth industry. The history of technical progress in the latter is a history of mechanization stretching from the twelfth century (or earlier) to the early nineteenth century, in the approximate order: fulling, spinning, weaving, carding and combing, finishing, together with such comparatively early applications of industrial chemistry as the use of chlorine in bleaching, improvements in dyeing and the like. In paper making, technical progress followed a very similar course over roughly the same period of time. The main processes in the order in which they were affected (which is also the order in which they take place) are: raw material preparation, bleaching, forming the paper, drying and finishing. This includes the same early application of chemistry to industry in the shape of chlorine for bleaching. In addition, there followed a further crucial innovation in the industry, providing a new raw material – the discovery of wood pulp.

Before the later nineteenth century, the major raw materials for paper making were linen, and to a lesser extent cotton, rags.[9] The pulping of the raw materials, which is the essential element in the first process, was originally carried out by hand, the rags being mixed with water and pounded. At what stage and where this process received its first mechanization, is not precisely known. The industry is said to have reached southern Europe by the eleventh and twelfth centuries, having come from China via

---

[8] For a note of the main secondary sources drawn upon in this section, see my article in *Economica*, February 1954, pp. 32-33 n.

[9] The essential chemical constituent of paper, be it made by hand or by machine, from rags, old ropes, straw, esparto grass or wood pulp, is cellulose, the main component of plant tissues. The essence of its manufacture, by hand or by machine, is that the cellulose fibres should be macerated until each individual filament is a separate unit, then mixed with water in such a way that, by the use of sieve-like screens, the fibres can subsequently be lifted from the water in the form of a thin layer, the water draining off and leaving a sheet of matted fibres. This thin sheet is paper.

the Middle East. It is claimed that in mid twelfth century Spain a stamping mill, operated by water power, was at work macerating the rags in a series of large mortars. Such a mill was certainly in use at Nuremberg at the end of the fourteenth century, and thereafter various types of stamping mill, normally driven by water but sometimes by wind, formed the vital feature of the European paper mill until the eighteenth century. It then began to be replaced by an improved type of beating engine; this was at first driven by water power but later by steam. With many improvements and variations in detail, the preparation processes of washing, beating and pulping remain in principle the same today.[10]

The introduction of chlorine for rag bleaching need not detain us long. It came into use in the 1790s and was an obvious corollary to the similar results in the textile industry of Scheele's discovery.

Meanwhile, until the introduction of the paper-making machine in the first decade of the nineteenth century, the actual forming of the paper was everywhere a hand process. The parallel with the textile industry is striking. Just as water power was applied to fulling and much later to spinning, whilst weaving remained an entirely hand operation, so was power applied to rag preparation whilst the forming of a sheet was still done by hand. The linking of rag preparation to water power meant that paper mills were to be found on fast running streams just as were so many mills, similarly powered, in other industries. To the striking technical resemblance between the fulling mill and the stamping mill there is added the tendency to determine location; indeed, when the paper industry was expanding in England from the sixteenth to the eighteenth centuries and the cloth industry geographically contracting, many former fulling mills were turned into paper mills.

By the end of the eighteenth century, paper making was a widespread European industry, Italy, France, Germany, Holland and Great Britain all having many mills. Water power and steam power (though the latter in only a very few places) had been applied to the first process and chemistry had made its mark on bleaching. In the first decade of the nineteenth century the paper-making machine was introduced in the English industry. In the technical changes which it introduced, striking resemblances are again noticeable to the comparable changes in the textile industry in spinning and weaving: it was a straightforward mechanization of hand processes. In the hand process, the size of the sheet is normally limited to what can be conveniently manipulated by the paper maker; production is slow and labour highly skilled. The machine simply mechanized the whole procedure by forming the sheet on an endless wire gauze or mesh, thus allowing theoretically endless sheets of paper to be made. The modern machine is

---

[10] The making of wood pulp is, of course, an entirely different procedure, normally carried on in or near the forest areas.

exactly the same in general principle though, of course, with many improvements in detail and very much larger and faster.

Once the making had been mechanized, the mechanization of the drying and finishing processes followed rapidly. By the mid nineteenth century, mechanization was complete. The output of the United Kingdom had multiplied about seventeen times since the mid eighteenth century and the stage was set for the next crucial development.

During the 1850s and 1860s, the gales of the free trade movement had swept through the paper industry as elsewhere and removed both the excise duties and the customs duties on the import of foreign paper. By this time machinery had been extensively adopted in the paper industries of other countries and these industries were expanding rapidly, notably in the U.S.A., Germany and France. The resulting substantial increases in international production and trade in paper meant in turn extreme pressure on raw material supplies. Unsatisfactory and peculiarly inelastic supply conditions had for long been tending to make rags costly and many attempts to find substitutes had been made. Not until 1860 was any appreciable success achieved when the use of esparto grass for paper making was patented and put into commercial operation. Of far greater significance, however, were the numerous experiments in the use of wood pulp, carried on in this country and elsewhere, which culminated in the perfecting of the chemical processes of producing wood pulp in the 1880s. The modern paper industry is substantially based on wood pulp, and the advent of this as the major raw material meant a reorientation of the industry in many ways, although not causing any radical revisions in the machinery by which paper was actually made. It had substantial international repercussions in that it brought a new stimulus to the opening up of the great softwood forests of Scandinavia and Canada, in which countries integrated pulp and paper mills have been developed; at the same time the English industry became dependent for the bulk of its raw materials on imported substances. The new international angle to the industry brought new types of integration in which press magnates appeared as the owners at once of forests, paper mills, printing presses and newspapers. On the technical side it brought the industry within the ambit of the chemical industry – for although the paper-making machine is still basically the same, the pulp-making processes are different and, moreover, the technical questions of the industry are of a nature to which applied chemistry may be expected to produce the answers. It has been said that today paper mills are 'built by engineers and run by chemists'.[11]

The industry's technical history thus has three landmarks: three crucial innovations – a medieval mechanization of the preparatory processes akin to the mechanization of fulling; mechanization of the making process

---

[11] J. Grant, 'Pulp and Paper', in *What Industry Owes to Chemical Science* (3rd ed., 1945).

during the classical industrial revolution; and the introduction of a new raw material. This last development has brought the industry into the ambit of what has been described as a 'second industrial revolution' (before the present tying of that label on to the expected consequences of the automatic factory) or, indeed, the fifth if we follow Schumpeter's numbering and terminology.[12]

What light does this shed on the various industrial revolutions?

To take first those for which there are relevant statistical series: those covering the period including the classical industrial revolution exhibit a highly characteristic pattern. Fig 2.1 reveals just the picture of steeply rising output which we have come to associate with large numbers of individual industries, with population growth, overseas trade, imports of raw cotton and so forth, during this period of English economic history.[13]

It is, in short, a typical picture.[14] The machine brought a great increase in productivity and did away with the great dependence on skilled paper-making labour. Mills became bigger, new and larger mills sprang up in Lancashire, near the coalfields and the new towns of the north; those in the remoter counties began to disappear. Increasing production was, as usual, matched by a declining total number of mills.[15] The whole picture, in short, is one of the classical industrial revolution *in one industry*: the first of the uses to which, as suggested above, the term is sometimes put.

What of the 'second' or 'fifth' or 'twentieth century' industrial revolutions? How does paper fit into what Schumpeter called 'the Kondratieff of electricity, chemistry and motors'? Fig.2.2 exhibits the same picture for this period as did Fig.2.1 for the earlier period.[16]

Here, then, in purely quantitative terms there appears to be a repetition of the 'industrial revolution' process as applied to one industry. And, moreover, we know too that it was accompanied by the major reorientation of the industry already described, by the new dependence on imported raw

[12] Op. cit., i, 397.

[13] Details of the sources from which these and the following graphs were constructed will be found in the Appendix (below, pp. 63-65)

[14] The shape of the curve showing the imports of raw materials reflects, particularly after the 1840's, both the growing world demand for paper-making materials and the existence of the foreign duties or prohibitions on their export. The widening gap between it and the output curve from about 1790 is accounted for partly by increasing home supplies of rags, from greater home production and consumption of cotton and linen textiles, partly by higher productivity in paper manufacture, and partly by the fact that chlorine bleaching permitted the use of a much wider range of coloured rags.

[15] In 1785 licences issued to paper and pasteboard makers in England totalled 381; in 1816 the figure of 522 corresponded to a total of 502 units at work; the number of licences reached its peak, at 643, in 1829 and declined thereafter as machinery left its mark; by 1860 there were only 306 mills at work in England and Wales.

[16] Imports of paper-making materials comprised rags, esparto and wood pulp.

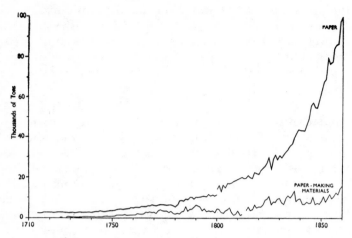

Fig. 2.1 English and U.K. paper production, 1714-1860, and
imports of paper-making materials, 1727-1860.

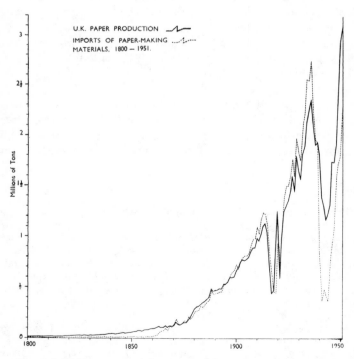

Fig. 2.2 U.K. paper production and imports of paper-making
materials, 1800-1951.

materials as reflected in the parallel movements of output and import curves, by changes in location and by increases in the size of mills. There was a continued and corresponding decline in numbers of mills in conjunction with steeply rising output; in the U.K. as a whole the number fell from rather over 400 in the 1850s to under 200 today, whilst during that century output had multiplied about 30 times. Behind the mere shape of these curves lies a complex pattern of changes in techniques, organisation and industrial structure. Today the industry and its imported raw materials are of major importance in the country's economy. The increases in output during the 1920s and 1930s were in striking contrast to the depression which affected so many industries. At once a very old industry, it also apparently behaved like a typical 'new' industry.

How are we to assess these patterns of industrial growth? If the use of the term 'industrial revolution' in its application to a single industry is allowed, then it seems clearly evident that we must say that the paper industry has passed through two such revolutions. But are we justified in accepting the figures presented in this way, each shaped, so to speak, in the comparatively small mould of a hundred or a hundred and fifty years? These are the conventional dishes in which the 'revolutions' are so frequently cooked. But if we take the long-period view, which our figures allow, and at the same time plot these figures as growth curves, the picture appears in a rather different light (see Fig. 2:3).

From this it is equally clearly evident that the second 'industrial revolution' in the industry offers nothing more, in quantitative terms, than a continuation of the rate of growth initiated during the classical industrial revolution period. Even this does not show up very clearly but it appears to start with two changes from the comparative stagnation of the early decades of the eighteenth century: one commencing between 1740 and 1750 and another between 1800 and about 1810. The introduction of wood pulp is scarcely visible.

Much has been written about the shape of industrial growth curves.[17] Professor Rostow has written: 'In general, although a phase of increasing rate of growth may occur in the very early stages of an industry, these growth patterns appear to follow roughly the course of a logistic curve; that is, they exhibit regular retardation'.[18] Warnings have been duly uttered to the effect that although 'we can see the curve of growth as logistic rather than exponential', this is not 'to suggest that all growth curves will be of this

---

[17] As well as Schumpeter, op. cit., see: S. Kuznets, *Secular Movements in Production and Prices* (New York, 1930); W.W. Rostow, *The Process of Economic Growth* (New York, 1952); R. Glenday, 'Long Period Economic Trends', in *Journal of the Royal Statistical Society*, ci, (1938); also W. Hoffman, 'The Growth of Industrial Production in Great Britain: A Quantitative Study', in *Econ. Hist. Rev.*, 2nd series, ii (1949-50), pp. 162-180.
[18] Rostow, op. cit., p. 100.

type'.[19] Indeed, Professor Kuznets and, deriving from him, Dr. Hoffman, have both noted the paper industry as providing an exception to the logistic curve.[20] Schumpeter, constructing his own elaborate model of economic movement, warned us against evolutionary theories of organic growth and emphasised that too much trust should not be placed in the gradient of any particular logarithmic straight line. This he saw as offering merely what he called a 'descriptive trend' or 'a piece of economic history in the form of a curve', though he did admit that we were on 'somewhat safer ground' in fitting particular types of curve to time series showing quantities of individual commodities.[21] It is not proposed here to consider the nature of 'laws of industrial growth' or whether indeed they exist, though it seems perhaps worth pointing out that the logistic curve might well be an expected proposition on the simple criterion that decreasing returns will appear at some stage, i.e. without postulating any specific 'law' of industrial growth as a whole. In the case of the paper industry it is clearly evident that it was only the discovery of wood pulp which prevented the regular retardation from showing itself earlier.

It is very questionable whether such quantitative data can be used as 'pieces of economic history',[22] without at the same time considering in detail the technical developments which lie behind them. The continuation of the same growth rate in paper was entirely dependent on the discovery of a *substitute*, in this case for raw material. If paper made from wood pulp were to be regarded as a different substance from that made from rags (which chemically it is *not*, see above, n.9), then there would already be a logistic curve for rag paper followed by another, still as yet of the exponential type but likely to show retardation as soon as the softwood forests begin to be exhausted. The curve of the imports of paper-making materials in Fig 2.3 gives some indication of this.[23] If figures existed for the production of papyrus, parchment and paper, one would *a priori* expect to see, for what might be called the 'Writing Materials Industry', a sort of family of successive logistic curves, the envelope of which would trace out a curve which

---

[19] Hoffman, loc. cit., p. 166.

[20] Kuznets, op. cit., pp. 22-24; Hoffman, loc. op. cit., p. 171. It should be pointed out that continuing growth is not here linked to rising exports. Paper exports form only a very small percentage of production and we remain net importers.

[21] Schumpeter, op. cit., and loc. cit., i, pp. 201-4, ii, pp. 491-94.

[22] Especially in the manner followed by Hoffman both in the article cited above and in the uncritical acceptance of various statistics (including those for paper in the eighteenth century) which go to make up his index of Britain's industrial production. See his 'Ein Index der industriellen Produktion für Grossbritannien seit dem 18. Jahrhundert', in *Weltwirtschaftliches Archiv*, 1934 (II), p. 383.

[23] This has, of course, a national coverage only and consequently the shape of the curve is partly due to the fact that increasing world demand for wood pulp, together with the growth of integrated pulp and paper mills in the forest areas, have to some extent put the English industry in an economically disadvantageous position.

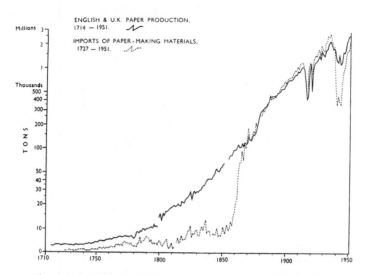

Fig. 2.3 English and U.K. paper production (1714-1951) and imports of paper-making materials, 1727-1951 (Log. Scale).

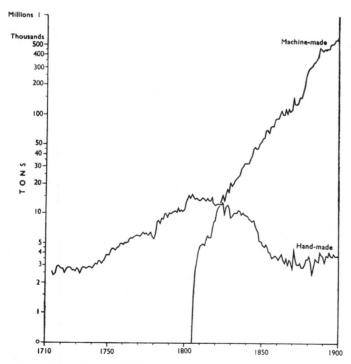

Fig. 2.4 English and U.K. producton of hand-made and machine-made paper, 1714-1900 and 1806-1900 (Log. Scale).

would not yet show signs of permanent retardation in growth. Fig 2.4 showing the output curves of hand-made paper and then its successor machine-made paper will serve as an illustration of this.

Two questions follow from this: how far can such an argument be generalised to apply to other industries, and – the old chestnut – what constitutes an industry? If we are willing to allow a certain common-sense elasticity in answering the latter, especially in the general direction of end uses to which products are put, it is not difficult to think of many examples which fit this pattern of industrial growth. The argument applies equally, for instance, to the development of the natural and then the synthetic fibre industry; at an earlier stage in the history of English and European textiles, the substitution of the 'New Draperies' for some of the older types of cloth offers a similar illustration. It applies also to the successive substitutions, first, of cheap iron (both cast and wrought), for wood, leather and other earlier constructional materials, and then after the 1860s, of steel for iron. The rise and fall of charcoal output, had we the figures, could be set against that of coal and the latter, in turn, matched with the statistics of the oil rush. The statistics of raw material imports and, in some instances, of exports in such industries as these would show appropriate changes comparable to those revealed above for the supply of paper-making materials.

Successive indices of this type reveal the constant change, the continual posing and solving of technical and economic problems in a manner in which national industrial growth curves, themselves composed of curves for conventional 'industries', do not. Indeed, the latter often conceal more than they reveal. What is the steel industry or the metallurgical industry or the transport industry or the textile industry for the purposes of tracing the course of industrial growth? Schumpeter noted 'the broad fact of great steadiness in long-time increase . . . both in the sense of a rough constancy of the gradient of the trend and in the sense of what, merely by way of formulating a visual impression, we may term the general dominance or trend over fluctuations'. He illustrated this by reference to industrial production indices relating to Great Britain for 1785-1914 and U.S.A. and Germany from the 1860s to 1914.[24] But in the truly long run, in the long focus of history, what exactly does this mean? Or again, what is the value to the economic historian of a production index in which even the classical industrial revolution can be made if not quite to disappear at least to appear a no more than a small change in the industrial growth rate?[25]

Now the studies, mostly by economists and statisticians, in which appear such quantitative analyses of industrial growth, have not paid over much

[24] Schumpeter, op. cit., ii, pp. 492 and 494.
[25] S. Kuznets, 'Statistical Trends and Historical Changes', in *Econ. Hist. Rev.*, 2nd series, iii, (1951), p. 269: 'in the overall indices of production in Great Britain prepared by Walter Hoffman, the Industrial Revolution does not appear as a truly revolutionary unheaval'.

attention to the question of how the concept of the industrial revolution, as otherwise used by historians, should appear in these series. But it seems clear that if we are to accept the arguments outlined above, the term 'industrial revolution', when referring to particular industries in their conventional forms, can be applied to every innovation which simply *maintains* the existing rate of growth of output.

If this appears to be a detraction from the significance of the term as normally understood and, indeed to be something of a *reductio ad absurdum*, then a remedy may perhaps lie in concentrating on *increase* in the growth rate, such as is registered in the paper industry, during the classical industrial revolution.[26] Should we, then, retain this crucial mechanization as indicative of the true 'industrial revolution in the paper industry'? Now if this is done, there seems to be no reason why we should not also accept earlier mechanization, however simple, which performed the same essential quantitative feat. And, moreover, if we examine that feat a little more closely it is seen to consist essentially of the mechanization or other crucial improvement of one process in the industry which, in turn, brings pressure to bear upon the other processes. If it could be shown to have thus operated, as is not unlikely, then the medieval application of water power to the rag-beating processes in the paper industry would seem to have a valid claim to the title. Doubtless, other industries might have similar pretensions: along with the stamping mill there may go the fulling mill, corn mill, the slitting mill, and the blast furnace with water-powered bellows, and more besides. Admittedly, figures are not available to prove that such innovations did in fact increase growth rates, but other sorts of evidence suggest that they certainly marked turning points in the development of the industries concerned and certainly had striking effects on industrial location. Professor Carus-Wilson is explicit about the nature of her 'industrial revolution' and the claims which she makes for it: 'the mechanizing of the first three cloth making processes during the eighteenth and nineteenth centuries is a commonplace of history, but the mechanizing of the fourth during the thirteenth century, though it gave rise to an industrial revolution *no less remarkable* has attracted scarcely any attention'.[27] (My italics).

So now even if the late nineteenth and early twentieth century 'revolutions' are rejected, we are still left with two 'industrial revolutions' in the paper industry, and indeed on these arguments the same would apply to many other industries at many other times.

Perhaps, then, the whole conception of an industrial revolution in a particular industry spells dangerous multiplicity. If safety does not lie this way, can

---

[26] Although if it were possible to extend the series further back in time, it is quite possible that this apparent increase would disappear.

[27] Carus-Wilson, op. cit., p. 40.

it be found in the wider use of the term: in its application to industry as a whole or to the economy as a whole? Outside the classical industrial revolution, the example best known to economic historians is perhaps Professor Nef's 'industrial revolution' of 1540-1640. In examining an era barren of detailed or continuous statistics, the assessment of its industrial development tends to be an admixture of various sorts of quantitative and non-quantitative evidence of one sort or another, the whole only too often amounting to a sample very far from random. Economic historians are indebted to Professor Nef for his fundamental researches into the coal industry, for pointing to industries once ignored and for unearthing the long roots of industrialisation. But there is a reason to suppose that the 'industrial revolution' which he has made his own owes more to the vigour and enthusiasm of his writing than to the typicality of his samples. The claims which he makes for his revolution have a familiar ring: 'The introduction of new industries and of new machinery, tools, furnaces in the old industries, had brought about technical changes in the methods of mining and manufacturing *only less momentous* than those associated with the great inventions of the late eighteenth and early nineteenth centuries'.[28] (My italics). In a more recent work this 'early English industrial revolution' is said to have marked 'the genesis of industrial civilization' and to have prepared the way for the eventual industrialization of the world.[29]

Although it is not feasible here to embark upon a comprehensive examination of these claims, it is possible to give some indication of the way in which this 'revolution' has apparently been built up.

According to Professor Nef, 'tens of thousands of work people' were swept into 'hundreds of new, capitalistically-owned enterprises', the introduction of which 'during the last sixty years of the sixteenth century opened an entirely fresh field for the growth of industrial capitalism'.[30] Amongst such industries was paper-making. For evidence on a scale of England's paper making at this time, Professor Nef relies on what has been written about John Spilman's mill, at work at Dartford in 1588. That the paper mill of this period, with its water wheels, stampers, buildings, and apparatus, represented something much more substantial in the way of fixed capital than the weaver's cottage and loom is scarcely open to doubt. But that any appreciable number of mills were of the size which Spilman's was alleged to be is very unlikely for a century or more after 1588. Professor Nef has to admit that Thomas Churchyard in his poem about Spilman's mill 'probably exaggerated when he spoke of 600 workmen', confining himself to the

[28] 'Progress of Technology', in *Econ. Hist. Rev.*, (1934) p. 22. See also Nef, *Rise of the British Coal Industry*, i, p. 165.
[29] *War and Human Progress*, p. 15.
[30] 'Progress of Technology', pp. 8 and 22.

assertion that 'the enterprise certainly employed scores of hands'.[31] But did it? And how many scores? And if it did, how many other paper mills were there that did? In early Stuart England the bulk of the paper used in this country was imported and continued to be for some time. Nor is there any reason to suppose that the average paper mill of the time represented a striking concentration of capital and labour. It was normally a building not much larger than a corn mill; it was leased from a landlord at a rent of round about £50 per annum; it probably employed about a dozen people in all, including the master paper maker himself, for a mill with one vat. And the majority were still one-vat mills: in the 1730s, the average number of vats per mill was about 1.2.[32]

Did such 'capitalistically-owned enterprises' as these really help to open 'an entirely fresh field for the growth of industrial capitalism'? As with shipbuilding,[33] so with paper-making: Professor Nef's claims seem to owe much to untypical examples. It seems highly likely that a careful examination of other industries which figure in his revolution – mining, metal manufacture, alum and copperas making, and so on – would reveal this same method by which a national 'industrial revolution' has been constructed out of a number of innovations in industry. This is not in the least to deny that the development of these industries marked a significant variation on domestic production or that they represented, taken together, an important phase in the slow growth of early industrialization; but this is quite different from inflating them into an 'industrial revolution' and equating this with the transformation wrought in the nineteenth century.

The main item, indeed, in many ways the basis, of Professor Nef's revolution is the coal industry. Here the evidence does not rest simply on increases in scale and capital outlay. The 'industrial revolution' he sees as ending with the Civil War; and thereafter 'although there was a recovery after 1660 and the production of British coal, cloth and paper grew during the eight decades that followed the Restoration of that year, it was not until at least the 1750s that the rate of increase in industrial output was again as rapid as during the period 1540-1640'.[34] No adequate statistical series are available to support this statement; it rests upon the type of non-quantitative evidence mentioned above, together with Professor Nef's own estimates relating to the growth of the British coal industry; these show a 14-fold increase between 1551-60 and 1681-90, a 3-fold increase in the following

---

[31] Ibid, p. 7.

[32] H.M. Customs and Excise Library: Treasury-Excise Correspondence, 1733-45, fos. 245-6 (see appendix below). Other evidence from Port Books, leases of mills and various sources, details of which will be given in the author's forthcoming work on the history of the paper industry.

[33] See below, chapter 3, for this aspect of Professor Nef's 'revolution'.

[34] *War and Human Progress*, p. 149.

century and a 23-fold increase between 1781-90 and 1901-10.[35] Further, the fact that there appears to be a 14-fold increase in one century and only a 3-fold increase in the next is used, together with its repercussions and other allied changes, as part evidence for an industrial revolution in the economy as a whole.

There is one obvious objection to this: comparatively large rates of increase will naturally appear whilst absolute amounts are small and/or whilst an industry is new. This can be clearly seen in the growth of such modern industries as oil, aluminium, synthetic fibres and many others: it is also reflected, as has been shown, in the early years of the growth of machine-made paper and in the import of paper-making materials into this country after the invention of wood pulp (see Figs 2.3 and 2.4). The charcoal-coal relationship is, indeed, just such a thing as is illustrated in Fig 2.4 and is consequently open to the same objections as a candidate for the title of 'industrial revolution', quite apart from its use as a basis for extending the revolution to the country as a whole.

In all this Professor Nef was supported by Schumpeter who, believing the term to be outmoded and misleading, held the classical industrial revolution to be 'on a par with at least two similar events which preceded it and at least two more which followed it'.[36] To Schumpeter these revolutions were long cyclical movements of the sort detected by Kondratieff. He firmly rejected the idea that the industrial revolution was a 'unique event or series of events that created a new economic order'.[37] Indeed, we can hear exactly the same sort of claims as those made by Professors Carus-Wilson and Nef: writing of the Kondratieff beginning in 1898, Schumpeter described it a being caused by an 'economic revolution *analogous in every respect* to the "industrial revolution" of text-book fame'.[38] (My italics.)

It is now time to take some note of the latest recruit to the ranks of 'industrial revolutions'. Not a great deal can be said of it as this new 'second industrial revolution' is still, to some extent, more a matter of prediction than of evidence. But it would not perhaps be difficult to find a place for it in a scheme of economic growth envisaging a series of 'industrial revolutions'. The invention of the vacuum tube or electron valve and its application to a variety of problems of communication, computation and control could be represented as the crucial technical innovation; on this could be based the development of 'automation' and the increases in industrial productivity and output associated therewith; the process would appear essentially as the substitution of automatic control for human control; the social and

---

[35] *The Rise of the Britsih Coal Industry*, ii, pp. 19-20.
[36] Op. cit., i, p. 253.
[37] Ibid.
[38] Ibid. i, p. 397.

economic effects arising from all this would, finally, provide the requisite justification for seeing it as an industrial revolution.

Quite outside this hypothetical pattern, those who speak of these developments simply as 'the second industrial revolution' put their whole emphasis upon the distinction between automatic operation and automatic control, between the 'first industrial revolution' in which mechanization replaced man's muscles and the 'second industrial revolution' which will make automatic work that was previously done by his brains:

> . . . the first industrial revolution, the revolution of the 'dark satanic mills', was the devaluation of the human arm by the competition of machinery. There is no rate of pay at which a United States pick-and-shovel labourer can live which is low enough to compete with the steam shovel as an excavator. The modern industrial revolution is similarly bound to devalue the human brain at least in its simple and more routine decisions. Of course, just as the skilled carpenter, the skilled mechanic, the skilled dressmaker have in some degree survived the first industrial revolution, so the skilled scientist and the skilled administrator may survive the second. However, taking the second revolution as accomplished, the average human being of mediocre attainments or less has nothing to sell that is worth anyone's money to buy.[39]

This view seems to be based on a number of fundamental misconceptions.

First, it is entirely misleading to represent the classical industrial revolution as the replacement of muscles by machines. This popular view almost certainly stems from an over-emphasis upon mechanization of textile manufacture. The power loom or the 'mule' do fit into this picture just as does the paper-making machine or the hydraulic press. But the major innovations in, for example, the iron, steel and chemical industries between 1760 and 1860 were not of this nature at all, and even the steam engine itself often replaced not human muscles, but water power or wind power.

Secondly, the distinction between automatic operation and automatic control is by no means clear – either in time or in nature of process. Such medieval mechanizations as the fulling or stamping mills can be represented as steps towards automatic operation just a the classical industrial revolution can be seen as marking a much larger and more rapid move in the same direction. It is possible to trace the principles and practice of automatic, continuous flow production, through the development of mechanical handling devices, back to the eighteenth century. Similarly, the use of various valves, governors, and other automatic control devices can also be traced back to the same period, or earlier. Since those days both automatic operation and automatic control have been extending in use, the latter especially in this century. The photo-electric cell, sister invention to the vacuum tube, has been used for some time both for various control processes, regulating or inspecting industrial products, and for various

---

[39] Wiener, *Cybernetics*, p. 37.

operational purposes, such as opening doors. Very high degrees of both automatic operation and automatic control (incorporating the use of electronic devices) have already been achieved in some industries, notably oil refining and motor vehicle manufacture.[40]

Thirdly, it is an obvious exaggeration to imply, as appears to be implied in the arguments of the 'second industrial revolution' enthusiasts, that the classical industrial revolution has enabled man, even today, to dispense with physical effort. Just as the existence of many complex economic, social and demographic factors (over and above the variations in production techniques mentioned above) makes nonsense of the picture of machinery simply replacing muscles, so does it seem equally unlikely that a world of automatic factories will be ushered in to replace all but the more advanced operations of the human brain. The classical industrial revolution got into its stride at a time of unprecedented population growth; yet in spite of the dislocation of labour which it involved, in spite of the hardship to many, a vast amount of far more regular employment came into being in the course of the nineteenth century than had ever been known amongst the underemployed masses of the pre-industrialised world. New jobs came into being, new categories of employment were opened up, new skills replaced old skills. The skilled mechanic did not 'survive the first industrial revolution'; he was created by it. The extension of 'automation' will doubtless give rise to serious economic and social problems. These are not the concern of this article, but it may not be out of place to suggest that a more careful consideration of these possibilities in the true light of the industrial revolution might prevent a stampede of grandiose claims and inappropriate terminology.

Fourthly, and perhaps most important from the economic historian's viewpoint, to represent the notion of 'automation' as something radically different from what has gone before, to cut it off and see it as marking a 'second industrial revolution', is to empty much of the real meaning of the term 'industrial revolution'. Of course, there is a radical difference between the potentialities of electronic devices and, say, the centrifugal governor, just as there was and is between electric power and the steam engine. But this is integral to the nature of industrial development, and of economic growth in the industrialised era, and that this should be so stems essentially from the nature of the classical industrial revolution.

How, then, are we to accept these various revolutions? What relation do they bear to the classical industrial revolution? Are they all identical phenomena? Although the Kondratieffs of Schumpeter's ingenious cyclical model may seem to be identical phenomena within that structure, they are not historically identical in any sense other than that in which certain not very adequate quantitative series can make them seem so. Nor again are they the

---

[40] 'Towards the Automatic Factory', *passim*.

same as a thirteenth-century revolution in the process of fulling, although such a revolution could form a vital constituent of a Schumpeterian 'industrial revolution'.

Perhaps it is time for a new 'historical revision' of the 'industrial revolution'. When H.L. Beales wrote his historical revision in 1929,[41] the dangers were not simply that it should be considered a unique phenomenon but that it was arbitrarily limited in time, without roots in the past and truncated in its development and application by the inadequacy of the word 'industrial' and the overtones of the word 'revolution'. Since then much has been done to show that the classical industrial revolution had its roots in the scientific thought and economic activity of the sixteenth and seventeenth centuries, and that it came to bear its fruit in decades long after the first Reform Bill was passed. But today the dangers are different: today we have too many industrial revolutions and too many ways of discovering them.

On its technical side *the* industrial revolution was the first major and large-scale success in man's efforts to apply his growing mastery of natural forces to economic production. It transformed this country in a way in which no country had ever before been transformed; and the process of industrialization which is still transforming once backward areas is the carrying abroad of this industrial revolution. Modern advances in science spring from the roots which first flowered so spectacularly in the seventeenth century, and modern advances in the interrelation of science and economic change (such as automatic controls) spring from that other first flowering which was the industrial revolution.

But, of course, it had aspects other than the technical. Professor Ashton has said of it that 'the changes were not merely "industrial" but also social and intellectual', and has justified his use of the term by noting that it 'has been used by a long line of historians and has become so firmly embedded in common speech that it would be pedantic to offer a substitute'.[42] And to keep it firmly embedded in common speech and give it a meaning which it deserves we should retain for it the significance which it was given by the earlier writers: by Porter,[43] for instance, writing in economic and technical terms of changes radically affecting not simply industry but the country's whole economy, its social structure and its modes of thought and action. The term should not be applied to certain technical or economic innovations in particular industries which either maintain or increase the growth rate, nor can we deduce an industrial revolution simply from observing the existence in the appropriate figures of an increase in the growth rate of several industries. It is necessary to go beyond the curves of industrial

[41] H.L. Beales, 'Historical revisions: The Industrial Revolution', in *History*, new series, 14 (1929), pp. 125-29.
[42] T.S. Ashton, *The Industrial Revolution*, (1948), p. 2.
[43] G.R. Porter, *The Progress of the Nation* (1851).

growth and beyond mere mechanization to the vital conjuncture of changes in which population growth, large-scale and extensive industrial invest-ment, and the remarkably pervasive effects of the application of science to industry are amongst the most important in producing the rapidly cumulat-ive process of industrialization. This use of the term – the third of those mentioned earlier – as well as conforming to the classical English industrial revolution, would at the same time approximately conform to the process sometimes now called, as by Professor Rostow, the 'take-off' into industriali-zation.[44] In this usage we avoid the danger of equating industrialization itself with industrial revolution, but reserve it for the initial and – in the long focus of history – comparatively sudden and violent change which launches the industrialized society into being, transforming that society in a way which none of the earlier so-called industrial revolutions ever did. At the same time we are retaining for the industrial revolution its uniqueness in the history of a country, but allowing its extension to others, as for instance in the conception of the Japanese industrial revolution, begun in the 1860s.

In this way, it should perhaps be possible to avoid depriving the term of its meaning, to avoid the path which at present seems to lead to the pointless notion of an economic history in which the absence of an 'industrial revolution, will soon be more significant than its presence. The qualitative changes wrought upon a society by the true industrial revolution would thus be emphasized. Though economic history may lean heavily on quantitative determinations, no amount of study of growth curves or the like will be adequate without searching examination of the technical, social, and econo-mic problems which lie behind them.

[44] Op. cit., p. 102.

Appendix 2.1
Statistical Sources

The sources of the figures from which the graphs were made were as follows:

Fig 2.1. The main source for the production curve was the printed returns in *B.P.P. 1857, iv*, supplemented by original compilations in the Library and Archives of H.M. Customs and Excise, London, especially those in the volume entitled 'Quantities, Rates and Amounts of Excise Duties, 1684-1798' and the evidence contained in the long series of letter books covering the correspondence in the eighteenth and early nineteenth centuries between the Commissioners of the Treasury and the Excise.

I am grateful to the Commissioners of the Customs and Excise for permission to consult these Records, and to the Librarian, Mr. R.C. Jarvis, and his staff for their co-operation in facilitating my work there.

For various reasons the printed returns before 1781 were unacceptable and further calculations became necessary in order to obtain figures even approaching reliability. The unreliability is apparent when the printed returns are compared with the amounts collected as revenue, with other series of the same sort, with other information known about the industry, and, above all, with the level to which these figures suddenly jump after the reorganization in the method of assessment which took place in 1781. This was primarily due to the fact that an increasingly large proportion of paper was charged *ad valorem*, instead of at one or another of a small number of specific rates for specified types of paper. This, in turn, was partly because a range of new types of paper was being made and partly because, with the exception of certain of the lower quality papers, it was advantageous to paper-makers to persuade the Excise officials to rate paper *ad valorem*. It is clear from the records of the Customs and Excise that not only was this done, but also that such papers were also generally undervalued. Amongst these records there are annual figures for this period of the value of paper rated *ad valorem*. The problem was therefore to find some factor with which to turn values into physical quantities and thus to obtain estimates of total production.

The following calculations designed to solve this problem were largely carried out by Mr. S.T. David to whom I am greatly indebted not only for this assistance but for his generous advice on statistical matters.

It was assumed that the printed Excise returns for the period 1785-1855 were tolerably reliable or at any rate consistent throughout. It was observed that the curve of the annual values of paper rated *ad valorem* showed, from 1740 onwards (before 1740 it was virtually stationary), the same rate of growth as that of the 1785-1855 curve. By fitting exponential curves to these latter figures and also to the *ad valorem* figures, and obtaining the closest fit for the latter over the period 1740-85, a factor was obtained, working out at rather over 2*s.* per ream, a low but feasible figure considering the general undervaluation. The curve of estimated total production shows a course of development conforming to that suggested by other evidence including some calculations made by the Board of Excise in 1785. Final figures in tons were thus obtained from the following formula:

$$[\text{Amount of paper charged in reams} + 2 \text{ (amount of paper charged in bundles)} \times 9.712 \text{ (value of paper charged } ad\ valorem \text{ in £'s)}] \times \frac{20}{2240}$$

1 bundle = 2 reams (as stated in 10 Anne C.18, imposing the duties);
1 ream   = 20 lb. (an average figure calculated for this period from various sources).

After 1781 the sources were as follows:
    1782-1799   *B.P.P.*, 1857, iv (England);
    1800-1855   *B.P.P.*, 1857, iv (U.K.);
    1856-1859   *B.P.P.*, 1860, xl (U.K.);
    1860   A.D. Spicer, *The Paper Trade*, London, 1907, App. IX.
Before 1800 all figures cover paper only; thereafter they include paste-board, cardboard, etc.

The import curve was derived from figures taken from the following sources:
    1725-1799   P.R.O., Customs 3 (London & Outports);
    1780-1789   P.R.O., Customs 17 (London & Outports);
    1790-1808   P.R.O., Customs 17 (England, Wales & Scotland)
                                    (Scottish imports about 8 per cent.
                                    of English);
    1809   P.R.O., Customs 4 (England & Wales);
    1810-1830   P.R.O., Customs 5 (England, Wales & Scotland);
    1831-1860   Appendix 3 to Select Committee on Paper (Export of
                                    Rags) *B.P.P.* 1861, xi (U.K.).

Fig 2.2 Production figures derived from the following:

1800-1860	As above.
1861-1903	Spicer, op. cit., appendix IX.
1908-1911	London and Cambridge Economic Service Annual Index
1913	of Production, Gp. VIII (Paper). The figures given there
1920-1923	covering paper made from imported pulp and esparto
1925-1929	only were adjusted by comparison with Census of
1931-1933	Production figures to obtain estimates of total
1936-1937	production.
1907	
1912	
1924	
1930	U.K. Census of Production (3rd, 4th and 5th).
1934	
1935	
1904-1906	Calculated from imports of pulp and esparto in the
1914-1919	same manner as the London and Cambridge figures (see
1938-1939	London and Cambridge Economic Service Special
	Memorandum 8, p.28) and then adjusted as before to
	cover total production.
1940-1951	Annual Abstracts of Statistics.

Figures for imports of paper-making materials from:

1800-1860	As above.
1861-1905	Spicer, op. cit., appendix I (from U.K. trade returns).
1906-1951	U.K. trade returns.

Fig 2.3 As for figs. 2.1 and 2.2.

Fig 2.4 As for Fig 2.1 and Spicer, op. cit., appendix IV.

3

Naval Dockyards Under the Later Stuarts*

The travellers and topographers of later seventeenth- and early eighteenth-century England often commented fulsomely upon the naval dockyards of the time, admiring their size and noting their growth since Tudor times.[1] As French wars succeeded Dutch wars, so did Portsmouth and Plymouth rise to importance alongside the existing yards at Chatham, Deptford and Woolwich.[2] In his 1695 edition of Camden's *Britannia*, Gibson observed

* The relevance of this topic in the context of the Industrial Revolution is certainly not evident from the title. It is included here in the hope that it may help to put changing patterns of industrial organization, and some of their immediate social consequences, in historical perspective.

The dockyards in question ostensibly present examples of large concentrations of capital and labour a century or so before the Industrial Revolution began the process by which, in time, such things became commonplace. In fact, however, as the article tries to demonstrate, these features were economic by-products of the state in pursuit of war. By the later decades of the seventeenth century not only had the Navy become of the country's bigger industries in its demands for both capital and labour but its dockyards had given rise to urban environments more familiar to a later age in their dependence upon concentrations of local employment. Nef's attempt to enlist shipbuilding as evidence for his invented industrial revolution of Tudor and Stuart times was as misplaced here, though in a rather different way, as his endeavour to build upon the example of Spilman's paper mill of the 1580s (see above, p. 56). The big concentrations of capital and labour represented by the naval dockyards owed nothing to the combination of market forces and technological innovation in the private sector. In this they were wholly unlike those concentrations which were to emerge in the later stages of the Industrial Revolution.

[1] This essay was written and submitted for publication before the appearance of J. Ehrman's book *The Navy in the War of William III, 1689-97* (Cambridge, 1953). No significant amendments have been made as a result of reading this work although a number of references to it have been incorporated in the text and footnotes. Mr Ehrman's highly detailed study of naval matters during the eight years in question seems to confirm the general tenor of the arguments used in the present article in reference to the whole period from 1660-1714. Two valuable later books bearing upon aspects of the topic are Ralph Davis, *The Rise of the English Shipping Industry* (1962), which deals authoritatively with the shipbuilding industry of the time; and M.W. Flinn, *Men of Iron: the Crowleys in the Early Iron Industry* (1962), which shows how the exceptional size of the Crowley enterprise was itself dependent on the similarly exceptional demands of the Navy.

[2] Harwich, Sheerness and Kinsale were also developed for naval purposes. For general information on the dockyards, see the Victoria Country History for the appropriate counties, especially the Maritime History section *V.C.H. Hampshire*, v, 359-467; *V.C.H. Kent*, ii, 243-388; and *V.C.H. Essex*, ii, 259-312. See also R.G. Albion, *Forests and Sea Power* (Cambridge, MA., 1926); and Ehrman, op. cit., chap. 3.

that the Navy had multiplied five- or six-fold in ships, tonnage and men since Camden wrote; he paid tribute to the corresponding expansion in the Chatham yard which, in due time, Defoe was to describe as 'monstrously great and extensive', resembling a 'well-ordered city'.[3]

What was the reality behind these and like observations?

It is the purpose of this essay to examine the nature of the naval dockyards as industrial entities,[4] to assess their economic significance in certain directions and to consider them in relation to civil shipbuilding. In the light of this it is proposed to discuss some of the conclusions reached by Professor J.U. Nef concerning the characteristics of shipbuilding in seventeenth-century England. An important pillar in the edifice of the 'industrial revolution' which Professor Nef has perceived as taking place in the period 1540-1640 is the growth of large-scale shipbuilding.[5] Writing of this country and that century, he has claimed that 'shipbuilding . . . had long been organized in large-scale units, for while smiths and carpenters, sail and rope makers might prepare the materials in their own households, the shipyards where these materials were assembled were large and costly establishments in which many workers laboured for wages'.[6] Expanding such themes as these and extending them in time, he has attempted to assess the comparative significance in such advances of the needs of war and the problems of peace. The growth of the English Navy in the sixteenth and seventeenth centuries is observed as leading to the 'establishments and expansion of large industrial plants such as those at Chatham, Portsmouth and Woolwich', but in general, commerce rather than war is seen as setting the pace in shipbuilding's progress. Professor Nef stresses the growing size of commercial vessels, most of which, he claims, were by early Stuart times 'coming to be built in sizeable shipyards owned by private capitalists'.[7]

Before considering the dockyards in any detail, it is perhaps worth

---

[3]   D. Defoe, *A Tour through England and Wales, 1724-6*, Everyman Ed., i, 105-10; *Camden's Britannia, Newly Translated in English: with large Additions and Improvements*, ed. Edmund Gibson (1695), p. 229. See also Defoe, op. cit. i, 97-9, 135-9, 230-1; *The Journeys of Celia Fiennes, 1685-1698*, C. Morris ed. (1947), pp. 53, 123; Thomas Philipott, *Villare Cantianum or Kent Surveyed and Illustrated* (1659, ed. 1776), p. 161.

[4]   Their administration will not be considered. See on this J.R. Tanner, *Samuel Pepys and the Royal Navy* (Cambridge, 1920); M. Oppenheim, *History of the Adminisration of the Royal Navy, 1509-1660* (1896); and Ehrman, op. cit. *passim*.

[5]   J.U. Nef, 'The Progress of Technology and the Growth of Large Scale Industry in Great Britain, 1540-1640', *Econ. Hist. Rev., v (1934), 3-24*. See also his 'A Comparison of Industrial Growth in France and England from 1540 to 1640', *Journal of Political Economy*, xliv (1936), 289-317 and 505-33, and 'War and Economic Progress, 1540-1640', *Econ. Hist. Rev.* xii (1942), 13-38.

[6]   *Econ. Hist Rev.*, v (1934), 20-1.

[7]   J.U. Nef, *War and Human Progress* (Cambridge, MA., 1950), pp. 84-88.

underlining the significance of two main factors relevant to the Navy and naval shipbuilding at this time. In an age of commercial rather than industrial rivalry between nations, the importance of the merchant marine was closely linked with that of the Navy. Sea-power and commerce, colonies and seamanship were motifs in a complex pattern in which the Navigation Acts and the fisheries, the coal trade and the naval dockyards all had their appropriate places. Consequently, the distribution of the state's expenditure tended whether directly through the deliberate fiats of policy or indirectly through the intrusive pressure of interests, strongly to reflect the power of such maritime matters. The succession of wars periodically brought naval spending to a very high proportion of total outgoings in the public sector, whilst even in more peaceful years the maintenance of a large fleet normally constituted a dominant item of expenditure.

Table 3.1 provides a rough quantitative illustration of this, showing the high relative figures, the variations between peace and war and also the rise in absolute amounts over the period. Hopes of peace after the second Dutch war saw £200,000 as an optimistic aim for annual naval expenditure of which £100,000 was to be for maintaining ships in harbour and the remaining half for setting them to sea.[8] Of an estimated annual cost in 1671 of £660,434, the 'charge of a year's fleet manned with about 60,000 men' accounted for £312,000 and the balance covered shipbuilding, maintenance, yards and the like.[9] The following forty years brought expenditure which made these earlier sums seem trifling, bringing too a corresponding extension in the Navy's economic demands.[10] Thus over the whole period, embracing both peace and war, an average of approximately a quarter of the state expenditure was directed to naval needs, exclusive of naval ordnance. Out of these totals, then, the construction and repair of ships, the maintenance of the dockyards and bases accounted, on the average, for about a half.

This leads to the second main point to be noted: naval ships and naval shipyards were very much larger than their civilian counterparts of the seventeenth century, or, indeed, of the eighteenth century. Today, a large merchant or passenger vessel and a comparably sized warship are clearly, from this point of view, of the same genre. They could be, and are, made in the same sort of yards. Many warships are today built on contract in private yards; in Pepys' time there were very few such yards which could build, let alone accommodate for repairs, a third-rate. From the Restoration to the

[8] Tanner, op. cit., pp. 41-42.
[9] J.R. Tanner (ed.), *A Descriptive Catalogue of the Naval Manuscripts in the Pepysian Library* (Navy Records Society, 1903-9), i, 105.
[10] Though not a *relative* increase as compared with that of the Army's demands.

Table 3.1*

PERIOD	TOTAL GOVERNMENT EXPENDITURE £	EXPENDITURE ON NAVY £	PERCENTAGE (II) TO (I)	SOURCE
1661-62	1,000,849	172,321	16	
1662-63	1,613,530	516,382	30	
1663-64	1,362,664	303,315	22	*Calendar of Treasury Books* (ed.
1664-65	1,268,261	300,484	25	W.A. Shaw), 1660-67,
1665-66	2,640,840	1,467,593‡	56	pp. xxxii-xxxiv
1666-67	1,928,924	166,372‡	8	
1667-72	No adequate figures available			
1673-74	2,565,134	865,312	34	Ibid., 1672-75, p.xxii
1674-75	1,848,072	549,106	30	
1675-76	1,268,533	236,506	19	
1676-77	1,832,650	516,528	28	Ibid., 1676-9, p. xv
1677-78	2,714,121	658,535	24	
1678-79	No adequate figures available			
1679-80	2,078,665	806,266	39	
1680-81	1,434,626	362,501	25	W.R. Scott, *Joint Stock Companies*
1681-82	1,163,983	357,081	31	*to 1720* (Cambridge, 1911-12),
1682-83	1,123,861	363,513	32	iii, 540
1683-84	1,145,577	331,791	29	
1684-85	1,250,124	368,950	30	
1685-86†	1,730,228	355,405	21	*Cal T.B.* 1685-89, p. xxix
1686-87†	2,093,827	444,805	21	Scott, iii, 542
1687-88†	2,333,220	469,980	20	
1688-91†	11,820,004	3,098,289	26	
1691-92†	4,501,108	1,239,209	28	
1692-93†	5,832,807	1,925,328	33	*Cal. T.B.* 1689-92, p.cciv-ccxvi
1693-94†	6,213,683	2,131,694	34	
1694-95	6,816,343	1,890,151	28	
1695-96	8,938,787	1,922,451	22	
1696-97	8,264,167	2,821,193	34	
1697-98	5,971,710	877,455	15	Ibid., 1695-1702, pp. ccxxvi-
1698-99	6,113,178	1,232,066	20	cccxxv
1699-1700	4,775,615	818,635	17	
1700-01	4,093,723	1,046,397	26	
1701-02	5,544,677	1,137,502	21	
1702-03	6,678,463	1,981,854	30	Ibid., 1703, pp. cix-cxliii
1703-04	7,648,937	1,871,702	25	Ibid., 1704-5, pp. cxxxiv-clxvii
1704-05	7,141,650	1,618,654	23	Ibid., 1705-6, pp. cxxxvii-clxix
1705-06	8,609,298	2,049,309	24	Ibid., 1706-7, pp. cxii-cxxxi
1706-07	9,868,863	2,251,890	23	Ibid., 1708 (Introduction),
1707-08	8,798,761	1,883,540	21	pp. cxxi-cxliv; ccxiii-ccxxvii
1708-09	10,209,830	2,022,446	20	Ibid., 1709, pp. cl-clxxix
1709-10	11,152,761	2,156,331	19	Ibid., 1710, pp. cii-cxx
1710-11	10,312,935	1,492,476	15	Ibid., 1711, pp. cxxxi-cxliii
	Average percentage		24	

* These figures are quoted in order to give an impression of the general order of magnitude. Closer examination reveals discrepancies and the degree of accuracy is sometimes questionable. For instance, for years marked † slightly different figures are quoted by Scott (iii, 541-43). see also Ehrman's comments, especially pp. 165-70, 462n., 470n., 470-2. Another set of slightly different figures for naval expenditure from 1689 will be found in *British Parliamentary Papers, 1868-69*, 35, pt. 2, p. 693.

Excluded from col. (ii) above are the figures for naval ordnance which, in the accounts of national revenue and expenditure, are included along with all other ordnance supplies under a separate general heading.

‡ These figures are almost certainly lower than the true amounts, for in 1665 there appears a new category of expenditure: 'Extraordinaries for the Dutch War' under which heading payments of £191,555 and £689,085 are noted for 1665-66 and 1666-67 respectively.

Revolution no man-of-war larger than a third-rate was built outside the
Navy's yards at Chatham, Woolwich, Deptford, Portsmouth and Harwich.[11]
    The tonnage of the majority of English ships plying in European trade
varied between 50 and 100 tons. The ordinary coasting hoy might be
anything from 4 to 80 tons; the coal trade between London and Newcastle
called into being some larger vessels ranging from 300 to 400 tons. A sample
of fifteen London vessels bound for the West Indies, North America, Spain
and Portugal, the Canaries and Madeiras and which took aboard further
cargo at, or off, Dover in 1633 shows an average tonnage of 178 and a range
of from 100 to 250;[12] other evidence suggests that such figures are not
unrepresentative of the general run of ships in the longer distance commerce.[13] Only in the African, American and Indian trades were there to be
found a few English-built ships that began to compare in size with the larger
men-of-war; by 1700 a handful of East Indiamen approached this position.
By contrast the thirty ships of the naval building programme of 1677, for
instance, were: one first-rate of 1,500 tons, two second-rates of 1,300 tons
each and twenty third-rates of 1,000 tons apiece.[14]

[11] See Table 3.2; for post-Revolution developments, see below pp. 88-91.
[12] Exch. K.R. Port Books, 190/661/13.
[13] See V. Barbour, 'Dutch and English Merchant Shipping in the Seventeenth Century',
Econ. Hist. Rev., ii (1930), 262-63; Albion, op. cit.; and L.A. Harper, *The English Navigation Laws*
(Columbia, 1939), esp. chap. 22.
    Average figures of tonnage are apt to be confusing owing to the variations as between
different types and areas of trade, to the presence of a small number of large vessels registered
at London and a large number of small vessels registered both at the outports and at London,
and to the wide ranges concealed by arithmetical averages.
    Thus a 1702 survey said to cover the whole of England gives an average figure of 76 tons, but
the variations of the same estimate relating separately to London and elsewhere give averages
of 150 tons and 62 tons respectively (Harper, op cit., p. 329 and n.) Other samples of English
ships entering the port of London, give averages of 112 tons for the years 1692-96, 100 tons for
1699-1701, 93 tons for 1702, and 114 tons for 1719. (Harper, op. cit., p. 347.)
    Exeter – by no means an insignificant outport – provides an example of what was probably a
typical picture of seventeenth- and early eighteenth-century shipping. Out of 145 ships
registered there in 1747, the average tonnage was 64, the range was from 12 to 240, and 119
ships, or 82% , were in the category from 20 to 100 tons. (W.G. Hoskins, *Industry, Trade and
People in Exeter, 1688-1800* (Manchester, 1935), pp. 169 and 182-83.
[14] *Cat. Pepys MSS*, i, 236. It should be noted, however, that the calculation of ships' tonnage at
this time was by no means reliable or consistent. Moreover, the distinction between tons
burthen, displacement tonnage and carrying capacity is not always clear. Nevertheless, the
magnitude of the discrepancies is not so great as seriously to modify the very real differences in
size between men-of-war and merchant ships in general.
    Some idea of the variations may be gathered from the fact that the seventeenth-century first-
rate *Royal Sovereign* was diversely described as of 1,631, 1,556 and 1,441 tons; a fifth-rate of 326
tons was estimated in 1684 to have a carrying capacity of 214 tons; a merchant ship launched in
1704 and calculated by its builder to be of 141 tons was described in its papers variously as 167

As might be expected only at London and Bristol were there private yards which could readily be put to the Navy's assistance for ships as big as a third-rate. Probably the largest of these were Henry Johnson's yards on the Thames at Blackwall and those of Castle at Deptford. In the century after the Restoration, with the continuing growth of the English merchant marine, these yards and others nearby underwent a major expansion and came in time to rival the naval yards in size and importance.[15]

Along with size went cost. An 80-ton hoy cost about £340 in the 1660s. At the same time, estimates by Christopher Pett for a second- and third-rate were £9,176 and £6,844 respectively.[16] In the following decade, a contract price for a third-rate was £9,000.[17] Such figures, moreover, exclude the costs of rigging, stores and guns. A 600-ton warship was said by Pepys to cost £4,800 'off the stocks' and £13,000 'set to sea'.[18]

Estimated values put upon the fixed assets of the Kentish yards alone give some impression of their size and of their growth under the stimulus of naval warfare:[19]

	1688	1698
	£	£
Chatham	44,940	56,059
Deptford	15,760	28,641
Woolwich	9,669	15,801
Sheerness	5,393	6,960
	£75,762	£107,461

These figures may serve to emphasize the extent to which the Stuart Navy posed a need for large-scale establishments and heavy capital expenditure such as was demanded by few forms of private enterprise in that age. Only in land and property owning as practised by the wealthiest classes and in a very few industries such as coal-mining, iron-smelting and founding, or alum manufacture were fixed capital assets on this scale to be found. The

---

or 170 tons. See, on these points: J. Charnock, *History of Marine Architecture* (1901), ii, 483, 488; *Notes and Queries* (1927), vol. 152, p. 327; vol 153, pp. 304, 340, 406; R.C. Temple (ed.), *The Papers of Thomas Bowrey* (Hakluyt Soc., 2nd ser. (1925), lviii, 125).

[15] Barbour, op. cit., p. 263; Albion, op. cit., p. 88; Defoe, op. cit., i, 346-8.

[16] *State Papers, Domestic*, Charles II, vol. 93, no. 27 and vol. 105, nos. 143 amd 145.

[17] Albion, op. cit., p. 93.

[18] *Cat. Pepys MSS*. i, 229. See comparable figures quoted in Ehrman, op. cit., p. 36. As he very pertinently remarks, 'the ship of the line was larger than the average country house of the day, and her construction far more complicated' (p. 38).

[19] *V.C.H. Kent*, ii, 355, 362. The relative growth over the whole period of the Portsmouth and Plymouth yards was, of course, far more spectacular. The provision of facilities for maintenance and major repair made the greatest demands, both in physical assets and in organization. See Ehrman, op. cit. pp. 80-1. The pressure of naval expansion brought into being a proposal in 1670 that new yards should be built at Erith and Greenhithe, covering some 24 acres and including two double dry docks, a wet dock, storehouses, etc., the cost of which was estimated at £63,000. The proposal was unfruitful.

Table 3.2

Places of Construction of the Warships Built between 1660 and 1688*

| | RATES AND NUMBERS | | | | | | | |
PLACES	1ST	2ND	3RD	4TH	5TH	6TH	YACHTS	TOTALS
Dockyards								
Chatham	4	1	6	2	1	—	4	18
Deptford	2	3	5	1	—	1	1	13
Woolwich	1	3	3	4	1	—	7	19
Portsmouth	3	5	3	1	2	2	3	19
Harwich	—	2	5	—	1	3	—	11
Private Yards								
Thames (Deptford)	—	—	—	—	—	—	—	—
Blackwall, Rother-	—	—	8	2	—	1	7	18
hithe, etc.)								
Bristol	—	—	2	2	—	—	—	4
Forest of Dean	—	—	—	1	—	—	—	1
Conpill	—	—	—	1	—	—	—	1
Woodbridge	—	—	—	1	—	—	—	1
Yarmouth	—	—	—	—	2	—	—	2
TOTALS	10	14	32	15	7	7	22	107

* *Cat. Pepys MSS*. i, 224. Cf. the similar story told by the more detailed information given in Pepys 'Register of Ships' in *Cat. Pepys MSS*. i, 226–84. Of the eight third-rates built on the Thames, five were products of Henry Johnson's yards at Blackwall and three were built by William Castle at Deptford.

contrast is further sharpened by the fact that shipbuilding is mainly an assembly process and that consequently (repair work apart) the value of the working or circulating capital was also on a like substantial scale.

The economic influence of the dockyards may be considered as operating through three main channels: through the employment of direct labour services; through the demand for a wide range of goods and indirect labour services; and through town-building, the yards forming the nucleus and dominating element in the communities which grew up about them.[20] It will be convenient to deal with the first and third of these together.

During the disturbed years of the later Stuart reigns, the numbers employed in the yards rose strikingly, as the graph in Fig 3.1 shows. Low though the January 1687 total of 1,185 seems by comparison with the 5,195 of March 1703, it may be contrasted with the figure of 980 to which total it was ordered that the numbers of workmen in all yards should be limited in 1654. In a half-century, then, the working force of the naval dockyards had risen over five-fold. The second Dutch war saw the movement under way: 238 were at work at Deptford in 1663, 302 at Woolwich in the following year; 1665 saw 800 busy at Chatham. Such figures are dwarfed by the 3,275 working in the Kentish yards alone in March 1704; by 1712, whilst the Treaty of Utrecht was being negotiated, these same yards still had over 2,500 at work.[21]

Thus in all the dockyard centres, and especially at Portsmouth and in the Medway towns, there is a clear picture of substantial concentrations of workers, labouring under conditions very different from those surrounding the 'domestic system'. To all the aspects of shipbuilding and repair there was added constructional work on the yards themselves, calling for the employment of the bricklayer or the house-carpenter or the plumber. So the totals cover a wide range of jobs: shipwrights and labourers normally constituting the largest single groups, followed by caulkers, joiners and carpenters, though the precise composition varied with different yards and different times. The total of 800 at Chatham in August 1665 includes, for instance, 440 shipwrights, 129 labourers, 47 house-carpenters, 41 joiners, 31 caulkers, 23 scavelmen, 18 bricklayers, 17 'ocam boyes', 15 boat-makers, and a scatter of plumbers and pump-makers, coopers and pitch-heaters.[22] Some idea of the scale of building – and this in modest terms compared with the big expansion carried out by William[23] – may be obtained from the construction work of the period April 1686 to October 1688. During that

---

[20] These three channels are not claimed as exhaustive. Just as it is not possible here to consider the administration of the yards, so the financial problems posed by them are ignored.
[21] *V.C.H. Kent*, ii, 367. See also *S.P. Dom.* Charles II, vol. 77, no. 68; vol. 449, no. 8; vol. 99, no. 125; vol. 106, no. 25; vol. 129, no. 69; vol. 191, no. 83; *Cat. Pepys MSS*. i, 69.
[22] *S.P. Dom.* Charles II, vol. 129, no 69.
[23] For some details of this, see Ehrman, op. cit., pp. 413-29.

time, twelve storehouses were built at Deptford, one at Woolwich, twenty-one at Chatham, twenty at Portsmouth as well as docks, dwelling-houses, mast-houses, boat-houses and so on to a total value of £32,000.[24]

The population of these dockyard towns was undoubtedly growing rapidly. Estimates based on the Hearth Tax Returns for 1664 suggest that at that time Deptford may have had a population of about 4,500 and Woolwich 2,500. The figure of some 1,800 for Chatham must be taken in conjunction with 2,400 for Rochester and 750 for Strood as the growth and close proximity of these towns had already created virtually a single urban area.[25] In 1686 it was claimed that Chatham's population had trebled in forty years.[26] The local J.P.'s reported, in 1702, that the Hundred of Blackheath (in which lay both Deptford and Woolwich) had experienced 'great Augmentation of building and Increase of Inhabitants'.[27] In 1711 the inhabitants of Woolwich itself were said to be 'chiefly compos'd of Workmen and others employed in Her Majesty's Dockyard, Ropeyard and Ordnance Service'.[28] Contemporaries were agreed in ascribing such increases largely to the dockyards and commented upon the intimate association of the towns with the Navy.[29]

It would, then, seem reasonable to suggest that during this period a large and increasing proportion of the families living in the dockyard towns were dependent upon direct dockyard labour. In so far as work was thus provided, the demand for labour may have tended to raise the general level of prosperity of those towns, just as did the demand for goods and services. Similar developments were taking place at Portsmouth, though rather later in their full incidence (cf. Fig 3.1). Defoe, indeed, speaks of that town as having been made prosperous by the presence of the Navy and so influenced by it that 'the inhabitants of Portsmouth are quite another sort of people than they were a few years before the Revolution'.[30] Some classes of these communities may well have enjoyed a consistent and continuing benefit, especially those providing goods and services always in some measure of demand. Some reflection of this is provided in the occupations of those freeholders qualified to serve on juries: in Chatham in 1696, for

[24] *Cat. Pepys MSS*, i, 95.

[25] Details of this and of the population estimates will be found in the author's unpublished Ph.D. Thesis (Univ. of London, 1951), 'The Economy of Kent under the Later Stuarts', chap. 1 and app. 1.

[26] Kent Country Archives: Quarter Sessions Order Books – Maidstone April 1686. It should, however, be added that as this estimate was included in a petition to the Lord Chancellor designed to secure financial assistance in rebuilding the church, said to be too small, it probably owed more to optimism than to accuracy.

[27] Ibid., Order Books – Maidstone, April 1702.

[28] Ibid., Session Paper 1711, bundle 140.

[29] See, for example, *H.M.C., Portland MSS*, ii, 277; Philipott, op. cit., pp. 104-5; D. Lysons, *Environs of London* (1791; 2nd ed. 1811), p. 458.

[30] Defoe, op. cit., i, 138.

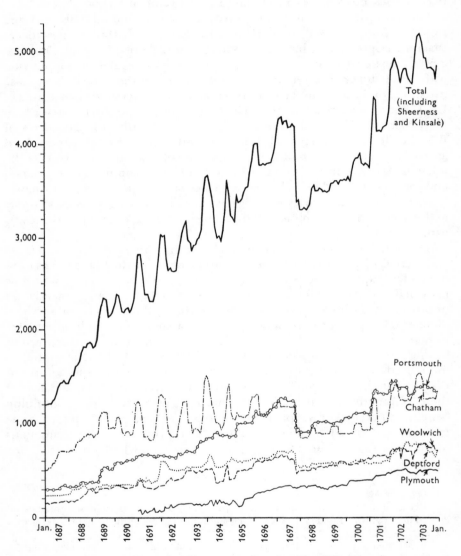

Fig. 3.1 Numbers of workmen employed at Naval Dockyards,
1687-1703. (British Library, Add. MS 9324, fos. 17-52)

example, out of a total of fifty so qualified, the accommodating title of 'gent' accounted for nineteen – and amongst these were several persons connected with the dockyards – whilst thirteen were shipwrights.[31] For many of the dockyard workers, however, benefits were not always so evident. Periods of vigorous, inflated employment, preceded by the furious recruitment of civilian labour by methods which included impressment, alternated with intervals of depressed conditions, during which labour was laid off, ships rotted and poverty was more noticeable than usual in a region with no other comparable source of employment. It is not, then, surprising to find that, in Kent at least, the dockyard towns show many symptoms of enjoying a generally higher prosperity than other areas of the county, both rural and urban, and yet at the same time, are the subject of periodic complaints of excessive poverty. Thus Chatham complains of the great charge of its poor relief;[32] at Woolwich the cost of the poor has risen along with the growth of numbers;[33] from Deptford comes that familiar pair of social groans: the parish cannot maintain its own poor, its landowners are 'unreasonably overrated and taxed'.[34]

Fortunately, perhaps, for the inhabitants of these areas they were kept fairly busy by the persistent warfare of the years from the restoration of the Stuarts to the arrival of the Hanoverians. But, as Fig. 3.1 indicates, such employment proceeded with great irregularity, both in the longer run with the alternation of peace and war and in the short run with seasonal variations.[35] The reality of the fluctuations in the shipbuilding programmes can also be seen – for the pre-Revolution – from Table 3.3. Although, of course, this takes no account of the demands of repair and maintenance, it is clear from the records pertaining to the yards that large dismissals of labour did in fact alternate with vigorous engagement. Thus, for instance, letters such as that from Commissioner Pett to Pepys in April 1664, stating that more workmen must be employed spinning hemp at Chatham and urging that they 'should work a day and a half each day', must be set against another letter received by Pepys, in March 1668, announcing that Sir William Coventry was 'well persuaded of the success of his project of

[31] K.C.A. Freeholders Lists.

[32] Ibid., Quarter Sessions Order Books – Maidstone, April 1686.

[33] Ibid., Sessions Papers 1711 bundle 140.

[34] Ibid., Quarter Sessions Order Books – Maidstone, October 1681, July 1689, October 1690, April 1691.

An indication of the employment opportunities and of the scope for increased prosperity in such urban areas as these is provided by the fact that although Deptford was one of a number of Kentish parishes complaining of being unable to meet the cost of poor relief at this time, the majority of such complaints came from rural parishes in East Kent or those in the economically declining city of Canterbury.

[35] See Ehrman, op. cit., pp. 89-91 for the background to these seasonal variations and further details of employment and its fluctuations.

Table 3.3

Naval Shipbuilding, 1660-88*

YEAR	1ST AND 2ND RATES	3RD RATES	4TH AND 5TH RATES	YACHTS AND 6TH RATES	TOTAL NUMBERS	APPROX. TOTAL TONNAGE COMPLETED EACH YEAR
1660	—	—	1	—	1	500
1661	—	—	—	2	2	200
1662	—	—	—	2	2	200
1663	1	—	1	1	3	2,000
1664	2	—	—	—	2	2,000
1665	1	—	1	1	3	1,500
1666	1	4	5	4	14	7,600
1667	1	2	1	—	4	3,900
1668	—	1	1	—	2	1,300
1669	1	—	—	—	1	1,100
1670	3	—	—	2	5	4,400
1671	1	—	1	2	4	1,900
1672	—	—	1	—	1	100
1673	1	1	—	4	6	2,800
1674	—	2	2	2	6	3,000
1675	1	2	3	2	8	4,900
1676	—	—	2	—	2	1,000
1677	—	—	—	2	2	200
1678	2	6	—	—	8	8,200
1679	2	12	—	1	15	14,300
1680	1	2	—	1	4	3,200
1681	—	—	—	—	—	—
1682	3	—	—	1	4	3,700
1683	1	—	—	1	2	1,200
1684	—	—	—	—	—	—
1685	2	—	—	—	2	2,500
1686	—	—	—	—	—	—
1687	—	—	4	—	4	2,000
1688	—	—	—	—	—	—

* Based on the table in *Cat. Pepys MSS.*, i, 222. Approximation for tonnages; 1st rate, 1,400; 2nd rate, 1,100; 3rd rate, 1000; 4th rate, 500; 5th rate, 300; 6th rate, and yacht, 100. The dates signify completion of building.

wholly paying off a good part of the men belonging to the Deptford yard.'[36] Reductions in establishment after the third Dutch war provided for the intended discharge of 1,616 men from the four main yards, retaining only 425 men in pay.[37] In June 1712, 400 men were dismissed from Deptford and Woolwich in view of approaching peace.[38]

Comparison of the wages paid at the dockyards with those prevailing elsewhere is not easy. Apart from the relatively small permanent salaried staff, wages seem normally to have been based on daily time rates, a procedure by no means invariable at the time. Rates of wages given in the Quarter Sessions Assessments are in some instances lower than those paid in the naval yards: carpenters, assessed in 1669 at 1s 8d per day, in summer, were receiving 1s 10d per day at Chatham in the summer of 1661; plumbers were being paid 2s 6d per day in the Deptford yard at the same time, whilst the comparable assessment stands at 1s 8d. Differences in the pay of labourers and shipwrights show only very slight margins. In any event, it is certain that for many civilian employments in many areas, wages actually paid exceeded assessed wages, so that, in fact, differences between dockyard and other rates may have been of trifling account.[39]

The whole subject of employment at the dockyards at this time was, however, complicated by the chronic financial want of the government, resulting in the total failure of the naval authorities to pay wages with any sort of regularity. This aggravated the vigour of fluctuations in work, helped to keep labour in a constant ferment, at once assisted in forging links of local credit relationships and strained them to the uttermost. When they reached an advanced state of tension further severe difficulties were encountered in securing labour and resort was again had to impressment.

It is not proposed to dwell for long upon the distress caused by this failure of naval credit.[40] It will suffice to note some of the main features of a situation which lasted throughout the period, though probably reaching its worst during the years of Charles II's reign. Wage payments were in arrears; workmen left to seek jobs elsewhere, presented petitions complaining of poverty and starvation and begging for payment. In November 1662 nearly £16,000 was due for wages at Chatham from July 1661 to September

[36] *S.P. Dom.*, Charles II, vol. 97, no. 17; vol. 236 no. 56.

[37] *V.C.H. Kent*, ii, 356.

[38] Ibid., p. 367.

[39] K.C.A. Wage Assessments by Quarter Sessions. That for 1669 is the closest surviving to the 1661 figures of dockyard wages; a 1661 assessment is unlikely to have shown higher rates, as the general tendency shown by later assessments was for wages to move slightly upwards.

The dockyard rates are in *S.P. Dom.* Charles II, vol. 46, nos. 38 and 39. See also H.M. Richardson, 'The Wages of Shipwrights in H.M. Dockyards, 1496-1788', *Mariner's Mirror* (1947), p. 265. For further details of wages and employment conditions, see Ehrman, op. cit., pp. 91-108.

[40] For some details of this and of the financial problems involved, see Tanner, *Samuel Pepys and the Royal Navy*, pp. 37-56, and *V.C.H. Kent*, ii, 336-88.

1662.[41] When the 400 men were dismissed in 1712, wages were once again fifteen months in arrears.[42] In June 1668 Sir William Coventry wrote to Pepys to inform him that £10,000 to £12,000 would be available to pay off men in the yards, some of whom were by then a year's wages in arrears. Coventry added that it would have two desirable effects. Those remote from their homes (labour was sometimes impressed and then dispatched post haste from one yard to another) and who made the greatest clamour and had the most hardship in finding credit would be paid off. Secondly – and this gives a clear indication of the conscious domination of the area by the dockyards – those 'who are inhabitants will be afraid of being discharged whilst hoping for the money, because then they must go from home to seek work and perhaps not find it'. Aware of its limitations, because of other employment available in the London area he added that, 'in Deptford and Woolwich this method will not have the same force, because the River Thames will be their home to furnish them work.'[43]

One of the effects of these economic and social conditions was to breed ill-organized combinations of labour. Men demanded higher wages as well as the payment of existing sums due: victuals were dear and credit not indefinitely elastic. The impressed men suffered most. The ropemakers petitioned as a body calling themselves the Company of Ropemakers and representing impressed men distant from their homes and allegedly in receipt of 'board wages'. In November 1665 they were six weeks in arrears: in March 1666 a further petition claimed that their board wages were then seventeen weeks in arrears; in June 1666 it had grown to nine months, credit at Chatham was drying up and the Clerk of the Ropemakers added to the petition that he did not believe they would be able 'long to subsist to doe his Ma:[ties] service without money to pay for necessary provisions'.[44] Between 1663 and 1665 discontent broke into strikes and mutinies; similar developments occurred in 1668 when shipwrights from Chatham presented themselves in a body at the Treasury.[45] Later in the century the significance of such events was stressed by Sir Edward Gregory, Commissioner at Chatham in 1693, who lectured the Navy Board upon the political consequences likely to follow delay in paying the dockyard workers, there being plenty of agents ready to excite discontent.[46]

In these various ways, then, the Stuart dockyard towns were coming to possess some of the characteristics of what are today called Special or Development Areas and were once Depressed Areas. For obvious reasons,

[41] *Cal. S.P. Dom.*, 1661-1662, pp. 234 and 554.
[42] *V.C.H. Kent*, ii, 367.
[43] *Cal. S.P. Dom.* 1667-8, p. 463.
[44] *S.P. Dom.*, Charles II, vol. 136, no. 121 (1665); vol. 151, nos. 34 and 110 (March 1666); vol. 160, no. 95 (June 1666).
[45] *Cal. S.P. Dom.*, Charles II, 1667-68, p. 456.
[46] *V.C.H. Kent*, ii, 363.

this analogy must not be pushed too far; but it may serve to put into economic and historical perspective the appearance of certain well-known features of industrial concentration.

Some idea may be obtained of the volume and range of demand for goods from the warrants for receipt of goods into stores according to contract, a reasonably complete series of which cover the period from February 1664 to December 1667.[47] The goods may be divided into nine main groups, the major constituents of which are indicated below:

1. *Timber and miscellaneous wood products.* English and imported hardwoods; Baltic deals; masts, spars, laths, barlings, etc; oars and barrels; handspikes, blocks, spiles and tree nails; boats, pinnaces, yawls, etc.
2. *Textiles.* French and East Anglian canvas; Holland duck and other linen; bewpers (bunting).
3. *Miscellaneous Naval Stores.* Hemp, cordage, cables, oakum, pitch and tar, train oil; rosin; brimstone.
4. *Ironwork.* Anchors, grapnels, nails.
5. *Armaments.* Cannon and shot.
6. *Leather and other animal products.* Hides and backs; ox and goat hair; leather scuppers and buckets; tallow.
7. *Wood fuel.* Broom, reed, faggots; charcoal.
8. *Building materials.* Bricks, tiles, lime and sand.
9. *Miscellaneous.* Ensigns and jacks, hammocks; brooms and brushes; candles and lanterns, etc., etc.

It is not possible to show total quantities and values of these because of the existence of imprecisely specified amounts and because of inadequate information on prices. As some indication of the scale of purchase, however, it may be mentioned that the value of timber and wood products supplied during that period probably exceeded £200,000 and included nearly 16,000 loads of hardwood timber; the value of textiles taken into store was about £30,000. Although these years were largely occupied by war, subsequent expansion and the later conflicts in all probability gave rise to much greater figures, thus suggesting that the picture offered may be not unrepresentative of the age.

Many of these goods were imported from overseas. All the masts and deals, as well as much of the plank and spars fall into this category and the trade in these commodities loomed large in the commercial relations between England, the Baltic countries and New England.[48] So, too, did the other main imported group of naval stores – pitch, tar, hemp, cordage; these also came primarily from the Baltic and Scandinavian countries. Textiles and iron also figured directly and indirectly amongst the imports:

---

[47] *Cal. S.P. Dom.* Charles II, 1664-65, p. 133; 1665-66, p. 131; 1666-67, p. 391; Addenda, 1660-85, p. 431.

[48] Albion, op. cit., *passim.*

many naval requirements were made in England from Spanish and Swedish iron;[49] foreign canvas continued for many years to be the main material of English sails.[50] These and other imported raw materials entered into all the major processes carried on in the yards. Without hemp from the Baltic the ropeyards could come to a standstill; a lack of deals or masts could slow down vital repair or building programmes.[51] On the effects of this upon international commercial and political relations it is not possible to dwell here.[52]

Amongst the home-produced goods which flowed into the dockyards, the outstanding items which alone gave weight to the English contribution to its own naval construction, were hardwood timber and guns. Most – but certainly not all – of the oak, elm and similar woods still came from English forests, though their dwindling strength was the subject of much contemporary comment.[53] Armaments were entirely produced by the English industry; East Anglia provided its modest quota of sailcloth. Local resources were responsible, too, for the miscellaneous building materials, wood fuel, leather and animal products, as well as much that appeared under the miscellaneous category. In the form in which these items were supplied is reflected both the stimulus to local industry and trade and the processes of the dockyards. Such commodities as handspikes and oars were sometimes bought in, as were blocks and barrels; small boats and pinnaces were regularly obtained from local shipwrights. Practice varied, however, no doubt with the differing pressures of peace or war, stagnation or reconstruction, and it is not easy to draw a line: though barrels and blocks were bought, blockmakers and coopers appear amongst those employed at Chatham in 1663 and 1665; local shipwrights supplied both Chatham and Deptford with such craft as 'boats, yawls and pinnaces', but nevertheless fifteen boatmakers were employed at Chatham in 1665. Ironwork seems to have been entirely drawn from outside – the Foleys being main suppliers of nails. Local anchorsmiths supplied the yards as required, and sometimes suffered thereby.[54] The presence of sailmakers at Chatham and Woolwich suggests that the sailcloth bought from the textile areas was made up into sails at the yards.

[49] See, for instance, *Cal. S.P. Dom.*, Charles II, 1670, pp. 64-65.

[50] Barbour, op. cit., pp. 269-70.

[51] See, for example, *Cal. S.P. Dom.*, 1665-66, p. 304; 1666-67, p. 209; 1670, pp. 347-8.

[52] Cf. Albion, op. cit., and A.T. Mahan, *The Influence of Sea Power upon History* (Boston, 1918).

[53] Albion, op. cit., chap. iii.

[54] See, for instance, the letter from John Ruffhead, anchorsmith, to Pepys in *Cal. S.P. Dom.*, Charles II, 1666-67, p. 72. Ironwork, e.g. nails, often came from domestic producers (see letter from Foley in *Cal. S.P. Dom.*, Charles II, 1661-62, p. 549) as did also sailcloth. These straightforward examples of a large organization buying supplies from small producers are used by Professor Nef in *War and Human Progress*, pp. 84-5, to minimize the extent of concentration represented by the dockyards; he observes that the 'production of naval supplies . . . was not centralized'.

As specific examples of purchases, during the 1664-67 period, which doubtless had their due reaction upon local producers, carriers and dealers, there may be noted the 208,000 bricks and tiles bought from Kentish makers, the 3,600 leather scuppers and buckets, or the 451,650 sheaves of broom, reed and faggots. But it is to the timber trade and the armaments industry that we must turn for our main examples of the influence of dockyard demand.

The numbers of guns carried by men-of-war varied from peace to war and as between home and foreign seas, but approximate maxima and minima for this period were: first-rate, 80-100; second rate, 54-84; third-rate, 52-72; fourth-rate, 36-54; fifth-rate, 26-32; sixth-rate, 10-18.[55] Thus, simply for the 107 ships built from 1660 to 1688, the total of guns needed, without allowing for spares or replacements, would have been approximately 5,600. Of these, 2,310 (or 4,101.2 tons of guns, as they were then measured) went to the 30 ships of the 1677 programme.[56]

This armament was bought from the gunfounders of the Kent and Sussex Weald and indeed it was probably only the Ordnance authorities' continued purchases from this source that kept in being the iron industry in that area. As the Midlands grew to importance in iron manufacture from the seventeenth century onwards, so the Wealden industry declined, gunfounding remaining its main support, and the long years of peace after 1713 did much to sap that final buttress.[57] Meanwhile, members of the Browne family continued to thrive on Ordnance demands under the later Stuarts as under the early Stuarts.[58]

'Fear not undoeing' wrote George Browne – holder of the office of Gunfounder to the King – to his partner Alexander Courthope in December 1664, during the urgency of rearmament for the second Dutch war, 'we have noe cause to complayne, which you will be satisfied in when your accounts are made up'. In January 1664/5 Courthope and Browne contracted to supply 1,500 iron guns. This represents 2,552 tons of guns, a total cost of £43,198. Many of these guns went, no doubt, to meet the Navy's requirements. Certainly, the Brownes played this role in the programme of 1677. By that time another John Browne was the current member of that dynasty and he received a share of a contract to supply the ordnance for fifteen of the new ships, his proportion amounting to 740 guns, totalling 1,310.6 tons.[59] Though naval demand provided a most profitable outlet for such enterprises it was attended with its customary risks. In 1681 Mary

---

[55] *Cat. Pepys MSS.* i, 233-34.
[56] Ibid., pp. 233-36.
[57] E. Straker, *Wealden Iron* (1931), *passim*.
[58] Ibid.
[59] The references to the activities of Courthope and Browne are derived from MSS. in the possession of Lord Courthope of Whiligh, for whose permission I am much indebted. See 'The Economy of Kent under the Late Stuarts', pp. 173-85 and app. 4.

Browne, 'relict of John Browne, his Majesty's Late Gunfounder' was peti-
tioning the Crown for moneys due, to the amount of some £27,000.[60]

Timber contracting and the gradual evolution of timber monopoly have
been traced by Professor Albion, who has shown how earlier methods were
superseded with the appearance of a 'class of middlemen or timber brokers
whose agents replaced the royal purveyors in treating for the small lots of
timber'.[61] In the importing branch of the business, the big dealer early
flourished and it will perhaps suffice to remind readers of the relations
between Samuel Pepys and Sir William Warren. The latter was not, however, alone in the field of major operators: such men as William Wood and
Peter Blackborrow (or Blackbury, as he appears in the *Diary*) were also
dealing in both home and imported timber on a large scale, and the big
yards which grew up on Thames-side during this period served both the
dockyards, especially those at Deptford and Woolwich, and the rising
private shipbuilding enterprises. Chatham, however, and probably also
Portsmouth, tended to rely for its hardwoods on the English timber and
local dealers. Both were well situated in this respect with accessible hinter-
lands stocked with oak and elm.[62] In this local supply, as in the imported
trade, the development of the timber merchant can be similarly traced and
the relations of one of these – John Mason of Maidstone – with the naval
authorities may serve to illustrate this aspect of dockyard influence.

Kent supplied an important proportion of the timber used in the
Chatham yard. In the period February 1664–December 1667, the total
quantities which, so far as can be ascertained, came from that county are
shown in Table 3.4.

Table 3.4
Intake of Timber from Kent, 1664-66*

GOODS	DESTINATION	TOTAL QUANTITIES	
Oak	Chatham	2,810	loads
Elm	Woolwich	80	"
Elm	Chatham	854	"
Oak and elm	"	1,891	"
Beech, ash, hornbeam, elm, oak	"	149	"
Compass and knee timber	"	450	"
Miscellaneous and unspecified	"	300	"
TOTAL	—	6,534	"

* *S.P. Dom.*, Charles II: vol. 108, nos. 236, 238, 259, 260, 284, 291, 307; vol. 141, nos. 55, 56,
59, 87, 90, 97, 128, 139, 145, 150, 153, 156, 160, 161, 227, 228; vol. 185, nos. 57, 60, 80, 81, 84,
88. *S.P. Supplementary*, vol. 137, no. 802. For the nature of 'compass and knee timber' see
Albion, *op. cit.*, chap. 1.

[60] *S.P. Dom.*, Charles II, Entry Book 67, p. 21.
[61] Albion, op. cit., p. 57.
[62] For Chatham, the Medway was the vital route from the Weald of Kent and Sussex, and the
trade therefrom in both naval timber and ordnance was an important stimulus to improvements in the navigability of the river.

By way of comparison with other counties and as an indication of the sources upon which the different yards relied – at any rate in this early Restoration period – this total may be set against the 6,050 loads from the three royal forests of Aliceholt, Whittlewood and Waltham sent to Deptford and Woolwich between December 1663 and September 1668.[63] Supply on this scale was propitious to the rise of middlemen and although many landowners are to be found amongst those tendering to the Navy, the professional timber merchant was clearly emerging. In such conditions 'carpenters' grew into 'timber merchants' and some aspired, in the documents of the time, to the dignity of 'gent'.

Mason – 'Mr. Mason of Maidstone' to the Navy Commissioners and one of the select company suspected of offering bribes to the not altogether incorruptible Pepys – was one of several shipwrights, carpenters, mariners who acted as intermediaries.[64] Indeed, almost anyone who could lay his hands on a piece of timber tendered it to the Navy. Of the 6,534 loads noted above, however, Mason alone sold 2,176 loads, followed by Robert Moorcock, a Chatham shipwright, with 1,890 loads, these two also supplying a joint contract of 40 loads.[65] Subsequently Mason became the main supplier of English timber to the Chatham yard and a potential monopolist.

After 1666, the relations between Mason and the dockyard authorities grew increasingly strained. On the one side were clear attempts to corner the market in English hardwood suitable for use at the dockyard, on the other was the government's failure to pay its debts. The latter was a factor relevant to the supply of all stores just as to the supply of labour, and its effects may be illustrated from the manner in which it affected Mason.

In July 1668, for example, he made a tender of 555 loads of urgently needed timber, but demanded up to 60s per load for it, with £500 in hand and ready money on delivery of every consignment.[66] After an unsuccessful effort to persuade Mason to lower his rates or to go to London to deal direct with the Navy Commissioners, Sir John Mennes had to report that Mason was 'so far from coming up to London about the same that he is indifferent whether you bargaine with him or not which makes me to judge

[63] *S.P. Dom.*, Charles II, vol. 257, no. 115.

[64] *Diary*, Feb. 24 1688 and Aug. 19 1668. On the former occasion Pepys was told of an accusation likely to be made that he had received £50 from Mason and remarked characteristically that, so far as he recollected, it was untrue but that he was troubled to have his name mentioned in the business 'and more to consider how I may be liable to be accused where I have indeed taken presents'. The second instance involved Will Hewer.

[65] Although Robert and John Moorcock continued to supply timber, John Moorcock was subsequently involved with Phineas Pett, the shipwright, in a disreputable affair in which the latter was found to be selling timber to the dockyards in contravention of the rule by which the King's Officers were prohibited from so doing. *Cal. S.P. Dom.*, Charles II, 1667-68, pp. 450, 501 and 607. See also Pepys's *Diary*, July 24 1668.

[66] *S.P. Dom.*, Charles II, vol. 242, no. 47.

hee is grown either very rich or hath many customers for the same'.[67] In the following years substantial contracts were signed for his timber but relations worsened. Mason demanded payment of his past bills and at the same time tried to force on the dockyards very large amounts of timber of all sorts along with their immediate requirements. Attempts, some successful and some not, to corner the market and raise prices alternated with grudging but necessary purchases of his timber. Not unnaturally, Mason's character and business habits periodically came under attack in the correspondence between the Commissioners at Chatham and the Navy Board.[68]

The arguments, the tactics, the sales, continued until Mason's death in 1679, though meanwhile he was much concerned with obtaining payment of his bills, ten letters of his on this subject appearing amongst the State Papers between 1668 and 1673.[69] In these letters – mostly blunt and ill-written – Mason often combined begging or demanding payment ('mony I want and mony I must Raise with my timber: and as for being paid in course I understand it not') with offers of more timber. In May 1671, for instance, along with a chiding for broken promises and an expressed fear of arrest for debt went an offer of 800 loads.[70] The general run of his actions suggests an eagerness to sell to the Navy – at his price. This in turn implied not only that naval contracts were profitable but that to an appreciable extent he was dependent upon them to make the scale of his buying worth while; for he bought up timber extensively in mid Kent and the Wealden area, Navy purveyors sometimes journeying to inspect the trees *in situ*, or on other occasions simply visiting his wharf and yard at Maidstone. It may then be suggested that in spite of increasing private uses for timber – shipbuilding amongst others – it was only the addition of large naval orders that brought into being local timber middlemen on this scale. Moreover, it is clear from Mason's and Warren's experiences alike that the periods in which substantial sums were owing to them by the authorities were amply balanced by the margin of profits contained in the payment when it arrived.[71]

Ships and yards, men, towns and stores – having now considered some

[67] Ibid., vol. 242, nos. 147 and 204.

[68] See, for instance, *Cal. S.P. Dom.* Charles II, 1668-69, pp. 529-30, 531-32, 534, 545, 554, 566, 568; 1670, pp. 398-99 and 460-61.

[69] *S.P. Dom.* Charles II, vol. 249, no. 148; vol. 255, no. 118; vol. 264, no. 123; vol. 283, no. 88; vol. 286, no. 115; vol. 296, no. 104; vol. 298, nos. 67 and 154; vol. 331, no. 68; vol. 345, no. 155. See also *Cal. Treasury Books*, 1679-80, p. 609.

[70] Ibid. vol. 298, nos. 67 and 154.

[71] Mason's activities were dwarfed in scale by those of Warren and so proportionately with their debts from the Crown, the former's running into thousands, the latter's into tens of thousands. But both alike prospered in their respective ways. On Warren's claims against the Crown, see H.M.C., *Earl of Lindsey*, pp. 116-54.

For the problems of material supply during William's reign, see Ehrman, op. cit., chap. 2.

aspects of these, the way is clear for a discussion of the naval yards in the context of shipbuilding in general.[72]

It is apparent that during the period in question, private shipyards in England were not normally of a capacity equal to the construction of ships of the larger naval tonnages. The very decision of the naval authorities to develop Harwich during the first Dutch war at a time when the dockyards were sorely pressed is indicative of the non-existence of private yards, certainly in the Thames or Medway estuaries, adequate to their needs. Allowed to decay, the Harwich yard was revived on the outbreak of the second Dutch war and in 1666 was launched the first man-of-war built there – a third-rate of 827 tons. Another period of decline followed, interrupted by the programme of 1677 which saw further enlargements and the contribution by Harwich of five of the thirty ships. After this, however, with the changing strategical focus of war the yard gradually fell out of naval employment.[73] The import of this evidence runs quite contrary to the suggestion made by Professor Nef, who, writing of the later seventeenth century, states that 'the private yards for building merchant vessels at Harwich and other English east-coast ports were probably as large as those for building warships.'[74] By the time of the third Dutch war, only the growing yards on the Thames and those at Bristol, as Table 3.2 indicated, were capable of building third-rates, though the smaller classes could be entrusted to yards as varied as Yarmouth and the Forest of Dean, Woodbridge and Lambeth.

The continuing pressure of war-demands, however, meant that during William's wars, as during the Dutch wars, the Navy – spurred by recurrent emergencies – had to turn to the private yards for help in the building programmes.[75] The dockyards, large as they were, could not shoulder satisfactorily the sudden burdens which the periodic violence of war laid upon them. The government was aware of this as it was aware of the limitations of the private yards. In 1677 Shoreham, for instance, was the subject of a proposition designed to make his harbour and shipyard suitable for the building of a third-rate, 'his Majesty being very desirous to increase

[72] For generous advice and criticism on the subject of merchant shipping and shipbuilding during this period, I am very grateful to Mr. R. Davis of University College, Hull.

[73] *V.C.H. Essex*, ii, 284-6, 292 and 306.

[74] Nef, *War and Human Progress*, p. 219. Immediately after this there is quoted the statement by the master attendant at Woolwich in 1671 to the effect that he had known so little to do at the yard that the docks were lent to owners to build or repair merchant ships. This is represented as support for Professor Nef's general argument; 'there were', he says, 'times when the English Naval Yards had to depend for work upon the progress of the merchant marine.' It would seem more reasonable to represent it as an obvious reaction to a period of temporarily reduced activity in any large-scale enterprise – pubic or private.

[75] The points made in this and the next paragraph are amply substantiated, with a wealth of detailed evidence, in Ehrman, op. cit., chap iii and pp. 429-39.

the number of building places'.[76] A Navy Board letter of May 1693 echoes the customary lament. Dockyard and merchant shipwrights alike are exhorted to 'use the best dispatch they can'; the Board 'labours daily under infinite difficulties to procure sufficient men and materials'; amidst the rising prices of shipbuilding timber, it is noted hopefully that 'Mr Winter of Southampton offers to set up a third-rate on that river at the same price as he built the last'. The net is being thrown over a widening area to catch all available shipbuilding resources. Table 3.5 gives some idea of its range, for a sample of ships under construction in 1693.

This could be interpreted as suggesting that a growing number of private yards were capable of building such large vessels as third-rates. This might, to some extent, have been so. More probably, however, it reflects the intense pressure put upon the dockyards and the more suitable Thames yards, and the consequent necessity to turn in desperation to yards hitherto regarded as unsuitable for naval purposes. Indeed, some private yards came, for a time at least, to rely largely on naval contracts and some private shipbuilders found themselves in a position having points in common with that of Mason.[77]

Since the initial development of the Navy, the building and maintenance requirements of men-of-war had consistently been so much greater than those of the normal run of merchant vessels as to demand large-scale shipbuilding and repairing yards. Ordinary trading ships – save for a very small number of East Indiamen – were not making comparable demands even by the end of the seventeenth century. Naval demands, by contrast, were outstripping the capacity of the Navy's own dockyards. The growth of the merchant marine was real enough, but it had been accomplished without any major qualitative change in the units of production. A quantitative change sufficed. In spite of commercial expansion and in spite of Henry VII's bounty for ships suitable for war service, which by Elizabeth's time settled into a grant of 5s a ton on vessels of 100 tons and upwards,[78] the tonnage of merchant vessels remained, as already shown, obstinately low for most of the seventeenth century. Certainly a few vessels of 400 tons or so were built in the late sixteenth or early seventeenth centuries, particularly in the East Anglian ports, some of which had their heyday of importance in civil shipbuilding during this age. Ipswich and Woodbridge, drawing on the timber of the hinterland, became for a time the shipyards of London and

---

[76] *Cat. Pepys MSS.*, i, 54.

[77] Ehrman, op. cit., p. 436. He quotes three examples in which 'large ships were being built in small *ad hoc* yards relying on naval assistance. Whenever that assistance was not forthcoming, the contractors suffered severely and at once.'

[78] *V.C.H. Essex*, ii, 274.

Table 3.5

Places of Construction of 25 Men-of-War in 1693*

	RATES			BOMB-VESSELS
PLACE	3RD	4TH	5TH	VESSELS
Dockyards				
Deptford	1	—	—	1
Chatham	1	—	—	2
Woolwich	—	—	1	—
Sheerness	—	1	—	—
Harwich	2	—	—	—
Portsmouth	1	1	—	—
Plymouth	—	1	—	—
Private yards				
Thames (Deptford, Rotherhithe, Blackwall, etc.)	—	5	—	1
Bristol	—	1	—	—
Southampton	—	1	—	—
Burseldon	1	—	—	—
Redbridge	—	—	1	—
Hull	1	—	—	—
Shoreham	—	—	2	—

* *Cal. S.P. Dom.*, William and Mary, 1693, p. 147. The Thames yards represented were those of Messrs Castle, Shish, Winter and Snellgrove. The exceptional position held by the Thames yards can be gauged by the fact that out of 106 warships (from third- to sixth-rates) built on contract between 1688 and 1709, they were responsible for the following proportions: 16 out of 26 third-rates, 27 out of 34 fourth-rates, 10 out of 27 fifth-rates, and 7 out of 18 sixth-rates. (Dates refer to the contract, not the launching.) B.L., Add. MSS. 9329, fos. 1-10.

built some vessels of 300-400 tons.[79] According to Defoe one of the main customers of the Ipswich yards was the London-Newcastle coal trade — a branch of commerce using larger ships than was usual for the time, and much used by Professor Nef as indirect support for the existence of large-scale capitalist shipyards.[80] Yet the evidence for any appreciable number of the larger vessels — bulky, 300-500-ton colliers specially evolved for the carriage of heavy cargoes — is slender indeed. The average size of a cargo of coal imported into London increased thus:

1592	...	...	...	56 tons
1606	...	...	...	73 tons
1615	...	...	...	83 tons
1638	...	...	...	139 tons
1701	...	...	...	248 tons

By 1731 the average shipment of coal from Newcastle had reached 312 tons.[81] Though the weight of a cargo was not the same as the tonnage of a ship, the inference from these figures would seem to be that even in the London trade, it was not until the end of the seventeenth century that the larger vessels became sufficiently numerous to affect the average tonnage.[82]

If, then, it is conceded that both in the coastal trade, including its coal branch, as well as in overseas commerce, the opportunities for large-scale shipbuilding, as reflected in the size of ships, were small before the later years of the seventeenth century, then the indirect evidence for this particular pillar of Professor Nef's 'industrial revolution' has vanished and the pillar itself crumbled away. For no direct evidence has apparently yet been brought to light.[83] Nor is there any reason to suppose that the construction of the normal merchant ships of the age needed any very large resources of capital and certainly nothing on the scale of the naval dockyards. Elaborate and costly equipment is not required to build vessels of the normal tonnage of that age any more than it is to build the similarly sized ships designed for very similar purposes which can be seen under construction in many a small yard on the shores of the Mediterranean today. In the seventeenth, and even in the eighteenth century only the biggest East Indiamen posed

[79] *V.C.H. Suffolk*, ii, 217-18. The largest vessel, for instance, in a list of 380 ships covering the years 1625-38, was a 400-ton ship launched at Woodbridge. From about this time, however, this region declined in importance as a shipbuilding centre.

[80] Defoe, op. cit., i, 42-43. Nef, *The Rise of the British Coal Industry* (1932), i, 174, 390-2; and *War and Human Progress*, p. 87.

[81] Nef, *British Coal Industry*, i, 39.

[82] Very much smaller average tonnages were found in the coal trade — other than between Newcastle and London — and in the coastal trade as a whole. See Willan, op. cit., chap. 2, and Nef, *British Coal Industry*, i, 392 and n.

[83] The sole evidence quoted by Professor Nef in his article in *Econ. Hist. Rev.* (1934), was that of Defoe and that in Nef, *British Coal Industry*, i, 174 and ii, 25-8, concerning the tonnages in the coal trade.

technical problems of construction and repair, similar to those of the larger men-of-war.[84] Such problems were instrumental in determining the size of the yards and it is not adequate to say simply, as does Professor Nef, that 'the construction of vessels of a hundred tons or more could not be undertaken without considerable capital'.[85] As late as the early nineteenth century, 'wooden shipyards were generally no larger than the workshops of other crafts. Very little capital sufficed . . . the plant required was limited to a large cross-cut saw, bolt cutters, borers and a derrick'.[86] Not only was the requisite physical capital small, but monetary problems arising from the need to purchase raw materials were solved by payment in instalments.[87] Thus was the small yard, producing small or moderate-sized ships, perpetuated.

Until other evidence is produced, then, the dockyards remain as the outstanding examples of large-scale shipbuilding in seventeenth-century England. By the end of that century, as has been demonstrated, their significance as a source of demand for a miscellany of stores and as centres of substantial employment was considerable. Being state undertakings they are not comparable from the point of view of private investment opportunity with such enterprises as that of Abraham Crowley at Winlaton,[88] but the scale of the needs represents nevertheless a significant intake of resources involving corresponding social and economic repercussions. The progress of the large man-of-war may or may not have influenced the progress of the merchant ship. Commerce may or may not have had a greater influence on sea-power than sea-power on commerce. It remains clear, however, first, that the maintenance of sea-power on the scale practised by England in the later seventeenth century demanded a substantial diversion of capital and labour from the private to the public sector.[89] Secondly, it would seem that such large-scale shipbuilding as there was in the England of that age owed its existence more to the demands of naval warfare than to the aspirations of peaceful commerce.

[84] Albion, op. cit., pp. 76-77, 88, 116.

[85] Nef, 'War and Economic Progress', *Econ. Hist. Rev.* xii (1942), 27.

[86] S. Pollard, 'The Economic History of British Shipbuilding, 1870-1914' (unpublished Ph.D. thesis, Univ. of London, 1951), chap 2, p. 50. The author points out that the predominantly small scale of shipyards, whilst wood was the main material of construction, has been obscured by the 'disproportionate prominence given to the handful of very large establishments' which, by the early nineteenth century existed on the Thames, the Tyne and the Clyde. Cf. the account in Ehrman, op. cit., pp. 71-3, of *ad hoc* construction of a warship at Southampton in 1696,

[87] *The Papers of Thomas Bowrey*, pp. 129-36. The agreement for the construction of a 141-ton merchant ship in 1704, the total cost of which was £732.5s. provides for the payment of £150 on sealing the contract, three more instalments of the same sum to be paid on completion of specified stages of construction and the balance on launching. Naval vessels built on contract in private yards were paid for in a similar fashion.

[88] A comparison which Professor Nef makes, *War and Human Progress*, p. 220. For details of Crowley's enterprise, see E. Lipson, *Economic History of England*, ii, 178-83.

[89] Cf. Mr Ehrman's comment (p. 174) that 'the Navy in 1688 was the most comprehensive and in some respects the largest industry in the country'.

4

*Growth and Decay during the Industrial Revolution: The Case of East Anglia**

The continuing debate on the standards of living in Britain during the first half of the nineteenth century has proceeded largely in terms of aggregates.[1] The battle is waged with national statistics of wages and prices, of consumption, income, and taxation; generalized statements (of not always well-founded generality) are lobbed to and fro. Not much heed seems to be paid to that diversity of the English economy of which the historian grappling with an earlier age is, or should be, almost painfully aware. The drama of *national* change has from the start attracted the critics and apologists alike, Engels as well as Ure. Conversely, those undramatic regions away from the centre of the stage have moved all but unnoticed. The

---

* This short piece is included here for two simple interrelated purposes: to emphasize the geographically limited area of the Industrial Revolution in its earlier stages; and to look at the experience of one region which it by-passed. Many statements about the Industrial Revolution have been couched in national terms; and quantitative aggregates are still much in fashion. Even by the 1830s, however, and despite the formidable impact upon contemporaries, its manifestations were still largely confined to parts of Lancashire, Yorkshire and the West Midlands with outliers in South Wales and Scotland. Examples of newly-mechanized manufacture were of course scattered over other areas and contemporary awareness of the phenomenon was nationwide; and by the 1840s the railways were diffusing their formidable impact ever more generally.

Meanwhile, regions which had once enjoyed pre-industrialized prosperity but which remained largely unaffected by the new industrialism often experienced stagnation and poverty. And that was much less commented upon by those contemporary observers who looked with disapproval upon current industrial change.

That the essay is only, as it says, 'a partial and preliminary survey' follows from the circumstances which gave rise to it. They perhaps need some words of explanation. It was written at rather short notice as a contribution to a *Festschrift* issue of the *Scandinavian Economic History Review*, with which I was then involved, to mark the sixtieth birthday of its founder and first editor, Professor Ernst Söderlund. It is based almost entirely on Parliamentary Papers. Further details, derived from other sources, of wages, employment and conditions of work in the silk industry in the area will be found in my *Courtaulds. An Economic and Social History* (Oxford, 1969), i, especially pp. 60-64, 96-101 and Chap. 9.

[1] See, e.g., R.M. Hartwell, 'The Rising Standard of Living in England, 1800-1850', *Econ. Hist. Rev.*, xiii (1961), and articles cited therein.

present essay, which is no more than a partial and preliminary survey, is about such a region.

Before the Industrial Revolution, the three counties of Norfolk, Suffolk and Essex had at various times been the scene of important industrial and commercial activity. Norwich, as the centre of a great worsted industry, made its influence felt over much of Norfolk and was the third city in the kingdom, second only to London and Bristol, right up to the era of industrialization. Further south, the widespread woollen industry of Suffolk and northern Essex reached the apex of its considerable importance in the late fifteenth and early sixteenth centuries, leaving for posterity a multiple monument in the shape of a score or more of splendid churches. When the 'New Draperies' came to England from the Low Countries, they came first to East Anglia. Norwich added a miscellany of 'stuffs' to its traditional worsteds, and Colchester acquired a fame for bayes and sayes. Though these two became the main urban centres for the manufacture and market-ing of the new fabrics, many smaller towns and villages, especially along the Essex-Suffolk border were busy with them. So although there were some changes in particular locations of industrial activity, in general the New Draperies brought jobs and incomes in the later sixteenth and seventeenth centuries to compensate for the declining manufacture of the older sorts of woollens. Along with this textile complex – with its ramifications of combing, spinning, weaving, dyeing and finishing, employing many thousands all over the countryside – went sundry other commercial and industrial activi-ties: trade in grain, butter, cloth, timber, and fish, from such ports as King's Lynn, Yarmouth, Woodbridge, Ipswich, Colchester; shipbuilding was sti-mulated by an active coastal trade, malting and brewing by acres of barley and a ready thirst for beer. The whole area was seemingly in the forefront of advance, prosperous in agriculture as in industry, accepting from the countries across the North Sea new ideas in farming as well as new men and new fabrics in textiles.

   Yet by the middle of the eighteenth century, before the Industrial Revolution had made its mark, much of the region's industrial and commer-cial life was already in decay. Norwich was beginning to feel the harsh winds which blew from the West Riding and its rapidly developing worsted industry; by 1801 it was not the third but only the tenth largest town in the country. The New Draperies were no longer new. Just as the ancient prosperity of Lavenham and Kersey, founded on woollens, vanished, so now the manufactures of Sudbury, Bocking, and Colchester were well on the downward path. Shipbuilding waned, the trade of Ipswich and Colches-ter declined, and as early as 1728 Defoe could sum up Sudbury as remark-able for nothing 'except for being very populous and very poor'.[2] Though

---

[2]   Daniel Defoe, *Tour through England and Wales* (1724-6, Everyman edition, 1928), i, p. 48.

Table 4.1

Expenditure on Poor Relief per Head of the Population*

	ESSEX		SUFFOLK		NORFOLK		AVERAGE FOR ENGLAND & WALES		LANCASHIRE		WEST RIDING OF YORKSHIRE		DERBYSHIRE	
	s.	*d.*	*s.*	*d.*	*s.*	*d.*	*s.*	*d.*	*s.*	*d.*	*s.*	*d.*	*s.*	*d.*
1801	12	1	11	4	12	5	9	1	4	4	6	7	6	9
1811	24	8	19	3	19	11	13	1	7	4	10	0	10	1
1821	17	7	17	9	14	10	10	7	4	8	6	9	8	1
1831	17	2	18	3	15	4	9	9	4	4	5	7	6	7
1841	9	9	8	10	8	11	6	2	3	6	4	7	4	6

* G.R. Porter, *The Progress of the Nation* (1847), pp. 94-95

Table 4.2

Percentage Increase in Population*

	ESSEX	SUFFOLK	NORFOLK	AVERAGE FOR ENGLAND & WALES	LANCASHIRE	WEST RIDING OF YORKSHIRE	DERBYSHIRE
1801-11	11	11	7	14.5	23	16	15
1811-21	15	15	18	17.5	27	22	15
1821-31	10	9	13	16.0	27	22	11
1831-41	8.6	6.3	5.7	14.5	24.7	18.2	14.7

* B.P.P. (British Parliamentary Papers), 1843 xxii, p.12.

yet another phase of rejuvenation in the long history of East Anglian textiles: the silk industry.

The use of silk yarn was not new to East Anglia, as mixtures of silk and worsted constituted an important part of Norwich's output of the New Draperies from the later sixteenth century onwards. By the early eighteenth century the Norwich industry was turning out large quantities of fabrics bearing such names as satins, damasks, camlets, crapes, and bombazines, all containing both silk and worsted yarn.[6] But the development of a pure silk industry, including the preparatory processes of winding and throwing, as

---

[6] Sir Frank Warner, *The Silk Industry of the United Kingdom: Its Origin and Development* (1921), pp. 265-96. M.F. Lloyd Prichard. 'The Decline of Norwich', *Econ. Hist. Rev.*, iii, (1951).

well as weaving, was new to eighteenth-century East Anglia. The celebrated introduction into England of Italian silk throwing machinery, its patenting by Thomas Lombe in 1718, and his subsequent erection of a large water-driven factory in the Derwent, near Derby, had stimulated the growth of similar mills. Very substantially protected, especially after the import of all manufactured silks and velvets was prohibited in 1766, the silk industry spread into various parts of the country; some large water- and later steam-driven mills were established, particularly in South Lancashire and Cheshire. Much of the thrown silk went to the old weaving areas – to the great London centre, Spitalfields, to Norwich, and to the ribbon-weaving town of Coventry – but increasingly it was absorbed by local weavers as the manufacture expanded in and around such towns as Macclesfield, Manchester, Stockport, and Derby. Spitalfields began to know the effect of competition; rising tension between masters and men, as the former attempted to reduce wages, led to the well-known Spitalfields Act of 1773. At a time when the practice of wage regulation had been virtually abandoned, this Act empowered the local Justices and the Lord Mayor of London to regulate the wages of the Spitalfields silk weavers.The move of the silk industry away from London was undoubtedly under way before the Act; the operation of the Act kept wages at a higher level in London than elsewhere, and so helped to continue this departure. It was under these various stimuli that London silk manufacturers, anxious to cut their costs, began to look more and more to nearby counties, and especially to Essex and Suffolk.[7]

A technically simple process, silk throwing could be, and was, carried out by the cheapest of all forms of free labour – children and young women. This was true before and after the introduction of silk-throwing machinery. The machines merely put the hand procedure on a larger scale, and provided for a new source of power; their owners still needed an ample supply of unskilled and juvenile hands to tie threads and do similar simple tasks. The adoption of the new machinery was therefore relatively slow, especially in areas where there were few competing jobs for such workers. In East Anglia and in the London area the old methods were still being used in the later decades of the eighteenth century though they were dying out as water-driven mills were set up in country districts; but even in the early nineteenth century, manually operated winding and throwing mills were still to be found in East Anglia, alongside water- and steam-powered mills.[8] In silk weaving the handloom predominated throughout the industrial

[7]   On the early silk industry, as well as Warner, *Silk Industry*, and Clapham, *Economic History*, *passim*, see W.M. Jordan, *The Silk Industry in London, 1760-1830* (unpublished London University M.A. Thesis, 1931) and N.K.A. Rothstein, 'The Silk Industry in London 1702-66' (unpublished London University M.A. Thesis, 1961); also *B.P.P.*, 1821, vii (House of Lords Committee on Foreign Trade: Silk and Wine) and *B.P.P.*, 1831-32, xix (Select Committee on the Silk Trade).

[8]   *B.P.P.*, 1834, xx, answers to questionnaire, *passim*; *B.P.P.*, 1840, x, pp. 217-18; C.H. Ward-Jackson, *A History of Courtaulds* (1941), p. 9.

revolution; by 1830 some power looms were beginning to appear though only in the weaving of the simpler fabrics.

An abundant supply of young women and children, unemployed hand-loom weavers from the woollen and worsted industries, some water power, a long textile tradition, proximity to London: with all these advantages for the entrepreneur, East Anglia seemed to promise well for the silk industry. Few of the new throwing mills appeared there before the end of the eighteenth century, but in the next quarter-century, aided by a sharp increase in import duties on foreign thrown silk,[9] water- or steam-powered mills were set up at Pebmarsh, Braintree, Bocking, Coggeshall, Colchester and Hadleigh – all in the old wollen textile area of the Essex-Suffolk border.[10] During the same period there were substantial increases in the handloom weaving of silk in the same region: Braintree and Bocking, Coggeshall, Colchester, Hadleigh, Halstead, Haverhill, and the important area in and around Sudbury, including such villages as Glemsford and Cavendish.[11] Many of the entrepreneurs associated with his business came from, or had connections with, London. John Hall who set up a mill at Coggeshall in 1818, and put out work to handloom weavers, was concerned with his partner Thomas Sawyer in a firm of ribbon manufacturers of London and Coventry; George Courtauld, who had been apprenticed to a London throwster, started up mills at Pebmarsh in 1800 and Braintree in 1809 on behalf of two different London firms; his son, Samuel, later started mills at Bocking and Halstead.[12] In the early decades of the century some of the throwing at these and other mills was done on the throwsters own account, some on commission for silk manufacturers at London or Coventry. Around 1820 many Spitalfields manufacturers were said to be employing country weavers;[13] and by 1840 almost all the employers putting out work to handloom weavers in the Essex-Suffolk area were London firms, such as Daniel Walters, Carter and Vavasseur, and T.F. Gibson of Spital Square. 'These towns are . . . as far as their silk manufacturers are concerned, merely outposts or dependencies of London, and they have all of them participated in the prosperity and shared in the calamities of the trade of the metropolis'.[14] Further north the influence of London was still present, though not directly related to Spital-fields. The Norwich industry turned more and more to silk as the old worsted trade declined; several thousand handloom weavers found employment

---

[9]   The rates went up from 4s. 11d. per lb. in 1781, by stages to 8s. in 1797-1801, thence by further stages to 14s. 8d. from 1814 to 1823. *B.P.P.*, 1831-32, xix, pp. 11, 265.

[10] *B.P.P.*, 1834, xx, pp. 369, 373, 375, 377; 1839, xlii (returns relating to factories); Ward-Jackson, *History of Courtaulds*, pp. 16-17; *Victoria County History: Essex*, ii, pp. 462-69.

[11] *B.P.P.*, 1840, xxiii, pp. 125-38.

[12] *B.P.P.*, 1834, Vol. xx, pp. 369, 373; 1831-32, Vol. xix, pp. 124-26, 372-84; Ward-Jackson, *History of Courtaulds, passim.*

[13] *B.P.P.*, 1821, Vol. vii, pp. 436, 441, etc.

[14] *B.P.P.*, 1840, Vol. xxiii, p. 125.

in this way. One large firm was instrumental in setting up mills for throwing and winding, as well as employing weavers in weaving shops. Joseph Grout went into the silk business in 1806 and by 1826 the firm of Grout, Bayliss & Co., silk manufacturers of Foster Lane, London, employed over 3,500 in Norfolk and Suffolk: they had throwing mills at Norwich, Yarmouth, Bungay and Mildenhall; employed handloom weavers, not only in Norfolk but in Essex as far afield as Sible Hedingham, Saffron Walden, Bocking and Braintree; and, according to Grout, had a capital in 1834 of £150-160,000.[15]

Until about the mid 1820s this expansion of the silk industry in East Anglia went some way towards compensating for the decline of the old industries, though, as the poor relief figures show, not very far. But between the 1820s and 1840s, along with some other centres of the British silk manufacture, East Anglia suffered shocks which brought further concentration to the area's industrial employment and, in the longer run, drastically changed the nature of what was to survive. The Free Trade ministrations, first of Huskisson and then of Peel, shattered the industry's protective shell. Although the duties on raw silk came down to a nominal penny in 1825 those on imported thrown silk were cut sharply, from 14s. 8d. per lb. in 1823 to a mere 5s. in 1825, and then to rates varying from 1s.6d to 3s. in 1829. What remained of these import duties was wholly repealed in 1845. Meanwhile, the prohibition on imported silk manufactures was replaced in 1826 by duties averaging about 30 per cent; and then in 1845 reduced again to about 15 per cent.[16] This exposure of both throwsters and weavers to competitive draughts put at an advantage silk manufacturers with large units, up-to-date throwing machinery, low costs, and a willingness to invest in power looms for weaving simple, standardized fabrics; it put at a disadvantage small, remote, old-fashioned throwing mills, and handloom weavers working on traditional designs and figured fabrics. To add to their troubles, throwsters were hard hit by furious fluctuations in silk prices, due allegedly to speculative buying in the course of 1836.[17]

All the industry felt the draught but the handloom weavers of Spitalfields and East Anglia, as well as remote and scattered producers in the West Country and Home Counties, suffered most; and those in the North-West prospered. This rough generalization needs qualification of course: inefficient producers went under in the North-West just as some particularly efficient producers consolidated their position and went ahead in East Anglia. But meanwhile in the short-run the outlook was poor for those dependent on the East Anglian silk industry.

[15] *B.P.P.*, 1831-32, xix, pp. 691-94; 1834, xx, p. 1109.

[16] *B.P.P.*, 1831-32, xix, pp. 5, 11, 265; Thomas Tooke & William Newmarch, *A History of Prices* (1838-57, ed. T.S. Gregory, 1928), v, p. 416.

[17] *B.P.P.*, 1840, xxiii, p. 129.

Its prospects in the task of adapting itself to changing conditions were not rosy. Although all silk throwsters were heavily dependent on the labour of young girls, East Anglian mills seem, from one report at least, to have used a particularly large proportion of this type of labour (Table 4.3).

Table 4.3

Employment in Silk and Cotton Factories, 1833*

	FEMALES AS PERCENTAGE OF ALL EMPLOYEES	FEMALES UNDER ELEVEN AS PERCENTAGE OF ALL FEMALE EMPLOYEES	FEMALES UNDER SIXTEEN AS PERCENTAGE OF ALL FEMALES EMPLOYED
Silk			
Norfolk, Suffolk & Essex	96	14	53
Somerset	80	12	39
Derbyshire	63	8	35
Cotton			
Lancashire	50	4	33

* Constructed from the figures given in Dr. James Mitchell's report – based on answers obtained from enquiries sent to factories – to the Factory Commissioners – *B.P.P.*, 1834, xix, pp. 291-94.

The county with the highest silk mill employment in the country, Cheshire (unfortunately excluded from this particular report), probably had a similarly heavy concentration of young female labour.[18] The numbers or proportions employed do not, however, tell the whole story. It is clear that in East Anglia some silk throwsters were able to use double sets of hands for night work. In contrast, the overwhelming majority of silk manufacturers in Cheshire and Derbyshire, as well as those in Lancashire and Staffordshire, found that their labour supply was inadequate for this. Samuel Courtauld used, for example, a double set and worked his mills day and night; but J. & T. Brocklehurst, at Macclesfield, did not work by night, and maintained that even when work was abundant, no second set could be found. Several manufacturers in the North-West pointed to the effect on wages which such attempts would bring about, and one Derby employer observed bluntly that for night and day working not enough children could be had at sufficiently low wages.[19]

[18] The figures for 1835 given in Porter, *Progress of the Nation*, yield results a little different from those obtined from Mitchell's figures, and suggest that Cheshire had a slightly higher proportion of young females than did the East Anglian counties.

[19] *B.P.P.*, 1834, xx, pp. 305, 314, 369, 374, 493, 495-96, 497, 573, 577-78, 581, 583, 591, 599, 627, 724; 1840, x, pp. 781-83.

In East Anglia the wages paid, for a twelve-hour day, were significantly lower than those in other areas. As the comparisons in Table 4.4 show, this was true within the same age-groups and was not simply a product of employing more young people.

Table 4.4

*Average Wages of Girls and young Women in Silk and Cotton Factories, 1833**

AREA	BELOW 11		11 TO 16		AGES 16 TO 21		21 TO 26		26 TO 31		31 TO 36		AV. POOR RATE PER HEAD IN 1831	
	s.	*d.*	*s.*	*d.*	*s.*	*d.*	*s.*	*d.*	*s.*	*d.*	*s.*	*d.*	*s.*	*d.*
Norfolk														
& Essex (silk)	1	5	2	7	4	0¾	5	0	4	11	4	4	16	11
Derbyshire (silk)	1	11	3	6½	5	11	7	0½	7	7	7	0½	6	7
Lancashire (cotton)	2	4¾	4	3	7	8½	8	5	8	7¾	8	9½	4	8

* *B.P.P.*, 1834, xix, pp. 291, 298

The lower the wage, the higher the poor rates. This correlation, for a few thousand female employees, would not prove much in itself. But the evidence of low wages amongst the East Anglian silk weavers provides powerful corroboration of the impoverished state of these textile workers. During the operation of the Spitalfields Acts the piece-rate wages paid to these weavers were generally about two-thirds of those paid in Spitalfields. Since their repeal in 1825, though there was apparently no settled relationship, the rates were uniformly well below those prevailing in London. It was generally maintained, moreover, that although rents were lower than in London, ordinary living expenses were not greatly different. Braintree, for instance, 'is sufficiently near London to be within the vortex; cheapness is not felt until farther down in the country: London is a sure market, and all articles of subsistence are drawn to it'.[20] Irregular employment often meant that many weavers' earnings were less than those of agricultural labourers. According to the type of fabrics, average weavers' earnings in the Essex-Suffolk border area, towards the end of the 1830s, varied from about 7*s.* to 13*s.* per week; agricultural labourers earned about 10s. plus some benefits in kind, e.g., beer or malt.[21] At about the same period, average weekly wages of men between the ages of twenty-one and forty-one working in Lancashire

[20] *B.P.P.*, 1840, xxiii, p. 128.
[21] Ibid., pp. 125-38.

cotton and Yorkshire woollen mills ranged from about 17s. to 22s 8d. per week.[22]

In brief, then, it seems probable that the opportunities open to entrepreneurs in the East Anglian silk industry for reducing costs by employing cheaper labour for longer hours were, by the 1830s and 1840s, virtually nil. The wages of both mill hands and weavers had already been reduced. According to Grout, the average rate of wages paid to all his employees had risen from 7s. 6d. in 1822 to 8s. 8½d. in 1825 and fallen to 3s. 8½d. in 1831.[23] Hall stated in 1832 that he had reduced the wages of the children he employed by 20 per cent in the past two years, 'a great and principal reduction in my annual expense'.[24] Although reductions were confined neither to East Anglia nor to the silk industry, the East Anglian silk industry wages were now running at levels which permitted of no further reduction. Competitive difficulties often made weaving work irregular, and it is quite clear that by about the 1840s there had been a substantial reduction in the total numbers employed in East Anglia as handloom silk weavers. In Norwich and vicinity in 1840 a census of handloom silk and worsted weavers showed 4,054 in employment and 1,021 unemployed. Wages there had fallen about 20 per cent in 1829 and remained at about that level thereafter, though increasing irregularity of employment had substantially reduced earnings.[25] In the Braintree area there was clearly a pool of underemployed weavers which served to keep wages down. Some firms had abandoned or contracted their weaving activities. Silk weaving at Coggeshall and Hadleigh had been given up by 1840.[26] Of Braintree and Bocking the report in 1833 for the Poor Law Commissioners noted 'a very dense population', formerly dependent on woollen weaving. The recently introduced silk weaving, the report observed, had at first paid high wages and given full employment, but now, since the reduction of the duties on foreign silks, many were unemployed and wages were made up out of the poor rates. At Braintree the rates per head were 18s. 2d., at Bocking and Coggeshall 18s. 6d. in the pound; by contrast at Chelmsford they were 6s. 6d. and at Saffron Walden 4s. 10d.[27]

In the throwing mills, manufacturers were complaining that it was no longer easy to get enough labour. Hall told the Select Committee on the Silk Trade in 1832 that were he to erect another mill it would not be at Coggeshall but 'in a situation where I should have more hands';[28] 'at Pebmarsh', Witts and Roddick testified in 1833 'the population is not

---

[22] *B.P.P.*, 1834, xix, pp. 291-92.
[23] *B.P.P.*, 1831-32, xix, p. 692.
[24] Ibid., p. 372.
[25] *B.P.P.*, 1840, xxiii, pp. 149-51.
[26] Ibid., pp. 126-38.
[27] *B.P.P.*, 1834, xxviii, p. 229A.
[28] *B.P.P.*, 1831-32, xix, p. 373.

superabundant for our employ; to induce fresh hands to settle would not be practicable'.[29] Grout at the same time bemoaned the shortage of children as having limited the extent of his works, at Norwich, Yarmouth, Mildenhall and Ditchingham: 'after having erected mills at one place . . . we have been obliged to go to another, having found it difficult to obtain a sufficient number of young females for our purposes'. He added significantly: 'The wages we are at present obliged to pay are so very low that no adult labour could be got for the money'.[30] The stick of competition and the carrot of profits combined, as usual, to bear hardest upon the weakest links.

The East Anglian firms which did survive from these difficult years were, not surprisingly, chiefly those which invested in power-loom weaving and concentrated on a narrow range of fabrics, indeed almost on one fabric. Both Grout and Courtauld were already in the 1830s weaving the simple gauzes, from which they both made all-silk crape, on looms driven by water- or steam-power.[31] In 1835, Essex and Norfolk had 406 power looms out of the 1,714 in the English silk industry as a whole.[32] As the numbers of handloom weavers contracted, so did the numbers working in the factories, mainly of these two firms, slowly increase. Paradoxically, then, in an area of long-term industrial contraction, the factory returns show a small increase in the total numbers employed in the East Anglian silk industry. (Table 4.5).

Table 4.5

Employment in Silk Factories

	ENGLAND AND WALES	EAST ANGLIA
1838	34,233 (U.K.)	4,180
1850	41,703	3,990
1857	55,300	6,235

* *B.P.P.*, xlii; 1850, xlii; 1857, xiv.

For three counties this is small stuff in the new age of industrialization when cotton factories gave employment in Lancashire alone to 149,769 in 1838, rising to 258,343 in 1857. But for East Anglia this was virtually all that was left of a once widespread and flourishing textile industry. These few

[29] *B.P.P.*, 1834, xx, p. 378.
[30] Ibid., p. 1110.
[31] *B.P.P.*, 1840, Vol. xxiii, pp. 126, 157-58; 1834, xx, p. 369; 1831-32, pp. 691ff.
[32] *B.P.P.*, 1836, xlv, p. 152.

mills represented concentrated and specialised outposts of factory industry in what had become by the mid-nineteenth century an overwhelmingly agricultural area. The intervening years had seen hope and failure, decay, revival, and drastic change. In the process, many wage-earning families had known greater poverty than that experienced by their counterparts who depended on the new factories of the North-West. Though the social and physical environment of those East Anglian families, free of the smoke and dirt of the fast-growing, over-crowded and unlovely towns of coalfield England, cannot but seem preferable, at least to us today, their monetary position was surely worse. Here, the '30s and '40s were for many both bleak and hungry.

5

*Proto-Industrialization: A Concept Too Many**

For about a decade now a new word has been rattling around in the corridors of economic history. Responsibility for the innovation seems to rest with Franklin Mendels, who publicized it in an article in the *Journal of Economic History* in 1972.[1] The word was 'proto-industrialization' and its intellectual appeal was such that it was soon popping up in sundry books and articles. Under the aegis of Pierre Deyon, for example, a whole issue of the *Revue du Nord* in 1979 was devoted to a consideration of it in relation to industry in northern France.[2] A neo-Marxist variation on the main theme came in the shape of a book by three scholars – Peter Kriedte, Hans Medick and Jürgen Schlumbohm – at the Max Planck Institute for History at Göttingen. Preceded in 1976 by a curtain-raising article in *Social History* by

---

* Despite the millions of words written about the Industrial Revolution nobody knows precisely why it began when it did. It was predictable that sooner or later research into the nature and organization of earlier sorts of industry would be undertaken with a view to producing a theory of change. It duly came in the 1970s under the name of 'Proto-industrialization', having been developed initially by an American scholar and then by French and German scholars. It was said to be 'a first phase with preceded and prepared modern industrialization proper'. The second phase was introduced by the industrial revolution, 'the theoretical instant when an economy enters into phase two'. (Franklin Mendels, 'Proto-industrialization: The First Phase of the Industrialization Process', *Journal of Economic History*, xxxii (1972), p. 241.

When it was selected as a main topic for discussion at an international economic history conference at Budapest in 1982 I found myself involved as a participant invited to comment upon the papers presented. Having read the numerous contributions I made some critical observations. They clearly found little favour with the proponents of the theory though perhaps securing a rather more sympathetic response from some English empiricists and other such eccentrics. This essay, which originally appeared as one of the Essays in Bibliography and Criticism periodically published by the *Economic History Review*, is an extended version of these comments.

Over the years since the Budapest conference various other commentators have criticized or supported, modified or enlarged the concept. A useful survey and bibliography will be found in L.A. Clarkson, *Proto-industrialization: The First Phase of Industrialization?*

[1] 'Proto-industrialization: The First Phase of the Industrialization Process', *Journal of Economic History*, xxxii, (1972), pp. 241-61.

[2] *Revue du Nord*, lxi, (1979), pp. 7-208.

107

Medick,[3] it was published in German in 1977 as *Industrialisierung vor der Industrialisierung* and in English as *Industrialization before Industrialization*.[4] In Scandinavia a whole issue of the *Scandinavian Economic History Review* was devoted to the topic;[5] in Britain the S.S.R.C. financed a small conference organized by Dr. Maxine Berg on 'Manufacture in Town and Country Before the Factory', which was held in Oxford in 1980.[6] The ultimate accolade for the notion came with the decision, made in 1979, that proto-industrialization should be one of the two main 'A' themes for discussion at the Eighth International Economic History Congress to be held at Budapest in 1982. Profs. Mendels and Deyon were appointed to convene the relevant session; contributions were solicited and a preliminary conference was held at Bad Homburg in May 1982. Finally, in August at Budapest, the topic of 'proto-industrialization; theory and reality' was subjected, with the aid of no fewer than forty-nine contributions and a General Report by Mendels, to a total of ten and a half hours of multilingual debate.

It is not my intention here to try to summarize either the contributions or the debate, even were that possible. Suffice to note that they embraced statements of faith in the theory and the provision of evidence in its support; statements of doubt or modification and the provision of evidence in its partial refutation; and statements of total disbelief. The forty-nine contributions were nothing if not wide-ranging. They included observations upon the alleged existence or otherwise of proto-industrialization within the confines of Africa, America, China, Denmark, England, Flanders, France, Germany, India, Ireland, Italy, Japan, Korea, Netherlands, Poland, Spain, and Taiwan, as well as theoretical constructs attached to no noticeable geographical base. My more limited aims are to indicate the origins and content of the theory; to look at some problems which arise when trying to apply it to England; and to offer some comments on the concept in principle.

Any examination of the theory must make an initial distinction between the Mendels version and the neo-Marxist version. Although they have a number of common elements, there are significant differences in argument, language and purpose.

The Mendels version started with his 1969 Ph.D. dissertation at the University of Wisconsin, 'Industrialization and Population Pressure in

---

[3] 'The Proto-industrial Family Economy: The Structural Function of Household and Family during the Transition from Peasant Society to Industrial Capitalism', *Social History*, i, (1976), pp. 291-315.

[4] P. Kriedte, H. Medick and J. Schlumbohm, *Industrialization before Industrialization*, translated from German by Beate Schempp (Cambridge, 1981). (Hereafter: K.M.& S., *Industrialization*).

[5] *Scandinavian Economic History Review*, xxx, (1982), pp. 1-99.

[6] The papers given at the conference were published under that title by C.U.P. in 1983.

Eighteenth Century Flanders'. This was a study of the relatively rapid population growth experienced in an internal region of eighteenth-century Flanders, where a peasant population combined agriculture with part-time linen manufacture, much of the output of which was sold on overseas markets. On this local base Mendels developed a general theory first adumbrated in his 1972 article. In the ensuing years the hypotheses there set out were variously amended, largely as a result of the discussions and publications which the article provoked. Indeed, even before the 1972 article had appeared Charles and Richard Tilly had, in their own words, 'lifted the term (and some of its supporting arguments)'[7] from Mendels' thesis and proposed the investigation of various aspects of proto-industrialization as a desirable activity for economic historians in the 1970s. Their proposal evidently had the desired effect. The task, undertaken jointly by Mendels and Deyon, of preparing a text for the preliminary conference at Bad Homburg and thereafter for the Budapest Congress stimulated further clarifications. The process culminated in an agreed joint definition set out in the General Report written by Mendels and made available to all participants in the Congress.[8] This text can thus be regarded as the authorized version.

It emphasizes a number of features which are seen as crucial to the proper definition of proto-industrialization. Five main features may be distinguished. 1. The unit of reference is the region. 'The hypotheses relating to proto-industrialization should stand or fall on the basis of regional not national or international analysis and data collection'.[9] 2. The central feature of proto-industrialization was the growth within that region of rural industry involving peasant participation in handicraft production for the market. It provided a necessary income supplement. It was seasonal, meshed in with the rhythm of agriculture, though in its 'extreme or ultimate form'[10] it could be a full-time family occupation. 3. The market for the goods produced by this activity was outside the region, often even outside the national frontiers. This element of the definition is to be stressed because thereby proto-industrialization is distinguished from the sort of petty industry which had long supplied local needs. 4. There was an essential linkage between proto-industrial activity and commercial agriculture. Not only did some other regions develop a food surplus which then met the needs of peasants unable to feed themselves from their small plots, but the latter supplemented their incomes both by proto-industrial activity

---

[7] C. Tilly and R. Tilly, 'Agenda for European Economic History in the 1970s', *Jnl. Econ. Hist.*, xxxi (1970), p. 187, n. 2.

[8] F. Mendels, 'Proto-industrialization: Theory and Reality. General Report': 'A' Themes. Eight International Economic History Congress, Budapest (1982), pp. 69-107. (Hereafter: Mendels, 'Report').

[9] Mendels, 'Report', p. 77.

[10] Ibid.

and by seasonal wage work on big farms. So within the general category of proto-industrialization came 'homogeneous regions where each village might have both a peasantry engaged in cottage industry and a class of larger food surplus producing farmers'.[11] 5. Towns within the region were associated with the process because of their marketing facilities and because they provided 'the merchants of the putting-out system [who] directed the manufacturing activity dispersed in the surrounding countryside'.[12]

So, in summary: 'Proto-industrialization is thus defined by the simultaneous occurrence of three ingredients within the framework of a region: rural industries, external destinations, and symbiosis of rural industry within the regional development of a commercial agriculture'.[13]

With the essential characteristics defining proto-industrialization thus set out, there follows a set of hypotheses, viz: 1. The generation of supplementary handicraft incomes will lead to an expansion of population, breaking up the self-regulating or homeostatic equilibrium of pre-industrial populations whereby the natural rate of growth is adjusted to local means of subsistence. 2. A region thus experiencing growing population and growing proto-industrialization will soon begin to encounter diminishing returns as dispersed industry creates difficulties in the collection of output and the control of quality. This will conduce to the concentration of manpower in workshops and then to the use of labour-saving mechanical inventions. 3. As a result of proto-industrial development, capital for these workshops or the introduction of machines will accumulate locally in the hands of merchants, commercial farmers or landowners. 4. Proto-industrialization will lead to the accumulation by merchants of technical knowledge as a result of their experience with inter-regional and international trade. In this way it provides 'a training ground in which the early industrialists were recruited'.[14] 5. The simultaneous development of proto-industrialization and a regional commercial agriculture will prepare the agricultural sector for the task of supplying food during the urbanization which accompanies the subsequent phase of industrialization.

These definitions and hypotheses together make up the essence of proto-industrialization as a theory, viz. that a region experiencing proto-industrialization will be propelled towards an industrial revolution by these mechanisms. Or at least, it will tend to be. This qualification is made because 'regional proto-industrialization sometimes proved to be a dead end'.[15] In such an event the region is said to experience 'de-industrialization'.

[11] Ibid., pp. 79-80.
[12] Ibid., p. 79.
[13] Ibid.
[14] Ibid., p. 80.
[15] Ibid.

So much for the general outline of the Mendels version. Before moving on to any further examination of it the neo-Marxist or Kriedte-Medick-Schlumbohm (K.M. & S. for short) variant demands attention. The book in which it is set out consists of two parts. Part I comprises an introduction and six chapters (two by each of the three authors) of exposition largely theoretical in character. Although these chapters do contain some illustrative material, much of the empirical content of the volume is provided in two different ways. One arrives in Part II, which consists of two reprinted articles: one by Mendels, 'Agriculture and Peasant Industry in Eighteenth-Century Flanders';[16] and the other by Herbert Kisch, 'The Textile Industries in Silesia and the Rhineland: A Comparative Study in Industrialization',[17] plus a brief postscript. The other route to empirical underpinning comes in the form of 129 pages of footnotes which guide the reader to an impressively wide range of secondary documentation.

Like a number of such works, the book has a conscious and welcome eclecticism, drawing upon the ideas not only of Marx but also of non-Marxist economists and economic historians, new and old, as well as such social theorists as Chayanov. Perhaps because of its multiple authorship, however, and its method of looking at one main idea from a series of different angles, it has much repetition and qualification; and the argument is not always easy to follow. Nor, alas, is enlightenment made easier by a prose style which, in Part I, is too often burdened by the millstones of a depressing jargon.

Here are some salient features of the broad line of argument. 1. K.M. & S. see their study as a further development of the Mendels theory (which they ascribe jointly to Mendels and to Charles and Richard Tilly). 'Proto-industrialization is here conceptualized as "industrialization before industrialization" which can be defined as the development of rural regions in which a large part of the population live entirely or to a considerable extent from industrial mass production for inter-regional and international markets'.[18] 2. It is a central feature of their argument, and indeed it is repeatedly stated, that proto-industrialization is part of the 'transition from feudalism to capitalism'. More specifically, it is said to belong to 'the second phase' of that transition.[19] 3. Proto-industrialization is said to have been concentrated in 'barren mountain regions' or 'harsh mountainous areas'.[20] This was so partly because the peasants there needed to increase their incomes as a result of the various ways in which 'social surplus labour' was appropriated; and partly because foreign markets were being opened up by 'merchant

[16] Originally published in W.N. Parker and E.L. Jones (eds.), *European Peasants and their Markets* (Princeton, 1975).
[17] Originally published in *Jnl. Econ. Hist.*, xix, (1959), pp. 541-64.
[18] K.M. & S., *Industrialization*, p. 6.
[19] Ibid., p. 7; see also pp. 8, 9, 40-41, 77, 94.
[20] Ibid., pp. 14, 24.

capital'. The latter was thus able to exploit a rural substratum living on poor or insufficient land, dependent on rural by-occupations but lacking the support of a gild, the power of the towns having been broken. 4. When the peasant household set out on the path of proto-industrialization it generated changes and contradictions in its internal roles and external functions. One of these changes was to favour early marriage and to stimulate the production of 'a maximal number of child labourers' by those people who were 'least capable of rearing them'. The imbalance and paradox can be explained only by the 'specific conditions of exploitation to which the entire family labour-power was subjected in proto-industrialization'.[21] Thus did proto-industrialization break through 'the demo-economic system which regulated the feudal agrarian societies of Europe'[22] and give rise to a 'dynamic of reproduction in proto-industrial families . . . anchored in a characteristic "generative structure"'.[23] 5. Proto-industrialization saw the transition from the *Kaufsystem* in which 'the sphere of production was ruled by the laws of petty commodity production' to the *Verlagsystem* which saw 'the penetration of capital into the sphere of production'.[24] 6. In England, although 'the laws of the family economy functioned as the engine of proto-industrial growth' they also 'stood in fundamental contradiction to the growth-dynamic of the overall system'. The only way out of the crisis was 'mechanization coupled with centralization':[25] hence the industrial revolution. In continental Europe, however, industrialization was primarily a response to the English challenge; consequently, the transition from proto-industrialization took longer. 7. Although proto-industrialization provided 'certain conditions for a capitalistic industrialization' they were not 'sufficient to actually introduce the process of industrialization'.[26] The proto-industrial system was marked by internal contradictions which gave rise to serious problems during its growth phase. If these were not resolved, and if the necessary 'general framework of capitalist industrialization'[27] was lacking or insufficiently developed, then the transition to industrialization might fail and de-industrialization take place.

The common ground occupied by the two variants is too obvious to need stressing. Both are variations on the familiar theme of a stage-theory of economic growth. For Mendels, proto-industrialization is 'the first phase of the industrialization process'; for K. M. & S. it is 'the second phase of the great transformation from feudalism to capitalism'. So, for the moment, let

---

[21] Ibid., p. 57.
[22] Ibid., p. 77.
[23] Ibid., p. 81.
[24] Ibid., pp. 99, 101 and chap. 4, *passim.*
[25] Ibid., pp. 136, 137.
[26] Ibid., pp. 145-46.
[27] Ibid., p. 147.

us put on one side the differences between the two and ask what happens if the theory as a whole is applied to England. By trying to see how it fits the origins and evolution of the sorts of industry comprehended within the term and by examining how they, in turn, may have conduced to industrial revolution it may be possible to consider the theory in the light of English historical experience. Obviously this can be attempted here only in the most general fashion, but it seems worth attempting if only because of the primacy of the English industrial revolution and the well-known existence of several areas of rural industry.

The timing of proto-industrialization is as good a place to begin as any. The proponents of the theory offer various times for various places, but the sixteenth and seventeenth centuries seem to be the favourite starting periods. This raises the first difficulty when looking at the English scene. From the thirteenth century onwards there is an increasing amount of evidence for the growth of a rural, domestic, putting-out textile industry, feeding overseas markets and experiencing, over six successive centuries, phases of expansion and contraction before finally going under in the face of mechanized production in the nineteenth century. When are we to say that proto-industrialization began in England and why? Several periods between, approximately, the 1380s and the 1750s offer ample evidence of a textile industry conforming to the general outlines of the Mendels model but doing so in differing demographic circumstances. For example, was that break-up of a homeostatic equilibrium, which proto-industrialization is said to bring, brought to the various textile manufacturing districts of England during the long growth phase which, with fluctuations, ran from about 1490 to 1630 whilst population was rising, or during the subsequent growth phase which many of them enjoyed between about 1660 and 1740, when population was nearly static? Or again, if it was in the 1490-1630 period that proto-industrialization was busily breaking through what K. M. & S. call 'the demo-economic system which regulated the feudal agrarian societies' creating in England 'a maximal number of child labourers', why did not those 'laws of the family economy' and their various contradictions contrive to bring about an industrial revolution in the seventeenth century?[28] Alternatively, if the break-through happened not in that period but in the eighteenth century, what meanwhile had happened to feudalism which, by any meaningful definition of that overworked word, had long vanished from England by the time that Blake was being troubled by dark Satanic mills? Or, yet again, if proto-industrialization developed because of the need for peasants to supplement their exiguous incomes one might reasonably expect this to happen at a time of falling real wages. Yet the English textile

---

[28] It is pleasingly ironic to note that the only candidate hitherto offered for an industrial revolution in that period – J.U. Nef's – was built upon virtually every sort of industry except those specified in proto-industrialization theory.

industry seems to have expanded in the period from the later fourteenth to the mid-fifteenth centuries and again in the later seventeenth to the early eighteenth centuries when real wages were rising, just as it did from approximately 1490 to 1550 and again from about the 1570s to the 1630s when real wages were falling.

Of course, these national swings, mainly derived from export trends, conceal the rise and fall of particular fabrics from particular areas. And so we come to the second big problem in the application of the theory to England. In what regions did proto-industrialization occur? Leaving aside Scotland and Ireland (from convenience rather than prejudice), about a dozen areas, all well-known to students of the subject, can be lined-up as runners in the English proto-industrialization stakes. They comprise the four main woollen textile areas of East Anglia, the West Country, the South-West and the West Riding of Yorkshire; some lesser woollen areas, viz. the Shropshire-Welsh border zone, the Westmorland industry centred around Kendal, the southern area embracing the Kentish Weald and parts of Surrey, Berkshire, and Hampshire, and a scattered central area covering manufacture in and around such towns as Coventry, Northampton and Lincoln. Two other different textile zones can also be clearly identified: Lancashire, originally with a woollen industry but later concentrating on linens and fustians; and the hosiery knitting area around the Vale of Trent, covering parts of the counties of Nottingham, Derby, and Leicester. Finally, there was the area primarily concerned with the making of small metal wares which was heavily concentrated in the West Midlands.

As soon as one asks whether these were all 'regions' in the sense required by the theory, one is immediately made aware that neither of the gospels provides a precise definition. Mendels offers a clue: 'the geographic space roughly coterminous with the traditional region defined by geographers'.[29] Following up the clue reveals that many of the familiar English areas do not coincide with single homogeneous geographical regions. For example, the Weald is an identifiable geographical region but the West Country is not; its textile industry was to be found in more than one region, though some of those regions did have certain similar geographical and farming character-istics. Likewise, the East Anglian area comprised both the Stour valley region and a quite separate zone in and around Norwich. According to the definitions used, so will the number of regions vary.

Were these regions harsh, barren and mountainous as the K. M. & S. version demands? Westmorland and the Welsh border come nearest to meeting this requirement and, with a little elasticity of definition, the edges of Dartmoor and the Pennines to which other well-known industrial areas spread, might also by thus accommodated. But by no imaginative stretching of definition could East Anglia or the putative Black Country be called

---

[29] Mendels, 'Report', p. 77.

harsh, barren or mountainous. And the nucleii of many rural textile areas seem to have been not in mountains but in river valleys: the Eden in Westmorland, the Wylye and the Bristol Avon in Wiltshire, the Stroud in Gloucestershire, the Stour and its tributaries in Suffolk, the upper reaches of the Aire and the Calder in Yorkshire, to offer but some examples. If 'barren and mountainous' can be translated to mean valleys and wooded uplands with mixed pastoral farming and easy access to grazing on the waste, only then could the English rural industrial scene begin to approximate to this requirement of the theory.

And did the indigenous population there turn to industrial by-employments because of poor soils and inadequate agrarian incomes (Mendels)? Or was it also because after the enclosure movement of sixteenth century England and the process of 'differentiation and polarization to which the peasantry was subjected', cottagers who lost their common land were 'practically forced into rural industry' (K. M. & S.)?[30] The latter explanation runs into the difficulty that many of the regions of rural industry were already enclosed before the sixteenth century and that much of the enclosure movement of that century affected other areas. Moreover, where enclosure and spreading rural industry did coincide, the prime agent was probably not enclosure but population growth.[31] The Mendels explanation seems likely to fit the facts better, though, as already noted, the expansion of rural handicrafts and putting-out was taking place certainly from the fourteenth century onwards in times of rising as well as of falling real wages. Furthermore, although it is clear that in some areas from the later sixteenth century onwards an increasing number of families were becoming dangerously dependent on industrial earnings, it cannot be deduced therefrom that their predecessors necessarily took up these by-employments because poor soils had made their agrarian incomes inadequate and because 'merchant capital' was waiting to pounce. In truth, any attempt to explain the development of rural industry and its distribution over the English countryside has to take into account a variety of causes, operating either simultaneously or at different moments of time: inheritance patterns, strength of manorial control, ease of settlement, use of water power, availability of raw materials, proximity of wasteland, type of agriculture, size of holdings, local population density. Even then it will be salutary to recall the warning given by Joan Thirsk in her pioneering essay on this whole topic: 'there is no certainty or finality in any explanation of the growth of a rural industry in one district rather than another'.[32]

---

[30] K.M. & S. *Industrialization*, p. 21.

[31] For a detailed example, see Victor Skipp, *Crisis and Development: An Ecological Case Study of the Forest of Arden, 1570-1674* (Cambridge, 1978).

[32] J. Thirsk 'Industries in the Countryside', in F.J. Fisher (ed.), *Essays in the Economic and Social History of Tudor and Stuart England* (Cambridge, 1961), pp. 70-88. I am grateful to Dr. Thirsk for her valuable comments on a draft of this article.

What of the most distinctive feature of both variants of the theory, viz. that proto-industrialization leads via earlier marriage to population growth? The greatest single difficulty here is clearly the absence of evidence. Without a statistically significant number of reconstitution studies of both industrial and non-industrial communities it is hard to see how the theory can be tested properly. Moreover, such studies will also have somehow to distinguish growth via in-migration from growth via earlier marriage; and they will need to be correlated with data on local real earnings. No existing studies are adequate to test the hypothesis satisfactorily. To make matters worse for the theory, the most recent findings on English population generally in the early modern period suggest that change was substantially a product of shifts in fertility consequent upon changes in the age of marriage; this in turn was apparently related to movements in real wages. When age at marriage began to fall around the beginning of the eighteenth century it did so in a phase of rising real wages and, furthermore, in 'agricultural' and 'industrial' communities alike.[33] So, for England at least, this particular argument of the theory looks unconvincing.

Do these various regions, however defined, support the hypothesis that proto-industrialization will lead dynamically to the mechanized activity of full industrialization? Omitting the central area on the grounds that it least conforms to the notion of a geographical region, and assuming that all the other areas are single regions for the purposes of the theory, then on a simple numerical count six regions did not move on directly to industrial revolution and four did.[34] In the negative category the southern region and the Westmorland area petered out well before the industrial revolution; others lasted longer, some of them changing the nature of their output from old to new draperies in the process and reaching a high point of prosperity around the end of the seventeenth century, only to decline slowly in the course of the eighteenth. The experience of those in the positive category needs no elaboration.

So this merely numerical evidence shows that more English regions experienced what the theory calls 'de-industrialization' than experienced the direct impact of industrial revolution. Incidentally, 'de-industrialization' must be the wrong term for this particular experience. De-industrialization is happening *today* in some parts of the older industrialized countries; in the context of the pre-industrial *past* the term must logically be 'de-proto-industrialization'. But presumably even the proponents of the theory boggled at that. 'Proto-industrialization' is bad enough; 'de-proto-industrialization'

---

[33] E.A. Wrigley and R.S. Schofield, *The Population History of England, 1541-1871* (1981), especially ch. 10 passim; and E.A. Wrigley, 'Marriage, Fertility and Population Growth in Eighteenth-Century England', in R.B. Outhwaite (ed.), *Marriage and Society* (1981), pp. 145-47.

[34] The six failures: East Anglia, West Country, South-West, Westmorland, Welsh border, and southern regions. The four successes; Yorks, Lancs, Trent and West Midlands regions.

is barbarous.[35] However, this counting in itself tells one nothing about causation or the route of transition. The process of change to full industrialization by no means invariably followed the routes specified in the hypotheses.[36] The obvious difference which separates the four which did receive the early impact of the industrial revolution from the six which did not is that the former were on, or very near to, coalfields. Nobody, however, would suppose that causation was as simple as that. But that the presence of coal and iron was of greater consequence in helping to determine the pattern of industrialization in England than was the existent distribution of so-called proto-industrialization is suggested by the industrial development of the North-East and South Wales. Neither area had any significant prior experience of what the theory recognizes as proto-industrialization, but both had coal and iron.

This observation will serve to introduce a further and related difficulty about the theory. Both versions seem to base it primarily, even solely, on rural, domestic, putting-out manufacture – cottage industry of one form or another. Virtually nothing is said about other types of rural industry, notably those involving some sort of centralized activity, e.g. in mines or mills, at furnaces, forges or boiling houses, in short, plant of any description. There is no examination of the different sex and age pattern of demand for labour in such industries; of how they fitted in with the peasant economy; of the agricultural activities of workers engaged therein; or, indeed, of the agrarian base of perhaps a majority of all workers in 'industry' in the widest sense. Nor does either version take significant heed of urban industry of either the domestic or the centralized variety, be it textiles, dockyards or soap-boiling. Digressing, for a moment, outside England to illustrate the effect of this narrow concentration, it is noteworthy that of the forty-nine contributions received for the Budapest Congress only one dealt with a wholly different form of industrial activity. Furthermore, in the special issue of the *Scandinavian Economic History Review* it is evident that much of the 'marked degree of scepticism'[37] about the usefulness of the concept for Scandinavian economic history arises from the difficulty of finding the sorts of industries and the requisite circumstances to fit the definition. If the purpose of the theory is to shed light on the way in which industrialization came about it is surely necessary to look at other sorts of

---

[35] This, however, may well fail to save it from appearing in the American fashion, without hyphens, as 'deprotoindustrialization'.

[36] For example, in the mechanization of the Yorkshire woollen industry the local mercantile community seems to have failed to play the role assigned to it by the theory. See R.G. Wilson, *Gentlemen Merchants: The Merchant Community in Leeds, 1700-1830* (Manchester, 1971), pp. 130ff.

[37] Lennart Jörberg, 'Proto-industrialization: an Economic Historical Figment', *Scand. Econ. Hist. Rev.*, xxx (1982), p. 2.

industrial activities and at urban manufacturing as well as rural in order to see if they conduced to or, equally important, failed to conduce to, industrialization proper.

The English scene again suggests that the sequence is far from simple and that blind alleys abound. For example, such towns as Manchester or Nottingham were seats of putting-out industry and their role in fostering industrialization was far more complex than the theory allows.[38] Or, to take a different example, the early industrialization of the Tyneside area – which can have had little experience of the proto-industrial family as defined in the theory, let alone of Chayanovian peasants – presumably owed something to the prior existence there of coal-mining and the coal trade (both coastal and export), glass-making and alkali manufacture not to speak of soap, salt, sulphuric acid and a real 'proto-factory' in the shape of the Crowley iron works. Or again, take the Kentish Weald. Its rural textile industry – with a full complement, as demanded by the theory, of clothiers, putting-out capitalism, peasant participation, a growing population, developing agricultural specialization and an esteemed export product – was at its apogee in the latter part of the sixteenth and the early seventeenth centuries. Moreover, this was only one industrial activity in a region which at the same time also had over fifty water-powered blast furnaces, constituting nearly 60 per cent of the country's total iron-smelting capacity. Yet its textile industry had failed by the end of the seventeenth century and its iron industry by the end of the eighteenth.

The pervasiveness of textiles in the theory and literature of proto-industrialization (forty of the forty-nine Budapest contributions dealt in some way with textiles) demands a particular comment. Fabrics, of whatever fibres, in England or elsewhere, readily became identified in pre-industrial manufacture with particular regions. It was not merely that they became widely known by names which were some variant of the place of production or of the port whence they were shipped, but it was the reality of a particular producing area becoming very heavily committed for long periods of time to the making of a particular type of fabric. Consequently, the more the products were sold on a widening international market and the greater the range of available substitutes, so competition by price, quality and type intensified and the more elastic became the demand. Meanwhile, however, the greater grew the difficulty of adaptation to such changes in demand in a putting-out system in which conservatism of method could almost be described as an endemic disease. Although the system knew little fixed capital it had much human capital, which means minds as well as hands; to re-tool a factory or scrap a plant is often easier than to bring about a fresh

---

[38] On the role of towns in early industrial development in England, see the article by J. Langton, 'Industry and Towns, 1500-1730', in R.A. Dodgshon and R.A. Butlin (eds.), *An Historical Geography of England and Wales* (1978), pp. 173-98.

approach in management or to re-train a work force with inherited ways of doing things. Of course, adaptation did take place: the new draperies are testimony to that. But adaptation has to be a *continuous* process in any economy which is not to be paralyzed into rigidity. Adaptation was the key to the survival of these textile-producing regions. And the mere existence of so-called proto-industrialization in such regions was no guarantee whatever of the appearance of the entrepreneurial skills or of the capital necessary to induce changes in production techniques as an adaptation either to changes in demand or to difficulties in supply.

Enough has been said perhaps to suggest that the theory looks a little unhappy when planted in English soil. But there are also objections in principle. The Mendels version insists upon precision: 'the theory of proto-industrialization consists of careful definitions and specific hypotheses'.[39] And yet at the same time it is to have very wide applicability. Its purpose of demonstrating and explaining a stage in the process of industrialization is to have potential validity from the middle ages to the twentieth century; in Europe, America, Asia or Africa; in past colonial territories and in the present Third World.[40] It is not clear how these two objectives can be reconciled. The more carefully the theoretical state of proto-industrialization is defined so as to achieve the specific hypotheses and the more widely it is then applied, the greater will be the probability that the hypotheses will not fit the facts. The more carefully defined it is to fit, say, eighteenth-century Lancashire the less likely it is that the resulting precise hypothesis will apply, to, say, nineteenth-century Japan. Conversely, the more variance permitted in order to give it flexibility the less valid it is as an explanatory device. If de-industrialization can be seen to follow proto-industrialization in a significantly large number of regions then the value of the theory is clearly put in question. The K. M. & S. version, in some ways more flexible though in others more deterministic, gives the game away in its provision for de-industrialization by specifying that something called 'the general framework of capitalist industrialization' is necessary in order that the conditions provided by proto-industrialization can lead to full industrialization. This may well be true, but it puts proto-industrialization itself in a wholly indeterminate position, leaving us unable to tell how much was caused by it and how much by all the other things comprehended within that

---

[39] Mendels, 'Report', p. 93.
[40] The hopes for this big spread were made abundantly clear in the preliminary text issued to participants when soliciting contributions for the Budapest Congress; and the response was evident in the geographical range of contributions received.

'general framework'.[41] We are back with that familiar collection of possible causes stigmatized by new economic historians as the 'shopping-list'.

The attempt to achieve precise definition is made in pursuit of the goal of rendering hypotheses 'falsifiable and refutable'.[42] This laudable aim is, however, perhaps more difficult to achieve than its proponents appreciate. For the theory is really very much more complex than brief summaries might suggest. Its variables are numerous and not all are readily susceptible to regression and correlation analysis. Some are measurable; some are not. A precise specification of such a model would be extremely difficult.[43] To expect it to perform successfully within parameters which would include widely variable cultures, climates and all manner of contexts from medieval Europe to modern Asia, is asking a lot. The answer to this may simply be that it is not that sort of model but just a suggestive hypothesis. Then the claim to precision and refutability goes out of the window; and a great deal of it becomes the familiar findings of various scholars dressed up in long words and sociological finery.

Of the two versions the more open to the latter charge is the K. M. & S. model with its talk of 'laws' and 'systems' and 'prerequisites'; of 'individualization and personalization' in relations between husband and wife; as well as of the 'whole problematic of the transition from feudalism to capitalism'.[44] This last certainly is a problem for Marxist historians. The insistence upon retaining this antique notion of two distinct growth stages, equivalent to supposed modes of production, called feudalism and capitalism, merely perpetuates the difficult task of filling in the interim of transition. Eric Hobsbawm's brilliant essay at doing the appropriate conjuring trick with the aid of the 'crisis of the seventeenth century' was one attempt to perform the task.[45] The K. M. & S. version of the Mendels proto-industrialization theory is essentially another such attempt to perform this particular Herculean labour demanded by Marxist theory.

[41] Cf. Prof. Pollard's comment on continental Europe: '. . . the concept [proto-industrialization] fails to deal with what ought to be one of the most fundamental aims of enquiry: the way in which some of the regions affected were able to convert to full industrialization, while others de-industrialized . . . The question still to be debated is whether we are dealing with a transitional phenomenon or with a dead end, and how far these alternatives were determined by inherent features'. See S. Pollard, *Peaceful Conquest: The Industrialization of Europe, 1760-1970* (Oxford, 1981), p. 76.

[42] Mendels, 'Report', p. 76.

[43] For example, it seems unlikely that the variables used by Almquist in his ingenious attempt to test the hypothesis for pre-famine Ireland would be adequate to meet the precisely defined version of the theory. See Eric L. Almquist, 'Pre-famine Ireland and the Theory of European Proto-industrialization: Evidence from the 1841 Census', *Jnl. Econ. Hist.*, xxxix (1979), pp. 699-718.

[44] K.M. & S., *Industrialization*, pp. 63, 94, 99, 136-37, 148, etc.

[45] E.J. Hobsbawm, 'The General Crisis of the European Economy in the Seventeenth Century', *Past and Present*, 5 (1954), pp. 33-53, and 6 (1954), pp. 44-65.

Irrespective of this specifically Marxist problem, both versions attempt definitions of proto-industrialization as a stage of growth towards industrial revolution or industrialization without much consideration of the meaning of these latter terms. So something specific is latched on to something vague. The very vagueness of these terms, however, is the reason for their common use. From its first, specific, British use the term 'industrial revolution' has been broadened out into a generalization, so that we speak of industrial revolutions in other countries. Its value lies precisely in its *not* having too careful a definition. It is, strictly speaking, a metaphor like so many of the terms which economic historians use. We cannot measure the industrial revolution. We measure component bits – output, export, productivity, capital formation, employment, wages, or the like – but not the totality. We recognize that the whole has immeasurable qualities far beyond its component economic bits. Similarly we know the qualities – for good or for bad – which industrialization brings to our lives today. But they are not necessarily founded on a predominance of industry within the region in which we live. Britain and Denmark, Switzerland and Japan, the U.S.A. and Sweden, or regions within those national entities, all enjoy the patterns and standards of living common to industrialized societies. Yet they are very different economies, by no means all based on the solution to problems of proto-industrialization by the establishment of mechanized industrial production. The benefits of industrialization may be built upon manufacturing industry or they may be imported in exchange for the export of agricultural products or oil or gold or by a variety of other routes. So what the theory of proto-industrialization is doing is to try to specify and define a route to a diverse and unspecific set of goals.

The only goal about which the theory is specific is that in which dispersed rural industry meets problems of costs and control, remedies these by setting up mechanized factory production, and gets the capital and entre-preneurship from those who had previously managed rural industry and sold its products. About that proposition three simple points may be made. First, there is nothing new about it; such topics have long been standard ingredients in texts on the British industrial revolution.[46] Second, some-times it happened that way and sometimes it did not;[47] and the theory of proto-industrialization, as its proponents admit, does not enable prediction to be made. Third, it is in any event concerned with only one small part of what we call industrial revolution or industrialization; it has no direct

---

[46] Mendels, 'Report', pp. 74 and 98 suggests that pre-industrial economies have been represented to students as static, 'feudal' entities separated from and contributing nothing to succeeding dynamic capitalist economies. To anyone who has worked and taught in the field of British economic history *c.* 1500-1850 such an accusation seems mildly astonishing.

[47] As Prof. Schremmer has put it in relation to Germany, 'the future development of a region with rural industry was in fact open-ended'. Eckhart Schremmer, 'Proto-industrialization: A Step Towards Industrialization?', *Journal of European Economic History*, x (1981), p. 670.

relevance whatever for the coming of steam power or the transformation of iron smelting and steel making, for railways, shipbuilding, mechanized papermaking and printing, gaslight, dyestuffs and all manner of familiar developments of the nineteenth century (let alone those of the twentieth) without which our notions of the industrialized society would not exist.

According to the *O.E.D.* the prefix 'proto', derived from the Greek, means first in time, earliest, original, primitive or, less commonly, first in rank or importance, chief or principal. Proto-industrialization, as defined in the theory, has no claim to conform to either of these definitions, especially to the more common meaning of being the earliest or original form of something.[48] To label a particular and carefully defined sort of rural industry in Europe from about the sixteenth or seventeenth century onwards as the earliest or original form of modern industry is to fly in the face of accepted meaning. And it does so not least because that particular sort possessed none of the more obvious characteristics of modern industry.[49] A more legitimate use of 'proto' is in the term 'proto-factory' in order simply to convey the idea of an early or original form of a concentration of workers in a plant.[50] But the proponents of the theory of proto-industrialization are clearly not content with that.

Should we be content and accept the concept as a valuable tool? The answer, or so it seems to me, is that we should be very grateful to Messrs. Mendels, Tilly, Deyon, Kriedte, Medick, Schlumbohm, and all other contributors to the debate for having stimulated so much thought and research on early modern economies; that we should certainly not abandon the region as a unit of study; that we should continue the hunt for common causes in the dawning of industrial revolution; but that we should not feel obliged to do so with the aid of the word and concept of proto-industrialization and still less with the notion of industrialization before industrialization.

[48] This point was made by Prof. Wolfgang von Stromer in a protest against the use of the term, which he circulated at Budapest.

[49] Curiously enough, the one characteristic of modern industry which putting-out manufacture sometimes developed, i.e. the possession of an industrial proletariat, albeit in an early form, is little stressed, even by K.M. & S.

[50] See, for example, H. Freudenberger and F. Redlich, 'The Industrial Development of Europe: Reality, Symbols, Images', *Kyklos*, xvii (1964), pp. 372-402; and S.D. Chapman and S. Chassagne, *European Textile Printers in the Eighteenth Century* (1981), pp. 194, 199.

6

*Gentlemen and Players**

The competence of businessmen in late Victorian and Edwardian England has come in for some hard knocks.[1] Some were handed out by contemporaries;

* In 1972, when this piece was written, the stream of publications trying to explain Britain's relative economic decline was not yet in spate. The successful challenges to the country's economic hegemony, mounted at the end of the nineteenth century by Germany and the U.S.A, had given rise to debate, both contemporary and subsequent, but more recent failings had as yet stimulated only a moderate outcry.

In its original conception, the purpose of the essay was to elaborate upon some nineteenth-century social features of the English business scene and to extend them into the 1950s and '60s. As should be evident, it is full of qualifications. It is concerned only with big public companies and leading businessmen; it dissents from the notion that there could be a direct casual relationship between attendance at Public Schools and something imprecisely called 'entrepreneurial failure'; it poses questions rather that stating conclusions. Nevertheless, these and like precautions did not prevent its use by others to support much more sweeping contentions. That the gentleman-and-players simile began also to pop up in sundry discussions of the general topic may perhaps have been helped along by a potted version of the essay which I gave as a B.B.C. talk. This was subsequently published in *The Listener* (vol. 90, no. 2333, 13 Dec. 1973) complete with cover photograph of a group labelled with the caption 'Gentlemen, Eton, 1870' and an inside picture called ' "Lord" Ted Dexter in action'. It showed the current cricketing hero in full flow. For the inclusion of this illustrative material I was of course in no way responsible. (The title of the original essay, incidentally, stimulated some requests for off-prints from departments of physical education at institutions as distant as Canada and Switzerland, countries not normally thought of as wholly devoted to cricket.)

Suffice to add in retrospect that the essay lays no claim to say anything about that great majority of English businessmen (let alone Scots, Welsh and Irish) who ran small companies and had never attended Public Schools and ancient Universities. Much information about historical British businessmen has now become available in the *Dictionary of Business Biography* (ed. David Jeremy, 5 vols., 1984-86). An extended version of some of the illustrations used in the article will be found in vol III (Oxford, 1980) of my *Courtaulds: An Economic and Social History*. A set of variations on the theme has been provided by Neil McKendrick's ' "Gentlemen and Players" revisited' in N. McKendrick and R.B. Outhwaite (eds.) *Business Life and Public Policy* (Cambridge 1986). A judicious survey of the Victorian entrepreneur will be found in P.L. Payne, *British Entrepreneurship in the Nineteenth Century* (2nd edn. 1990); and James Raven's 'British History and the Enterprise Culture', *Past and Present*, 123 (May 1989), pp. 178-204 gives a very useful run-down on the spate of publications on the whole topic.

[1] One of the necessary items in the travelling baggage of the university teacher today is the seminar paper, ready to be produced on request. The present essay started life in this way and is simply a final presentation of many preliminary drafts or short versions which have been given to sundry groups and seminars. I am grateful to those who, in ensuing discussions, have

others have been added by later generations of historians and economists. For the most part the chronicle of alleged defects is limited to the period running, approximately, from 1860 to 1914. Why this limitation?

Before 1860, whatever criticism might be levelled at industrialism or the social consequences of the new men, none could be aimed at their enterprise *per se*. The reason was the simple one that there were no standards; nobody had seen the like of it all before. So foreigners came to envy and returned to emulate; and home-bred lyricists such as Andrew Ure and Samuel Smiles celebrated economic advance and found moral purpose in business endeavour. Thereafter, historians have been so preoccupied with trying to find out why it happened, or with striking economic and social balances of its effects, that they have barely had a chance to consider the quality of this early business enterprise. Its quantity has apparently been all too obtrusive.

For the years after 1914 neither the shortcomings nor the achievements of English businessmen receive much attention in the standard economic history texts. The sequence of war, depression, recovery, more war, and then readjustment of the British economy in a new and rapidly changing world: these have been and still are the dominant themes. Despite a mounting pile of books about management techniques and sundry Anglo-American productivity comparisons unflattering to the English, the student of our economic history over the last fifty years is not offered any such vision of drooping deficiency as he is for the preceding half-century.

Some of the reasons for the disparity are obvious enough. For the later nineteenth century, the shock to native pride induced by the discovery that, in some respects at least, this country was being overtaken by those unfortunate enough to live outside Victoria's rule generated a violence of reaction which the historian can hardly miss. In later years the shocks were of a different order; and comment correspondingly so. Furthermore, though historians of industry have been busy amongst all sorts of pre-1914 records, only a very few firms have allowed the inquiring eye of the scholar to peer into their post-1914 files. There is also a reason of a different sort. The influence alike of the ideas of Keynes and of the overpowering facts of depression, recovery, and war have combined to push our approach to the economic past into certain distinctive routes. Obsessed since the Second World War with the problems of economic growth, we ask aggregative, or at most sectoral, questions about the economy ever since the First World War. Impressed by the need to measure, equipped with the tools of post-Keynesian economic theory, and supplied with an abundance of statistics,

variously contributed to the final form. An earlier version was read, separately, by Mr. Arthur Knight and by Mr. Malcolm Falkus, and I would like to thank them particularly for many helpful comments. They bear no responsibility, however, for the opinions expressed herein.

For some readers the title perhaps needs one piece of explanation: the Gentlemen *v* Players cricket match was played at Lord's Cricket Ground, London, annually (with only a few breaks) from 1806 to 1962.

we advance on pre-determined lines. The ideas and behaviour of men have come to be regarded as virtually irrelevant. Nor has this approach been confined to the post-1914 period. Arguments based especially on factor-endowments and the rates of growth of markets – treated as independent variables over which businessmen, either as salesmen or as lobbiers of governments, had no control – have also been applied to the classic period of alleged entrepreneurial decline. Their effect has been to downgrade the importance of businessmen's behaviour in attempts to compare the economic performance of Britain and other countries. Prof. Habakkuk, affirming that he knew 'no way of forming more than a general impression of the relative importance of . . . non-economic influence', plumped for certain economic factors as adequate to explain this country's lag behind America in the adoption of new industrial methods during the later nineteenth century.[2] No sooner had Dr Aldcroft canvassed the idea of general 'entrepreneurial failure' in Britain, 1870-1914, than Prof. Temin rejected it as a cause of British decline, relative to the U.S.A. and Germany; in the steel industry during the period 1880-1913.[3] Comparative factor-endowments and growth-rates are thus combined to exonerate businessmen from deficiencies once held against them.

But what are we to do when faced with such comments as the following, so widely spaced in time? Here is the U.S. Consul in Bradford in 1879:

> The Channel of commerce is changing . . . instead of changing with the stream, English manufacturers continue to sit upon the bank of the old water-course and argue from plausible but unprofitable scientific and commercial premises that it had no right to alter . . . [4]

And here is the U.S. Minister for Economic Affairs at the U.S. Embassy in London in 1955:

> An American Observer in Britain is struck by the apparent prevalence of basic attitudes towards industry in considerable contrast with those at home . . . There is the familiar point of industry's somewhat uncertain social status . . . There is a sense of doubt concerning the social utility of industry and the legitimacy of profit . . . Profits are often considered somewhat shameful . . . [5]

The immediate message is not the same, but there is a common underlying

---

[2] H.J. Habakkuk, *American and British Technology in the Nineteenth Century* (1962), p. 220.

[3] D.H. Aldcroft, 'The Entrepreneur and the British Economy, 1870-1914', *Econ. Hist. Rev.*, 2nd ser. xvii (1964); P. Temin, 'The Relative Decline of the British Steel Industry, 1880-1913', in H. Rosovsky, ed. *Industrialization in Two Systems* (New York, 1966), p. 154.

[4] Quoted in J. Potter, 'The British Timber Trade since 1850' (unpublished M.A. thesis, Manchester, 1949). I am grateful to my former colleague for telling me about this observation quoted in his thesis.

[5] Quoted in R.S. Edwards and H. Townsend, *Business Enterprise: Its Growth and Organization* (1961), pp. 566-67.

view. Though the 1879 comment seems here to spell out complacency and conservatism, and that of 1955 adds allegations of guilt about profits to the well-known theme of industry's social inferiority, both carry with them the implication that in American eyes English businessmen are deficient in the pursuit of profit.

It is of course possible to take the view that observations of this sort – and many more could be quoted – should be used only as evidence about American attitudes and not about English attitudes. In practice such auster- ity has proved only too resistible and all manner of literary comment, native as well as foreign in origin, has been pressed into service in the debate about Britain's comparative decline, especially during the so-called 'Great Depres- sion' period, 1873-96.[6] Precisely because such observations can be given no quantitative value and because the debate has been conducted largely in terms of comparisons between the performance of various countries, so has the reaction against such evidence, and the influences to which it allegedly testifies, proceeded apace. The notion of adverse 'social attitudes towards entrepreneurship' as a major factor causing retardation in economic deve- lopment in nineteenth-century Europe has been scathingly dealt with by Prof. Gerschenkron.[7] Prof. Landes has continued to mount a powerful rearguard action, incorporating entrepreneural attitudes in his study of European industrial advance.[8] But economists and econometric historians have little time for business history or, indeed, any sort of inquiry not employing the techniques of an economic science seen primarily as some- thing capable of prediction.

Such evidence as the attitudes of businessmen or the performance of particular firms and industries admittedly presents substantial methodolo- gical problems for the economic historian. They come to the fore in the attempts to compare national economic developments. How is entrepre- neurship (even if it can be isolated) to be treated as an assessable factor? How can it be allocated a degree of contribution to national failings or achieve- ments? Comparisons at an international level are of course extremely difficult: only too rarely do we possess enough information to make them with the degree of confidence which is only too often granted to their conclusions. But even if we abandon such premature claims and confine our

[6]   For some examples, see A.L. Levine, *Industrial Retardation in Britain, 1880-1914* (1967); for an admirable survey of the debate, complete with bibliography, see S.B. Saul, *The Myth of the Great Depression* (1969); and for a still more recent discussion of the entrepreneur, see Donald N. McCloskey and Lars G. Sandberg, 'From Damnation to Redemption: Judgements on the Late Victorian Entrepreneur', *Explorations in Economic History*, ix (1971).

[7]   A. Gerschenkron, 'Social Attitudes, Entrepreneurship and Economic Development' in his *Economic Backwardness in Historical Perspective* (Cambridge, MA. 1962), pp. 52-71.

[8]   David S. Landes, 'Technological Change and Development in Western Europe, 1750- 1914', in *Cambridge Economic History of Europe*, vi, especially pt. 1 (Cambridge, 1965), pp. 563-84; and in his *The Unbound Prometheus* (Cambridge, 1969), pp. 352-58 and 526-28.

attentions to examining the attitudes and achievements of English business-men in a national context only, we have still to decide – and to make clear our decision – by what criteria their views and performances are to be judged. Let us assume that the attitudes indicated by the two comments from American observers in 1879 and 1955, quoted above, have some correspondence with reality, that they truly tell us something of English businessmen, quite independently of what they may reveal about American ways of thinking. Or let us suppose that we have contemporary letters, diaries, account books, or the like, showing the views and performances of particular English businessmen and firms. We may judge evidence of this sort by various yardsticks. For example: (*a*) by certain standards of efficiency and productivity in the firm involving assumptions about continuous profit-maximization and choice of best practice, such as we might use today; (*b*) by criteria obtained as a result of taking into account social costs and/or benefits, including various types of externalities, not all of which are readily measurable or customarily considered;[9] (*c*) by strictly contemporary standards, i.e. we may try to purge our minds as far as possible of current teachings, and consider our evidence in the light of what contemporaries saw as the relevant criteria. Whether (*a*), (*b*), or (*c*) should be used depends on our purpose. In an ideal world some combination of all three would perhaps commend itself. Here, I shall concern myself with (*c*), regarding this as a necessary first step before which no really valid historical or economic judgement can be made, even though for certain purposes it may well be inadequate and should eventually be replaced by a more complex standard.

So the intention of this essay is to consider certain social and historical aspects of English business behaviour,[10] as suggested by the two quotations of 1879 and 1955 in the light of national and contemporary criteria, and firmly eschewing international comparisons.

What have been the recognized goals of success for the English business-man? What has a man hoped to do with a business fortune?

Prof. Perkin is surely right in stressing that social ambition provided an immensely powerful motor of business activity at the time of the industrial revolution. One does not have necessarily to accept his more comprehensive claims ('the pursuit of wealth *was* the pursuit of social status'; or 'underlying causes were social causes').[11] Yet it remains a fair deduction from the life-patterns of such as the Arkwrights, Strutts, Crawshays, Marshalls, Wilkin-sons, Wedgwoods, or Courtaulds that social advancement was one of the

---

[9] See, for examples, E.J. Mishan, *The Costs of Economic Growth* (1967), *passim.*

[10] English, *not* British. This article does not claim to sat anything about the Scots, Irish, or Welsh even though some may be mentioned *en passant.*

[11] H. Perkin, *The Origins of Modern English Society, 1780-1880* (1969), pp. 63, 85.

most prized possessions to be bought by an English business fortune. There is nothing new about this; nor, it must be stressed, was it in the least new for the industrial revolution period. A long line of Cannings, Springs, Greshams, Baynings, Ingrams, Cranfields, Hickses, Childs, Banks, Claytons, Hoares, and many more stretches back into the English socio-economic past. Those of the later centuries differed from their predecessors merely in adding manufacturing industry to commerce and finance as the likeliest path to success. They acquired, controlled, and deployed their capital in rather different ways; they faced different problems in reaching similar ends. As a first step in getting into perspective the quality, rather than the quantity, of English business enterprise at the time of the industrial revolution it is perhaps worth emphasizing that making things (and often with less fixed capital than was once popularly supposed) instead of dealing in things is a difference only of means, not of ends. No more then than today was the maximization of profits an end; it neither was, nor is today, the only means employed.[12] 'A realistic analysis', it has been said of modern business, 'must avoid the presumption of a profit motive, let alone a maximization of profit motive'.[13] The ends are more intangible and varied: profits are a path to prestige, power, status, personal satisfaction, adventures made, purpose and achievements gained. Here is a mid nineteenth-century statement on the subject:

> It is not, so far as I know, by any means to mere *money* gain so much as success in well-contrived and well-conducted action that our interest and satisfaction in our business is found; the money gain is a legitimate result, and no doubt enhances the interest and satisfaction; but it is not the spirit and soul of it, infinitely less is it the *measure* of it.[14]

This is not to be dismissed as mere Victorian hypocrisy even though the man who wrote it – Samuel Courtauld in a letter to his nephew in 1856 – had been helped to the £20,000-£30,000 a year profits which he was then making out of the provision of silk crape for Victorian mourners, by a powerful urge for personal social betterment. Despite its sententious manner and retrospective form it is not perhaps so very different in its implications from Lionel Cranfield's appeal to Arthur Ingram in 1607 that they should join in the purposive exploitation of all that fate might offer:

---

[12] The progressive erosion of the orthodox belief in profit-maximization as a description of modern business behaviour can be traced in various works, empirical and theoretical. For a small sample, see R.A. Gordon, *Business Leadership in the Large Corporation* (Washington D.C. 1945, 2nd edn. Berkeley, 1966) especially chaps. 12-14; P. Sargant Florence, *The Logic of British and American Industry* (1953), especially pp. 292-334; Edith T. Penrose, *The Theory of the Firm* (1959), especially chaps 3 and 8; and Robin Marris, *The Theory of 'Managerial' Capitalism* (1964), especially chap. 2.

[13] P. Sargant Florence, op. cit., p. 297.

[14] Quoted in D.C. Coleman, *Courtaulds: An Economic and Social History* (Oxford, 1969), i, 175.

> One rule I desire may be observed between you and me, which is that neither of
> us seek to advance our estates by the other's loss, but that we may join together
> faithfully to raise our fortunes by such casualties as this stirring age shall afford.[15]

It was to take Cranfield's and Ingram's successors, some two centuries later,
longer than is commonly supposed to discover the true implications of the
new 'stirring age'.[16] It is possible that they were assisted in their failure by
their continued pursuit of certain very English non-economic ends, and by
the evolution of certain very English patterns of education.

The social structure of pre-industrial revolution England had only one
really important division: between those who were Gentlemen and those
who were Players. For all the elaboration of status and hierarchy distinguished in the seventeenth and eighteenth centuries, the line of greatest
consequence was that older division which distinguished gentility from the
common people. And the great game of life to be played by anyone
possessed of ambition but born on the wrong side of the line was to cross that
divide. Whether certain societies or certain groups within societies nurture
abnormally vigorous growths of such ambitions; and if so, why, when, and
under what stimuli: these are questions which have been the object of much
speculation but few definitive answers.[17] What at any rate seems certain is
that in later eighteenth-century and early nineteenth-century Britain a
changing economy greatly extended existing opportunities for crossing the
great social divide.[18] In one sense the industrial revolution was a revolution
of those who were not gentlemen. And, as usual in partial revolutions,
sooner or later the values of the revolutionaries succumb to those of the
surviving elite who, in turn, modify their own standards to fit the new
situation. When the business and technological drive of the English industrial revolution loses some of its momentum in the later nineteenth century
perhaps, in part at least, it is because too many of the revolutionaries are too
busy becoming gentlemen.

The gentleman, both as idea and as reality, was a much elaborated topic of
sixteenth- and seventeenth-century England. The origins of the concept are
of course much older, drawing upon classical and Christian ideals and upon
the notion of chivalry, as well as the hard facts of medieval political power.

---

[15] Quoted in Menna Prestwich, *Cranfield: Politics and Profits under the Early Stuarts* (Oxford, 1966), p. 72.

[16] Below, p. 138.

[17] See M.W. Flinn, 'Social Theory and the Industrial Revolution', in T. Burns and S.B. Saul (eds.), *Social Theory and Economic Change* (1967).

[18] One remarkable testimony to this is the otherwise astonishing popularity of Debrett's *Peerage of England, Scotland, and Ireland* (which went to 22 editions between 1802 and 1839) and Burke's *Peerage and Baronetage* and *Dictionary to the Landed Gentry*. See W.L. Burn, *The Age of Equipoise* (1964, paperback edn., 1968), p. 254n.

In the sixteenth century, however, the dissemination to this country of renaissance culture from France and Italy, bringing with it *inter alia* the translation of Castiglione's *Courtier*, helped to give birth to a progeny of native works setting out the approved behaviour and ideals of the English gentleman.[19] More economic opportunities and growing wealth brought more social mobility to Tudor England. As aspirations to gentility and grants of honours alike multiplied so did the literature of definition and the machinery of heraldic approval. The gentleman became an English institution.[20] Sir Thomas Smith's famous words of 1583 go a long way to define all that appeared to be necessary:

> as for gentlemen, they be made good cheape in England. For whosoever studieth the laws of the realm, who studieth in the universities, who professeth liberal sciences, and to be short, who can live idly and without manual labour, and will bear the port, charge and countenance of a gentleman, he shall be called master . . . and shall be taken for a gentleman.[21]

The comment is shrewd enough and it comprehensively embraced much of what was, and long remained, the ostensible nature and practice of English gentility. The ideals which lay behind it were also of great consequence. For they were to inform, however crudely and coarsely, however imperfectly, the teachings of numerous later generations amongst whom, in the nineteenth and twentieth centuries, were a growing number of England's business leaders.

Here is a definition of 1608:

> the means to discern a gentleman be these. First, he must be affable and courteous in speech and behaviour. Secondly, he must have an adventurous heart to fight, and that but for very just quarrels. Thirdly, he must be endowed with mercy to forgive the trespasses of his friends and servants. Fourthly, he must stretch his purse to give liberally unto soldiers and unto them that have need; for a niggard is not worthy to be called a gentleman . . .[22]

The cultivation of elaborate manners could easily be transmuted into the foppish wits of Restoration drama; and the possession of the qualities suggested by 'an adventurous heart to fight' readily led to those bullying squires who litter the eighteenth-century scene, and to that admiration for well-bred ignorance and contempt for education which Defoe so deplored

[19] R. Kelso, *The Doctrine of the English Gentleman in the Sixteenth Century* (Illinois, 1929).
[20] On the relation between this development and the patterns of English education at the time, see L. Stone, *The Crisis of the Aristocracy, 1558-1641* (Oxford, 1965), pp. 672-724; and Joan Simon, *Education and Society in Tudor England* (Cambridge, 1967), pp. 333-68.
[21] T. Smith, *De Republica Anglorum* (ed. L. Alston, Cambridge, 1906), pp. 39-40.
[22] W. Vaughan, *The Golden Grove* (2nd edn., 1608), bk 3, chap. 16.

in his *Complete English Gentleman*.[23] Yet the stress on justice, magnanimity, and generosity is as important as the wealth and position which they imply. Along with the well-known enthusiasm for certain sporting pastimes they too were to become embedded in the character-training activities of the English Public School system, during its great nineteenth-century efflorescence. The concept of the English gentleman, as evolved in the sixteenth century, is said to have put more emphasis upon a moral code than upon the military prowess which figures so largely in some continental models.[24] At some points this moral code merged into the gentlemanly code of honour. In its most extreme form this meant the idiocies of duelling which did not finally peter out in England until the 1850s.[25] But, more important, it also provided the basis for a luxuriant undergrowth of unwritten and unspoken rules of behaviour. The observance of such rules helped to give great coherence to the gentlemanly elite. So, naturally, they came to be peculiarly embedded in the practices and attitudes of the schools to which were sent the children not only of the existing elite but of those parents whose accumulated profits thus enabled the family crossing of the great social divide to be completed. At other points the moral code merged with the sense of *noblesse oblige* to lay high esteem upon the performance of unpaid public service.

The purgings which the gentlemanly concept received at the hands of the nineteenth-century religious revival, in its varied and often conflicting forms, left an ideal which was in many respects remote from the new world of competitive industrialism. Though they disputed as to means, both John Henry Newman and Thomas Arnold wanted not an ancient knight or a bullying squire or a modern tycoon but a Christian gentleman. Here is Cardinal Newman's concept of the gentleman, significantly to be found in one of the essays of his *The Idea of a University*, published in 1852:

It is almost a definition of a gentleman to say he is one who never inflicts pain . . . He has his eyes on all his company; he is tender towards the bashful, gentle towards the distant, and merciful towards the absurd; he can recollect to whom he is speaking; he guards against unseasonable allusions, or topics which may irritate; he is seldom prominent in conversations, and never wearisome. He makes light of favours while he does them, and seems to be receiving when he is conferring. He never speaks of himself except when compelled, never defends himself by a mere retort, he has no ears for slander or gossip, is scrupulous in imputing motives to those who interfere with him, and interprets everything for the best . . . He has too much good sense to be affronted at insults, he is too well employed to remember injuries, and too indolent to bear malice. He is patient,

---

[23] D. Defoe, *The Compleat English Gentleman* (ed. K. Bülbring, 1890), p. 237. For the gentlemanly ideals of the eighteenth century, see George C. Brauer, Jnr., *The Education of a Gentleman: Theories of Gentlemanly Education in England, 1660-1775* (New York, 1959).

[24] Kelso, op. cit., p. 48.

[25] Burn, op. cit., p. 257.

forbearing, and resigned, on philosophical principles; he submits to pain, because it is inevitable, to bereavement, because it is irreparable, and to death, because it is his destiny. If he engages in controversy of any kind, his disciplined intellect preserves him from the blundering discourtesy of better, though less educated minds . . . [26]

And so on. This aggregation of sentiments must surely have made Newman's ideal gentleman an egregious bore. But however admirably virtuous, he hardly sounds ideally equipped for the economy of industrial capitalism, the perfect transmitter for sustained economic growth. In this paradigm the only qualities which might be thought to be relevant to the world of competitive industrialism – leadership and an 'adventurous heart to fight' – are now the least stressed.

Samuel Smiles, too, tried to purge the gentlemanly ideal of its ancient knightly obsession with a code of honour, with duelling, riches, and rank. It was to be made respectable. Yet it was to remain; and to remain moreover as the ultimate crown to be worn by those who had helped themselves. Hardly a better tribute could be paid to the persistence, with suitable modification, of the ideal than its appearance in the final chapter, 'The True Gentleman', of Smiles's *Self-Help* of which, let it be remembered, nearly a quarter of a million copies were sold in England between its publication in 1859 and the end of the nineteenth century.[27] Smiles turned the gentleman into the embodiment of virtuous character:

> The True Gentleman is one whose nature has been fashioned after the highest models . . . His qualities depend not upon fashion or manners, but on moral worth – not on personal possessions but on personal qualities . . . Humanity is sacred in his eyes: and thence proceed politeness and forbearance, kindness and charity . . .
> . . . The true gentleman has a keen sense of honour, scrupulously avoiding mean actions. His standard of probity in word and deed is high. He does not shuffle or prevaricate, dodge or skulk; but is honest, upright, and straightforward. His law is rectitude . . .
> . . . Riches and rank have no necessary connexion with genuine gentlemanly qualities. The poor man may be a true gentleman – in spirit and in daily life. He may be honest, truthful, upright, polite, temperate, courageous, self-respecting, and self-helping – that is, be a true gentleman.[28]

Whether or not this is best described as 'the entrepreneurial ideal of the self-made man',[29] it still seems scarcely the most likely formula for those ruthless, driving, dynamic tycoons who so impressed Schumpeter and who so fascinate business journalists today.

[26] J.H. Newman, *The Idea of a University* (new edn., 1893), pp. 208-10.
[27] Samuel Smiles, *Self-Help* (ed. Asa Briggs, 1959), p. 7.
[28] Ibid., pp. 372-4.
[29] Perkin, op. cit., p. 278.

We do not have to suppose that such ideals everywhere coincided with reality; nor to imagine that Thomas Arnold and his numerous imitators and successors were uniformly successful in moulding the characters of all their charges to conform to the prescribed pattern of the English gentleman. But we should be foolish to belittle the persistence and continuity of these attitudes of mind well into the twentieth century. 'Since Arnold's time', wrote Taine in 1862, after visiting Eton, Harrow, and Rugby, 'the object of their education has been to turn them out as Christian Gentlemen.'[30] He was far from complimentary about either the curricula or the fagging but he recognized the ultimate aim. So too at the ancient universities: 'the thing that matters is always the ethical content, morale, cast of mind, the dominant inclination of the men in question'.[31] Fascinated by the peculiarly English concept of gentility, he saw the English picture of the ideal:

> a truly noble man, a man worthy to command, a disinterested man of integrity, capable of exposing, even sacrificing himself for those he leads; not only a man of honour, but a conscientious man, in whom generous instincts have been confirmed by right thinking . . .[32]

For all of Smiles' pious hopes for the poor man with the proper sentiments, it was the passage through the educational procedures of the Public Schools and ancient universities which was to grant membership of the right club. Taine recognized the universities as essentially clubs: 'An English University is in many respects a club for young men of the nobility and gentry, or at least of wealth.'[33]

The concept of the gentleman's club, be it the right school for the young, the right university for the adolescent, the right club for the adult, was an integral part of the gentlemanly ethos in practice, just as was the unwritten code of behaviour. Both as concept and as practice it has shown a powerful talent for survival.

As Dr Reader has shown in his recent work on the origins of I.C.I., the 'Winnington Hall Club', started at Brunner Mond's Cheshire works towards the end of the nineteenth century and continuing into the twentieth, was a management club with a membership chosen on a basis which mirrored the nature of English society:

> Election to the Club was narrowly restricted. Technical men of graduate standing – meaning, for practical purposes, chemists – could perhaps take it for granted: no one else could, least of all engineers and commercial men . . .[34]

[30] H. Taine, *Notes on England* (trans. and ed. by E. Hyams, 1957), p. 105.
[31] Ibid. p. 117.
[32] Ibid. p. 145.
[33] Ibid. p. 118.
[34] W.J. Reader, *Imperial Chemical Industries: A History*, i, *The Forerunners 1870-1926* (Oxford, 1970), p. 218.

The whole structure rested on class distinction. University men and professional men (amongst whom engineers were by no means automatically included) were gentlemen: the rest were not, unless they achieved the status by consent of those already holding it.[35]

Here was a highly successful firm in a science-based industry adopting, in a suitably modified form, the essential tenets of Sir Thomas Smith's definition of three centuries earlier. Nor were such attitudes confined to this particular branch of 'new' industry. The gentleman's club was still providing a model for the chairman of the dominant firm in the British rayon industry ninety years after Taine had commented on the social scene. Here is an observation of 1952:

> For a long time there has been no fundamental change in the Board . . . The Executive Directors have directed and managed, and on the whole they have been successful. There has been a Gentleman's Club atmosphere in the Board Room, and I believe it is true to say that over the years this has spread to all the departments of our business. It is, in fact, part of the goodwill of the company which we must safeguard. On the other hand great care must be taken to avoid inefficiency.[36]

Whatever the merits of the gentleman's club, even this advocate obviously saw that its relationship to business efficiency could be tenuous. Why? The answer is *not*, I think, to be found simply in that neglect of science which was the all too common reaction to gentlemanly education when it came under criticism in the later nineteenth century.

Insofar as the great debate on English education touched upon the world of business at all, it did so through the concern for the country's deficiencies in scientific and technical education. As is well known, this was much paraded, in books and speeches by prominent persons and in evidence given to a series of committees and commissions, stretching roughly from the 1860s to the 1890s. The great importance which the Public Schools and ancient universities had long attached to classical learning seemed obviously suited to a class who were to 'live idly and without manual labour'. Furthermore, the contempt with which the intellectual leaders of Greek and Roman society had regarded the 'mechanic arts'[37] readily fused with the concept of a classical 'liberal' education to create the image of the educated amateur, his wits sharpened by contacts with antiquity and thus rendered capable of

---

[35] Ibid. p. 219.

[36] Courtaulds' Archives: private memorandum by Sir John Hanbury-Williams, Chairman of Courtaulds, sent to four of his senior directors, 25 July 1952. Quoted by kind permission of Courtaulds Ltd.

[37] See, e.g., A.J.P. Ubbelohde in C. Singer and others (eds.), *A History of Technology*, iv, (1750-1850) (Oxford, 1958), pp. 665-6.

turning his mind to any task suitable for his social status. It was an essential part of this educational process that on no account should it contain elements of functional training directly aimed at a specific vocation.[38] Training was for Players; Gentlemen were educated. Gladstone put it unequivocally in 1861: 'the classical training' was the basis of a liberal education. But, this classical training:

> can only apply in full to that small proportion of the youth of any country who are to become in the fullest sense educated men. It involves no extravagant or inconvenient assumptions respecting those who are to be educated for trades and professions, in which the necessities of specific training must more or less limit general culture.[39]

It was integral to this approach that whilst there might be something to be said for pure science as an intellectual exercise, there was very little to be said for technology. For a time, in the later seventeenth century, and in certain walks of life during the eighteenth century, the first fine enthusiasm of the scientific revolution had diffused ideas of the new science and brought interests in its practical uses amongst all manner of men.[40] But in the nineteenth century reaction against it set in; the academies declined; the hold of the classics was strengthened; and by the 1860s the advocates of change were having to 'awaken interest in scientific education as if it never existed before'.[41]

A corollary of this failure of science to establish itself in education was a sharpening of the distinction between 'pure' and 'applied' science. The abstract study of the nature of things – science – had been much pursued by the cultivated amateur; but the making of things, albeit with the assistance of new methods of inquiry, remained manual labour and thus to be comprehended within the proper tasks not of the gentleman but of what came to be called the 'practical man'. So there evolved and sharpened in the course of the nineteenth century two parallel distinctions: between pure and applied science; and between the 'educated amateur' and the 'practical man'. Both are social phenomena, both have continued until very recent times and perhaps are only now disappearing. In industry the cult of the practical man has been the essential obverse of the cult of the amateur. They were complementary; and they both owed much to two historical influences: to the embodiment in English education of the idea of the gentleman; and to the social nature of the English industrial revolution.

[38] For an adaptation, to another field of inquiry, of the theory behind this process, see M. Oakshott's essay, 'The Study of Politics in a University', in his *Rationalism in Politics* (1962). See also G. Kitson Clark, *The Making of Victorian England* (1962), pp. 263-64.

[39] Parliamentary Papers 1864, xx, 395.

[40] See A.E. Musson and Eric Robinson, *Science and Technology in the Industrial Revolution* (Manchester 1969), especially chaps. 1-4.

[41] N. Hans, *New Trends in Education in the Eighteenth Century* (1951), p. 210.

Neither the improvements in the educational standards of the English nobility and gentry in the sixteenth and seventeenth centuries nor their increasing involvement in urban and courtly life removed from the concept and practice of gentility its original associations with military prowess and rural life.[42] Certainly the stamp of gentility came to be given to many persons wholly unconnected with matters military or rural. But this elite very rarely included amongst its members those who were to become the pioneers of industrialism.[43] The prosperous merchants of eighteenth-century Leeds, for example, who had already achieved gentlemanly status, were not lured by the promise of profits into new and socially dubious adventures in manufacturing.[44] It was, on the other hand, precisely from the ranks of 'practical men' that these entrepreneurs were drawn. They came, in the main, neither from the gentry nor from the bottom of society. They were 'not typically very poor men who struggled to greater affluence through their creative efforts'.[45] They came instead from what might be termed the middle order of Players, those just on the other side of the line: yeomen, traders, skilled artisans; from the 'respectable farming family' which spawned the ironmaster Richard Crawshay; from the linen-draper father of the great flax-spinner, John Marshall; or from amongst the successful London silversmiths who were the ancestors to the future textile Courtaulds.[46] This middle stratum had its existence not simply in an urban business world, but also in that rural and military world with which the concept of gentility was so closely associated. Just as non-commissioned officers carried out practical work which it was not deemed appropriate for the officer and gentleman to do, so did the steward, bailiff, or tenant farmer see to those practical matters of farming or agrarian improvement in which landowning gentlemen might take an active interest but did not physically execute. The 'practical man' was the essential concomitant of the gentleman. But he remained a Player.[47]

---

[42] See L. Stone, 'The Educational Revolution in England, 1540-1640', *Past and Present*, 38 (1964).

[43] The practice of primogeniture amongst the upper class may well have contributed to a flow of younger sons into commerce but, before the nineteenth century at least, it was probably only their sons in turn who would produce some recruits into manufacturing industry.

[44] R.G. Wilson, *Gentlemen Merchants: The Merchant Community in Leeds, 1700-1830* (Manchester, 1971), pp. 121-34.

[45] Everett E. Hagen, *On the Theory of Social Change* (1964), p. 301.

[46] J.P. Addis, *The Crawshay Dynasty* (Cardiff, 1957), p. 4; W.G. Rimmer, *Marshalls of Leeds, Flax-Spinners, 1788-1886* (Cambridge, 1960), p. 13; Coleman, op. cit., i, 3-8. In general, see the list in Hagen, op. cit., pp. 303-9.

[47] One especial usefulness of 'practical men' was evident in the early days of the Gentlemen *v.* Players matches. Players, whose who received payment and who had originally been drawn from amongst 'men engaged in rustic occupations',were lent to the Gentlemen in order to equalize the strength of the sides; Sir Pelham Warner, *Gentlemen v. Players, 1806-1949* (1950), pp. 13-14. I am grateful to Malcolm Falkus for this reference.

As the industrial revolution went its successful way, so did the 'practical man' come into his own. Respect for practical achievement mounted; the acknowledged virtue of the 'practical man' grew greater. The leadership role exercised by the Gentlemen in the countryside was now assumed in industry by the Players. But it was also universally seen and acknowledged that the ultimate goal of the 'practical man', the Player, was still to cross the social divide and become a Gentleman. As industry consolidated its success and emerged as a recognized possible route to this ancient goal, so did further social developments follow. New occupational patterns were extruded: the industrial 'practical men' were to be found amongst, for example, the ranks of mill and factory managers; in general, amongst the layer which, in time, was to stretch downwards to top foremen but upwards to stop short of the board room. Partners and directors, if rich enough, could become gentlemen; gentlemen might decently become directors. The 'practical men' continued to look after practical, technological matters; they continued to be seen as needing training but not education. They remained Players. Promotion from the ranks was always possible. So the layers of 'practical men' came to constitute a reservoir from which might be drawn directors and thus, eventually, Gentlemen. The partnership, in English manufacturing business, of the 'educated amateur' and 'practical man' had been formed, in concept and in deed.

The 'mystique of practical experience', to use Prof. Landes' words,[48] grew apace in the course of the nineteenth century. When contemplating the quality of much of the early entrepreneurial achievement, the unusual must not be allowed to dazzle us too much: not every pioneer industrialist possessed Wedgwood's remarkable combination of commercial and organizational skills,[49] there was a great intellectual gulf between the world of Watt and Black, and that of a host of small, imitative factory masters;[50] in the textile industry, as Prof. Wilson has observed, 'the new machinery . . . involved no principles that an intelligent merchant could not grasp.'[51] Moreover, those practical Players from whom so many of the early entrepreneurs had been drawn, as had so many businessmen of earlier centuries, were peculiarly those who grasped the practical problems which they had to solve a well as, if not better than, the principles. They saw the industrial revolution as a triumph of practice rather than principles, of applied technology rather than scientific theory. It was the trumpeting of Smiles or Ure rather than the analysis of Babbage, which sounded the popular, and influential, response. Sir William Fairbairn's view in 1861 of the pioneer civil

---

[48] *Cambridge Economic History of Europe*, vi, pt. I, 572.

[49] See various articles by Neil McKendrick, notably *Econ. Hist. Rev.* 2nd ser. xii (1960) and xxiii (1970).

[50] See E. Robinson and D. McKie (eds.), *Partners in Science: The Letters of James Watt and Joseph Black* (Cambridge, MA., 1970).

[51] Singer and others (eds.), *History of Technology*, v, 799.

engineer of the industrial revolution gives a remarkable picture of the ideal of the 'practical man':

> The millwright of former days was to a great extent the sole representative of mechanical art . . . he was an itinerant engineer and mechanic of high reputation. He could handle the axe, the hammer, and the plane with equal skill and precision; he could turn, bore, or forge with the ease and despatch of one brought up to these trades, and he could set out and cut in furrows of a millstone with an accuracy equal to or superior to that of the miller himself. Generally, he was a fair arithmetician, knew something of geometry, levelling and mensuration, and in some cases possessed a very competent knowledge of practical mathematics. He could . . . draw in plan and section . . . construct buildings, conduits, or water courses . . . build bridges, cut canals . . . [52]

No doubt many fell short of such an ideal. But how vastly remote from the paradigm of the gentleman, his upbringing, and his doings! Indeed, the two concepts exhibit clearly the contrasting contemporary views of these two elements, present in English society, and in time, to come together in the organization and direction of industry.

It was one of the essential characteristics of the entrepreneurs of the industrial revolution period that few of them perceived the longer-term implications of what was happening. Naturally, there were exceptions in whom a vision of the continuous application of science to industry trans-cended the monetary and social ambitions of most of the new businessmen. But the majority probably saw innovation as a once-and-for-all event rather than the beginning of an era in which invention and innovation were to be built into the whole process of business life. They saw it, in short, as 'practical men'. And when in time they had made good and they or their successors and equivalents were faced with the challenge of competition in the post-1860 world they paraded the empirical virtues they knew. Here is John Whigham Richardson in 1911 inveighing against the improved technical education which many contemporaries saw as suitable for those who were not destined for the gentlemanly education:

> technical education can surely only mean the teaching of an art . . . I can conceive of no better school than the workshop. You have there the experience and skill of the best artisans . . . you are in the very atmosphere of your craft . . . you are learning by doing . . . [53]

When combined with invincible ignorance and the more fatuous sort of patriotism, the 'practical man's philosophy' achieved a rich idiocy. Here is one of the Players batting, for Lancashire, also in 1911:

[52] W. Fairbairn, *Treatise on Mills and Machines* (1861), preface, p. v.
[53] Quoted in W.H.B. Court, *British Economic History, 1870-1914* (Cambridge, 1965), pp. 171-72.

My lad, never again let anybody in Lancashire hear you talk this childish stuff about foreign competition. It's right enough for Londoners and such like, but it puts a born Lancashire man to shame as an ignoramus. It's just twaddle. In the first place, we've got the only climate in the world where cotton piece goods in any quantity can ever be produced. In the second place, no foreign johnnies can ever be bred that can spin and weave like Lancashire lasses and lads. In the third place, there are more spindles in Oldham than in the rest of the world put together. And last of all, if they had the climate and the men and the spindles – which they never can have – foreigners could never find the brains Lancashire cotton men have for the job. We've been making all the world's cotton cloth that matters for more years than I can tell, and we always shall.[54]

Although the flow of industrialists' sons to the Public Schools started early in the industrial revolution, it was not until after the mid-nineteenth century that the flow became a flood. Moreover, it was normally not the first generation of sons who were thus despatched to learn the gentlemanly arts, but the second, i.e. the grandsons or grand-nephews, as the whole family moved up the scale of wealth and status. One of the most striking examples of this lag is provided by the educational pattern of Matthew Boulton and his sons.[55] The father attended an academy near Birmingham but his education apparently included little formal instruction in sciences. He took considerable pains about his son's education, as did his partner James Watt, both men trying to ensure that those who were to succeed them in the business should be well-grounded not only in the 'liberal arts' but also in mathematics, science, engineering, and foreign languages. Matthew Boulton, junior, did not go to a Public School. But, before he died, in 1842, he had sent his son to Eton. The urge to gentility and improved social status had been present in the father and in the sons. As Dr Robinson has observed, James Watt, though confessing himself a self-made man, was proud of his status as a 'gentleman' which his genius had obtained for him; and his partner exhibited the familiar English class-worry that his son might acquire the wrong sort of accent, in this case that of Birmingham, described by the boy's schoolmaster as 'a vicious pronunciation and vulgar dialect'.[56]

The pattern is familiar elsewhere. Thus, although Sir Richard Arkwright became a landed grandee in his own lifetime, it was the progeny of his only son, also Richard, who went to Eton or Harrow, followed by Christchurch or Trinity, Cambridge, thence to set up branches of the new landed gentry

---

[54] A reminiscence of a Lancashire cotton manufacturer's retort in 1911 to a comment on the growth of Japanese cotton spinning capacity, in B. Bowker, *Lancashire under the Hammer* (1928), p. 22, quoted Court, op. cit., p. 123. Meanwhile, as Bowker himself commented (p. 23), 'Lancashire was sending out public-school man after public-school man to keep up British prestige, to refuse to learn Chinese for fear of losing caste, and to wait for trade to come to him.'

[55] Most interestingly described by Dr. Robinson in Musson and Robinson, op. cit., pp. 200-15.

[56] Ibid., p. 201.

family.[57] John Marshall's eldest son was educated by a private tutor and then sent to the Inns of Court; the younger sons went into the family business at an early age. But their children, from the 1840s, went to Arnold's Rugby and Trinity, Cambridge, to Harrow or Cheltenham.[58] The Dissenting strain sometimes lasted out longer against the allurements of gentility. The Unitarian Kenricks, successful but less wealthy than the Marshalls or Arkwrights, persisted with Dissenting schools and the new London University until the third generation. So it was not until the 1880s that Kenricks began to go to Rugby and Balliol to read classics.[59] Similarly in the Unitarian Courtauld family, though richer than Kenricks, two generations went to Dissenting schools before, in the 1880s and thereafter, Rugby and Cambridge began to be the chosen venues.[60] The paper-maker, William Balston, married late in life, in 1806, and promptly fathered a large family. The eldest son had to go straight from the local school up to the mill. But the rest went in turn to Tonbridge, Rugby (2), Eton, and Westminster, all followed by Oxford or Cambridge.[61] When Balston sent his third son to Eton in 1829 he dispatched the boy with an accompanying remark which adequately sums up much of the whole process: 'Always remember, Edward, that you are not a gentleman.' It is one of the nicer ironies that in 1862 the Headmastership of Eton passed to Edward Balston.[62]

Once Arnold had done his work at Rugby, between 1828 and 1842, and the reforms demanded by the Clarendon Commission in 1864 had been put in hand, the way was open for the dissemination of the idea of the gentlemanly education. The recommendations of the Taunton Commission of 1868 helped to push a number of grammar and proprietary boarding schools into the Public School world. The Public Schools multiplied; and more and more of those who were to lead British business in the first half of the twentieth century went through their character-forming procedures. Despite the attractions of the professions, an increasing percentage of school leavers went direct into business: 6 per cent from Marlborough in 1846 but 23 per cent in 1906; 6 per cent from Merchant Taylors in 1851 but 42 per cent in 1891; 9 per cent from Clifton in 1867 but 25 per cent in 1907; even Winchester sent 12 per cent of its leavers straight into business in 1893.[63]

Meanwhile, however, the attacks on the schools and ancient universities

---

[57] E.L. Jones, Industrial Capital and Landed Investment: The Arkwrights in Herefordshire, 1801-43', in E.L. Jones and G.E. Mingay (eds.), *Land, Labour and Population in the Industrial Revolution* (1967), pp. 33-34.

[58] Rimmer, op. cit., pp. 114-15, 225.

[59] R.A. Church, *Kenricks in Hardware* (Newton Abbot, 1969), pp. 80-81, 144.

[60] Coleman, op. cit., i, 207-9; ii, 210.

[61] T. Balston, *William Balston, Papermaker, 1759-1849* (1955), pp. 131, 133-35, 141.

[62] D.C. Coleman, *The British Paper Industry, 1496-1860* (Oxford, 1958), p. 245.

[63] W.J. Reader, *Professional Men* (1966), pp. 212-14.

for their neglect of science increased in intensity and included formidable indictments by such men as Lyon Playfair or T.H. Huxley who stressed the importance of science to business. Huxley, for instance, told the Samuelson Committee of 1867: 'If I intended my own son for any branch of manufacture, I should not dream of sending him to the university.'[64] Those who were prosperously engaged in business had to decide: should they send their sons to Public School and ancient university, to gain the gentlemanly education and the habits of confident social superiority, and thus to give them a good start in a stratified society; or should they attend to the dictates of their own experience or conscience which, in some cases at least, told them a different tale? Prof. Checkland has recently shown how, earlier in the century, the successful merchant and businessman, John Gladstone, 'frequently and poignantly', as he said, aware of the inadequacy of his own education, determined that Eton was the place for his elder sons. Although he had to wrestle with his strict Evangelical conscience, because of the 'very awful state of the Church' at Eton, the urge for the family's social advancement and his hopes for political careers for his sons triumphed. But when it came to the education of another son, intended for the business life, it was soon decided that Eton should be replaced by Glasgow.[65] Later equivalents to John Gladstone, though less troubled by religious laxity at the reformed Public Schools, found themselves in a similar situation. The recollections of S.R. Lysaght, of the steel-making family of that name, as set out in an autobiographical novel of 1925, go back to the 1870s. His fledgling steelmaster is made to begin his business career without taking a degree and is told by his employer that that would be 'of no commercial use' and that 'university life was too easy and pleasant'.[66] The sentiment was precisely matched in real life by the Courtaulds. Concerned about the education of one of his sons, the second George Courtauld, with over thirty years of business life behind him, remarked in a letter to his brother Samuel, in 1856:

> I have had some little experience now; and my feeling is very strongly that, for the great majority of young men in our position in life, a college course is not fit preparation for a business life.[67]

A year later, when discussing the education of another of George's sons, Sam Courtauld, himself the main entrepreneur of the family, expressed regrets about his own education which nicely echoed those of John Gladstone, thirty years earlier, and posed a familiar dilemma:

[64] Singer and others, eds. *History of Technology*, v, 790.
[65] S.G. Checkland, *The Gladstones: A Family Biography, 1764-1851* (Cambridge, 1971), pp. 129-37.
[66] S.R. Lysaght, *My Tower in Desmond*, quoted in C. Erickson, *British Industrialists: Steel and Hosiery, 1850-1950* (Cambridge, 1959), p. 35.
[67] [S.A. Courtauld, ed.] *Courtauld Family Letters, 1782-1900* (Cambridge, 1916), vii, 3785.

I, through all my life, have so painfully felt the want of scholarship that I may perhaps over-estimate its importance.

His prescription for a nephew who was expected ultimately to go into the family business was:

to let Sydney at 17 go for his degree. He ought, I fancy, to be able to gain this starting-point in an Englishman's life . . . at the London University, if not at Cambridge . . . And as between Cambridge and London, my feeling is that the atmosphere of . . . London would be more favourable . . . [68]

But this was still a generation brought up in the original Unitarianism. The cry for a 'liberal education' for the sons of businessmen was mounting. In 1867, as an Oxford don observed:

At present wealthy manufacturers and merchants are much disposed to send their sons to the best liberal schools, though not to the Universities,if they are intended for trade. But if liberal schools will not teach modern subjects, and if the Universities will not fully recognise their importance, there is a risk in such quarters as these of losing liberal education altogether.[69]

The risk and the danger were averted: a little reform and a little science, and social ambition did the rest. Despite some modifications, their curricula remained heavily weighted towards the classics. The whole tenor of their thinking utterly rejected what John Gladstone's most famous son, William Ewart Gladstone, after Eton and Christchurch had left their mark upon him, was to call the 'low utilitarian argument in matter of education for giving it what is termed a practical direction.'[70]

The reforming ideal, flourishing between the years 1870 and 1914, got some science; the preserving ideal – by now a nice amalgam of the institutionalized gentlemen of the sixteenth century, of Newman, Arnold, the Clarendon Commission, and compulsory games – ensured a measure of continuity with the past. Only Edwardian England could have nurtured so bizarre a phenomenon as Henry Newbolt's Public School poetry. Here the ancient themes of chivalry, military prowess, and a code of honour have been transmuted into a world in which cricket, moral virtue, and patriotism are identical. In the 1920s and 30s, despite debate and criticism and change, many of the essential educational ingredients remained. The Public Schools

---

[68] Ibid., vii, 3834-7.

[69] C.S. Parker, 'On the History of Classical Education' in F.W. Farrar (ed.), *Essays on a Liberal Education* (1867), p. 78.

[70] P.P. 1864, xx, 394, quoted Brian Simon, *Studies in the History of Education* (1960), p. 307.

were not 'moved to give a practical education of direct usefulness to business men'.[71]

In 1951, a sample inquiry showed that approximately 58 per cent of the directors of the larger public companies in Britain had been at Public Schools.[72] The average age of the directors in the inquiry was about fifty-five, though 62 per cent were aged fifty and over.[73] No correlation between age and attendance at Public School was given, but it seems at least probable that a substantial proportion of the directors had been at an English Public School before the First World War or during it. The directors in the sample were asked to give their fathers' occupations. Of those directors whose fathers were described as 'gentleman or landowner', 90 per cent went to Public Schools; so did 81 per cent of those whose fathers were also directors.[74]

This linkage of class, education, and business leadership – at least among the bigger companies – was a phenomenon which grew in strength during the years from the 1860s through to the 1940s.[75] In the 1920s and '30s the top posts in business – as, more noticeably, in the Civil Service, Church, Government, and the Forces – tended to be filled by members of an extended club. The essential qualification for membership was a certain sort of education – though there were, of course, honorary members. During the industrial revolution period there had been a partially analogous pattern in the new business world of that time, as many of the Nonconformist pioneers consistently recruited their business partners from other Quaker or Unitarian families. It, too, had been a club of sorts; it lost its unique qualities in the historical scramble for social position. By the end of the nineteenth century, the vigorous social climbing of the earlier period had probably slowed down; a big business plutocracy emerged.[76] Dr Erickson's inquiry into the leaders of the British steel industry shows a steady increase in those educated at Public Schools: for those in office in 1865 only 10 per cent had been at Public Schools; for the period 1875-95, it rises to 16 per cent; and then sharply to 31 per cent for 1905-25 and 33 per cent for 1935-47.[77] Likewise, during these same years of gain for the Public Schools, Oxford and Cambridge drew ahead of other universities as the favoured venues for the minority of those leaders who had been to universities: in 1865, 4 per cent had been to Oxford or Cambridge, 9 per

---

[71] See Edward C. Mack, *Public Schools and British Opinion since 1860* (New York, 1941), pp. 112ff. and *passim*; also Kitson Clark, op. cit., pp. 267-74.

[72] G.H. Copeman, *Leaders of British Industry* (1955), p. 101. The companies sampled were those with net assets of £1 million and over in 1950.

[73] Ibid., p. 106.

[74] Ibid., p. 127.

[75] For some evidence on this see P. Sargant Florence, op. cit., pp. 206-7, 303, 329-33.

[76] Perkin, op. cit., pp. 425-37.

[77] Erickson, op. cit., pp. 33-5.

cent to other universities; in 1953-47, 21 per cent had been to Oxford or Cambridge, 10 per cent to other universities. And most who had been to the ancient universities had read arts subjects, not science. Her inquiry into the Nottingham hosiery industry showed by contrast that only a few Nottingham hosiers 'received the education of the *élite*'.[78] The leaders of this much smaller-scale industry, with its firms operating in a competitive, provincial environment, never achieved the social wealth and social status of the steel-makers. It seems likely indeed that, during the years, the larger the business the more likely would it be that its leaders had attended Public Schools or the ancient universities.

Analysis of the educational origins of Courtaulds directors as the firm grew through the First World War and into the 1930s reveals a picture very similar to that of Dr. Erickson's inquiries into the steel industry:

Directors of Courtaulds Ltd

	ORD. & PREF. CAPITAL	NUMBER OF DIRECTORS	DIRECTORS AT PUBLIC SCHOOLS		AT OXFORD OR CAMBRIDGE	AT OTHER UNIVERSITY
			NUMBER	PER CENT		
1914	£2m.	6	3	50	2	1
1927	£20m.	10	6	60	3	1
1938	£32m.	17	14	82	6	1

By 1938 the average age of the Board was fifty; 56 per cent of all the directors were fifty years of age and over; all but one of those who had attended Public Schools had been at school before or during the First World War.[79] And in 1952, after another World War had intervened, it was one of those directors, Sir John Hanbury-Williams, who made the observation, quoted above, praising the 'Gentleman's Club atmosphere' and seeing it as part of the goodwill of the company.[80]

To return to the questions posed earlier in this essay. What *may* have followed from this long-enduring concern by English businessmen to push themselves and their families across the social divide, and from the powerful role played by an especial pattern of education in furthering this ambition?

It is of course possible that nothing at all flowed from these developments. To argue thus must imply certain assumptions. First, it could rest on a contention that the findings marshalled here were so unrepresentative of the English business community as a whole, or even of the leading parts of it, that they were not worth considering. This point can perhaps be settled by further empirical inquiry in business history. For the present, however, I shall assume that such historical evidence as we have is enough to warrant

[78] Ibid., p. 115.
[79] Courtaulds archives.
[80] Above, p. 134.

belief in its representative character, at least in the larger units of English business. Second, it could pre-suppose that all that has been claimed for a Public School education as a device for shaping character in a particular way, be it for good or bad, by supporters or detractors, was wrong; in short, that it did not work. This supposition seems improbable: improbable because of the very nature of the upbringing, because of the specific purposes for which it was designed, and because of its long historical association with gentlemanly status. It was a type of education peculiar to England (though occasionally copied elsewhere because recognized as distinctive); it aimed to create men with a specific outlook and approach to life. Are we to believe in its persistent failure, despite the very success signalled by the contemporary recognition of such men and such attitudes in 1950 as in 1850? Obviously it did not always succeed; obviously there were many who did not conform to type. But we can consider its likely influence only in general terms.

A third assumption which might be used to provide a basis for dismissing the case poses much more difficult problems. What if all the effects of the gentlemanly education, however real in some aspects of life, had virtually no effect upon the process of making business decisions? In brief, would business decisions, though not necessarily all other decisions, have been the same whatever the upbringing of those making them? The possibility has the merit of focusing attention upon the question of the channels by which it is supposed that such influences made themselves felt. Patently it is not enough simply to show that the educational processes in question embodied a powerful admiration for the idea of the gentleman; to note that the values thereby inculcated seemed to be incompatible with those inherent in business success. To do this in no way demonstrates any positive, casual relationship with the quite different phenomenon alleged to exist at the time and called 'entrepreneurial failure'. Just such a casual relationship between Public Schools and industry has, however, been assumed to exist. Of British entrepreneurs, and especially those in the older industries, Mr David Ward has stated categorically that 'one reason for their failure in the late nineteenth century lay in the growth of the public schools'.[81] Having marshalled the evidence about their values he concluded that they 'facilitated the transmission of the culture of the landed and gentry classes to the industrial classes'. This produced a 'haemorrhage of talent' which helps to 'explain the poor performance of these [traditional] industries'.[82] But the notion of 'entrepreneurial failure' is notably imprecise; it cannot simply mean 'poor performance'. Moreover in the sense of successful English businessmen retiring to the land and ensuring that their sons acquired 'the culture of the

[81] David Ward, 'The Public Schools and Industry in Britain after 1870', *Journal of Contemporary History* ii, (July 1967), 38.
[82] Ibid., 52.

landed and gentry classes' a 'haemorrhage of talent' had been going on for such along time that it begins almost to look like a candidate for explaining not the failure of English business after 1870 but its *success* before 1870 and well before that.

Indeed, a plausible hypothesis can be set up on these lines. It would argue that because manufacturing business was not seen as an occupation fit for gentlemen and because successful businessmen regularly withdraw their children from the business world by sending them through the gentlemanly educational process, the field was continually being cleared for a succession of thrusting, ambitious Players. Some part of their very driving power, it might be argued, came not simply from social envy but from a sense of deprivation: deprivation socially, educationally, in some cases politically and in matters of religious worship. If, to take two of the examples quoted earlier, John Gladstone and Samuel Courtauld had in fact enjoyed the education the lack of which they lamented in later life, they would probably not have become businessmen but would simply have joined other gentlemen in the scramble for office, political power, professional activity, landownership, or whatever was considered meet for their social status. If successful businessmen, before and during the industrial revolution, had not been so anxious to attain a life of rural gentility might there not have ensued a much more rigid, inflexible, and unadventurous course of business enterprise than in fact there was? Might, indeed, the industrial revolution not have occurred when and where it did?

The pursuit of such hypotheses is not the concern of this essay. But they may serve to demonstrate how close we are, in thus attempting to examine the relationship between business action and attitudes of mind engendered by a socially orientated educational process, to another intellectual location. This is one which is very familiar to economic historians. The location is that in which some scholars have carefully nurtured two other concepts thought to be causally related: Protestantism and Capitalism. That debate has surely gone on long enough to demonstrate the inadequacy of simply invoking the nature of certain Protestant doctrines, or parading a multitude of sermons. Those unwilling to go all the way with Kurt Samuelsson[83] and deny any correlation have recourse to a variety of more complicated transmission mechanisms, ranging from class conflict to toilet training. So it is with the present discussion. If the contention that business decisions might, after all, have been just the same without Public Schools is to be rebutted, we have to consider rather more complex patterns of transmission than one-to-one relationships between values and actions. The difficulty of the supposed one-to-one relationship can be seen in the many men who, having been through the gentlemanly mill, showed no lack of ability in areas of business

---

[83] K. Samuelsson, *Religion and Economic Action* (1961), especially pp. 150-54.

life removed from manufacturing industry. Banking can hardly be successfully run without a good eye for profit; and English merchant banking, with
its especial mix of finance and diplomacy, was, until only very recent times,
almost a preserve of the older Public Schools; it was also very successful. So
were many other financial activities of the City of London, so much so that
they often sustained the British balance of payments when the balance of
commodity-trade was in the red. Are we to suppose that bill-brokers and
stockbrokers, Lloyd's underwriters, and bullion dealers all achieved their
profits because they were free from the damaging intrusions of those who
had been to Public Schools? So if in manufacturing industry there is a
stronger case for suggesting an influence upon economic performance, it
cannot be made to rest simply on the transmission of certain ideals supposedly incompatible with successful profit-making.

It is also necessary, on the other side of the equation, to refine the crude
notion of 'entrepreneurial failure'. The joys of defining 'entrepreneurial'
could fill a whole volume. For the moment, however, here are three broad
categories of entrepreneurial action:

1. The exploitation of innovations, technical and/or organizational, by
   the setting up of new businesses.
2. The exploitation of innovations, technical and/or organizational,
   within existing businesses.
3. The continuous adaptation of the technical and/or organizational
   structure of an existing business to small changes in the market both
   for factors and for final products.

The first two categories comprehend the familiar examples which come
easily to mind, from Arkwright to Ford, from Bessemer converters to Marks
& Spencers shops. But to leave it at that is tacitly to assume that entrepreneurship is confined to the big, spectacular, and comparatively infrequent.
But much activity with an equal right to be called entrepreneurial is carried
on in short- or medium-term situations, doing what is defined in the third
category. That process of adaptation is not simply managerial; it is one of
the essential entrepreneurial functions of a board of directors, often in
practice dominated by one man who is the modern equivalent, within the
joint-stock company, of the 'classical' entrepreneur of the history books.
Even in category (1) the innovation exploited may be quite a small matter of
organization, either in production or in selling, in a small firm; but if it leads
to higher productivity and profits than in existing larger firms in the same
industry, then the small firm's subsequent growth in size and prosperity is a
reflection of entrepreneurial ability.

After this digression it is possible to return to the questions posed earlier.
They can now be reformulated. Is it possible that certain sorts of entrepre-

neurial activity were adversely affected by the gentlemanly ethos and the Public School education, and if so through what channels?

It seems at least a reasonable hypothesis that these educational patterns and social attitudes helped to perpetuate, well into this century, and longer than they might otherwise have continued, the twin cults of the 'educated amateur' and the 'practical man'. Any consideration of the possible effects of the one implies examination of the other: they were, so to speak, in joint supply. Entrepreneurial activity in the first of my categories, i.e. the exploitation of innovations by the launching of new businesses, in manufacturing industry, had long been peculiarly a preserve of those who, in the shorthand of this article, I have called Players. So if we are to suggest that the gentlemanly ethos and the growing numbers of Public Schools later affected entrepreneurial activity, by directing talents elsewhere, then it is likely that their influence would have made itself felt by stengthening and continuing the repulsion which gentlemen had long felt for activities in category (1). Probably this did in fact occur; for the statistics quoted earlier suggest that the smaller and newer the company the less likely was it to have Public School men on its board. Therefore the task of innovation in manufacturing industry was still mainly left to the 'practical men'. It is important to stress, however, that this does not *in itself* tell one anything about 'entrepreneurial failure'. For, as suggested earlier, a plausible case can be made out for arguing that, in the English social structure before about 1870, the ranks of those deprived of certain social and educational advantages, yet imbued with ability and ambition, provided a full reservoir from which successful businessmen were continually drawn, much to the country's economic advantage. Can it be said for the later period, and relative to industry's needs, either that those ranks suffered depletion or that the quality of those coming forward was lowered? It is a topic worth investigating; and the relation between business recruitment and the ordinary grammar and secondary schools needs to be a part of the inquiry. The standard answer is to point to the poverty of technical education and the inappropriateness of Public School education; but this is clearly inadequate. Yet it is also possible that the perpetuation of the duality, in education and social attitudes, may have had an adverse effect on entrepreneurial recruitment.

In my second and third categories of entrepreneurial action, where evidently more Public School men were to be found as companies grew bigger, the joint supply of 'educated amateurs' and 'practical men' is still in evidence. For both sorts sat on boards of directors. The Players had owed their ascent either to successful activity in category (1) or to recruitment from the ranks. But once they had been merged at the top with those whose route thence had been different, individual responsibilities for business decisions were likewise merged. The historian is faced with a real problem of identification; and usually only access to documents far more revealing than board minutes will offer any answers. Certainly there is no reason whatever to suppose that the distinction between 'thrusters' and 'sleepers', detected in one recent survey of British management,[84] was in any way historically coincident with that other boundary line between 'educated amateurs' and 'practical men'. Suffice it to suggest that if, during the period 1870-1950, there was 'entrepreneurial failure' in categories (2) and (3) and if the influences here considered helped to bring it about, then the most likely channel of transmission seems to have consisted of two mutually reinforcing tendencies inherent in the joint 'educated amateur-practical man' situation.

The first of these was the creation, or at least the strengthening, of a certain hostility towards innovation. It is important not to exaggerate the extent of this; and still more to note that it was not a unique product of the regard for the social *status quo* inherent in a traditionalist education. In Courtaulds in the 1930s for example, it was the 'practical men' at board and managerial level, who were both the most stubborn opponents of new ideas and scientific research and the least willing to recognize trades unions or the need for change in the face of labour unrest.[85] It was the Public School- or university-educated leaders who showed initiative in bringing in scientists or in making organizational changes which the practical men opposed. At its worst, however, the combination could and did perpetuate inertia in business because both parties to it had a built-in distrust not simply of 'science', but of any theoretically based knowledge. Economics, management techniques, industrial psychology: all were frequently looked upon with grave suspicion, for they represented attempts to professionalize an activity long carried on jointly by 'practical men' and gentlemanly amateurs.

The second of the mutually reinforcing tendencies which may have constituted a possible route of influence depends in part upon a question of age. The average age of directors in the samples quoted earlier was fifty to fifty-five; those who had reached the boards of big companies by the route of success as Players in smaller companies were unlikely to have been younger and more likely to have been significantly older.[86] In the social context discussed earlier they were therefore more likely to have been interested in the immediate gratification of social ambitions, in the playing out of certain social roles, than in direct profit maximization or innovational activity. What of the Gentlemen who sat with them around the board-room table? If at this stage we introduce the possibility of that direct connexion between educational influences and business decisions, then we *may* suppose that the long historical exposure to the gentlemanly concept and education produced a tendency somewhat to depreciate the aim of maximizing profits and somewhat to appreciate the aim of securing stability and order. These

[84] Political and Economic Planning, *Attitudes in British Management* (Harmondsworth, 1966).
[85] Coleman, *Courtaulds*, ii, 222-43, 437-49, and *passim*.
[86] The position in 1938 in Courtaulds was: average age of directors educated at Public Schools, fifty; of those not educated at Public Schools, fifty-six.

tendencies were sometimes made manifest in an attitude to business relations which emphasized careful strategical moves and the making of deals
and agreements which lessened the intensity of competition. This last
feature is complex in origin and in action hard to demonstrate. Obviously,
such arrangements were made in other countries by persons whose education had been quite different. Obviously, it was likely in practice to be
intertwined with short-term responses to the course of the trade-cycle and,
especially, to the troubled and depressed circumstances of the inter-war
years in Britain. Yet if it could be separated out from these more immediate
influences it could perhaps be shown to have longer roots. It perhaps owed
something to the social consciences of the radical dissenters who founded so
many of the businesses which survived and prospered in nineteenth- and
twentieth-century Britain: something to the tradition of public service, and
to the unwritten roll of things done and not done embedded in the
gentlemanly code; and something to both the Christian sense of guilt about
money-making and profits, and to the liberal influences which had borne
upon the Public Schools over the years. It added up to a vague but persistent
belief that some things were indeed more important than profits. Such a
notion had a hard time to survive the influx of the plutocracy in the late
nineteenth and early twentieth centuries; it was frequently extinguished by
a crass, jingoistic materialism; it was sometimes sustained simply by the wish
to enjoy more leisure in a gentlemanly fashion, to pursue foxes rather than
profits. However variously motivated, it seems to have existed. As shown by
earlier quotations, it has perplexed American observers. In its ultimate
result it is not uniquely English;[87] in its origins and forms it is. And it can
hardly have failed to reinforce the sentiments of elderly Players that their
main task in life was now to ensure that they and their heirs should behave
like Gentlemen rather than like the successful innovators they had once
been. Such a combination may then have acted to ensure a lower level of
performance as entrepreneurs in categories (2) and (3) than might have
been achieved in the absence of these social and educational constraints.

The counterfactual hypothesis poses questions peculiarly difficult to
resolve. The social influences here considered bore historically upon English businessmen as upon other Englishmen. They bore, either not at all or
in different environments or through different mechanisms, upon men in
other economies. It seems unlikely that future generations of students will
be told of some firm-seeming conclusion that x per cent of the entrepreneurial lag in English manufacturing business during the period 1870-1950
was attributable to y per cent of the entrepreneurs having been educated at
Public Schools. Nevertheless, it is well to examine the assumptions which lie

---

[87] See, for example, the comments on some other European countries' failure to conform to
American notions of an entrepreneurial ideal in the 1960s, discussed in Landes, *Unbound
Prometheus*, pp. 526-27.

behind the too easy judgements which are readily made. Today, continuously told of an urgent need to attain maximum economic efficiency, we are also told that the class-conscious and socially divisive effects of the old Public School education have not been conducive to those ends. Yet we need to pause to ask what, historically, might have been the likely alternatives to the attitudes thus allegedly engendered. Here is a typical judgement:

> The public school system, while producing first-class administrators, produced also an educational climate unfavourable to industrial advance. The second and third generations in manufacturing families were not always able or willing to maintain the single-minded drive of their fathers and grandfathers, preferring to devote themselves to public life or to establishing a position in society. Energy which might have gone into real ventures was diverted into more socially acceptable channels.[88]

Whatever the truth of these brave words from Sir Alexander Fleck, then chairman of I.C.I., in 1958, they carry the built-in assumption that new business ventures have a value which transcends the maintenance of certain social patterns; that somehow businessmen are failing if they behave as other men; that 'public life' or 'a position in society' are, *ipso facto*, inferior goods. But how, historically, were the successful businessmen of Victorian or Edwardian England suddenly to learn to renounce the long traditions by which their predecessors had abandoned their counting houses and climbed into the gentry? And if, by some unlikely magic, they had turned themselves into single-minded, constantly profit-maximizing entrepreneurs, what sort of world might have resulted? If it is true that one of the costs of the Public Schools producing 'first-class administrators' was some lag in industrial advance, how can we know that the price was not worth paying?

To pose these questions is neither to defend nor to attack the Public School system but rather to insist that if one condemns it as having been historically inimical to business efficiency, one must also take heed of the external costs, social as well as economic, of any historically likely alternative. Furthermore, as this essay has tried to emphasize, just as it is important not to ignore the long historical roots of the class-bred gentlemanly education designed to shape character and to imbue certain moral ideas so it is also important not to base explanations on supposed one-to-one relationships between educational values and business actions. Today, the leaders of British industry include many men who were not at those schools, so ironically called Public, and, amongst those who were, many whose

[88] Singer and others (eds.), *History of Technology*, v, 821. These sentiments echoed those of Prof. Sargant Florence's work of 1953: 'This pervasive gentlemen-ideal . . . is not a favourable climate for the provision of efficient business leadership' (op cit., p. 330) and 'while England has perhaps the ablest lawyers and civil servants in the world, her businessmen are on the average of lower attainments and keenness than their opposite numbers in the United States' (op. cit., p. 332).

educative years were passed in the shadow of the depression, the dictators, and the Second World War. Many of the Public Schools themselves are changing; university expansion has altered the special position of Oxford and Cambridge. Even in the 1930s, the sentiments of Newbolt's Public School poems were good for a laugh; today they are the sober evidence of history. The end of the Gentlemen *v* Players cricket matches in 1962 was perhaps symbolic. The joint cult of the 'educated amateur' and the 'practical man', of Gentlemen and Players, may perhaps at last be dying, as professionalism advances in business. 'The change-over to modern professional management', it is claimed, 'is a crucial phase in the development of a firm.'[89] We need to ask the question: What will be the social cost, as well as the economic benefit, of that? In learning to ask, and in seeking to answer, such questions we are likely to be helped by a more careful understanding of the social and economic history of that curious but unloved species: the English businessman.

---

[89] *Attitudes in British Management*, p. 61.

7

Adam Smith, Businessmen and the Mercantile System in England*

At the heart of *The Wealth of Nations* lies a strange paradox. A book which has been notably influential, especially in English-speaking countries, in stimulating policies designed to give maximum freedom for private enterprise, also exhibits a remarkable hostility to the agents of that enterprise.

This hostility to businessmen does not merely surface in an occasional remark. It is unequivocal; and is diversely damning. Smith deprecated businessmen's behaviour as 'the sneaking arts of underling tradesmen'; and referred contemptuously to merchants and artificers acting 'in pursuit of their own pedlar principle of turning a penny whenever a penny was to be got'.[1] Moreover, he presented businessmen as historically disastrous:

> The capricious ambition of kings and ministers has not, during the present and preceding century, been more fatal to the repose of Europe, than the impertinent jealousy of merchants and manufacturers The violence and injustice of the rulers of mankind is an ancient evil, for which, I am afraid, the nature of human affairs

---

* The concept of the mercantile system is of no *direct* relevance to that of industrial revolution or even of the Industrial Revolution. Businessmen, however, as agents of change are of very real relevance to it. Because Smith saw them as the creators of the mercantile system it is in that context, mainly in Book IV of the *Wealth of Nations*, that most of his observations about them are to be found. Proponents of both the catastrophic and the entrepreneurial versions of the Industrial Revolution have invoked his name, with ascriptions of influence or responsibility varying according to taste. But few such enthusiasts have taken much notice of his opinions of businessmen even though historians of economic thought have often commented upon them.

The article here reprinted began as a paper read to a Colloquium on 'Economic Concepts and European Thought in Historical Perspective' held in Vienna in May 1986. I am grateful to Professor Donald Winch for pointing out to me that my observation (below, p. 156) that Smith 'endowed his unintended consequences . . . with the moral capacity of bringing benefit to society' is not an entirely accurate representation of Smith's argument as it was not invariably associated with benefit. The 'unintended consequences' could be undesirable as well as desirable; losses could be registered as well as gains. See Donald Winch, 'Adam Smith's "Enduring Particular Result": A Political and Cosmopolitan Perspective' in I. Hont and M. Ignatieff (eds.), *Wealth and Virtue* (Cambridge 1983), p. 266.

[1] Adam Smith, *An Inquiry into the Nature and Causes of the Wealth of Nations*, ed. E. Cannan, Modern Library edn. (New York, 1937), pp. 391, 460.

can scarce admit of a remedy. But the mean rapacity, the monopolizing spirit of merchants and manufacturers, who neither are, nor ought to be, the rulers of mankind . . . [2]

It was not simply that he saw businessmen as possessed of these deplorable and pretentious characteristics. Worse still, and he rubbed this in on more than one occasion, they were humbugs:

> Our merchants and master-manufacturers complain much of the bad effects of high wages in raising the price, and thereby lessening the sale of their goods at home and abroad. They say nothing concerning the bad effects of high profits. They are silent with regard to the pernicious effects of their own gains. They complain only of those of other people.[3]

Their own interests were, claimed Smith, commonly opposed to the public interest. Consequently they had 'an interest to deceive and even oppress the public, and . . . accordingly [had] . . . upon many occasions, both deceived and oppressed it'.[4] The very liberty of the subject had indeed been sacrificed to the 'futile interests of our merchants and manufacturers'.[5] Presumptuous humbugs, pursuers of monopoly, deceivers and oppressers of the public, they were, not surprisingly, damned by Smith as peculiarly bad rulers. 'The government of an exclusive company of merchants is, perhaps, the worst of all governments for any country whatever.'[6]

This comprehensive hostility has, of course, been noted and commented upon, but its origins and intensity, its function in the historical framework of the *Wealth of Nations* and its implications have not been much examined. Clearly, Smith could not have absorbed these sentiments from any hostility to merchants which his father might have built up as Comptroller of Customs at Kirkcaldy, for the good reason that his father died shortly before his birth. W.R. Scott offered the vague supposition that Smith's acquaintance with Glasgow merchants may have induced them, but nothing survives in Smith's correspondence to support this or indeed to suggest any other explanation.[7] It seems not to have been a product of Smith's having himself become a Commissioner of Customs because that appointment was made two years after the *Wealth of Nations* first appeared; all the hostility was evident in the first edition, and later editions simply add detail on tariffs, bounties, the East India Company and aspects of colonial trade rather than

---

[2] Ibid., p. 460.
[3] Ibid., p. 98. He said it again, in slightly different words, on p. 565.
[4] Ibid., p. 250.
[5] Ibid., p. 625.
[6] Ibid., p. 537.
[7] W.R. Scott, *Adam Smith as Student and Professor* (Glasgow, 1937); E.C. Mossner and I.S. Ross (eds.), *The Correspondence of Adam Smith* (Oxford, 1977).

in any specific way intensifying the anti-businessman sentiments.[8] He may have been consciously giving the public (or at any rate a growing section of it) what the public wanted to hear. On this hypothesis, Book IV in particular becomes a polemic against that emotively charged thing: monopoly.[9] Certainly to attack monopoly was a well-known route to approval. It remains, however, neither easy nor feasible to relate his attitude of hostility directly to his general knowledge of the Scottish economy of his time.[10]

The difficulty of explanation lies particularly in the ambivalence in Smith's attitude towards the commercial society which he championed. Joseph Cropsey has offered an answer in terms of Smith's concern with justice. 'Justice, the substitute for and ouster of benevolence, is at the same time the soul of commerce'.[11] So the moral defects of commercial society are the price to be paid for freedom and civilization. And it is evident that, as Dr. Phillipson has put it, 'Smith's critique of the capitalist and the spirit of monopoly was animated by a desire to legitimize a particular conception of a commercial polity.'[12] Some part of the intensity of Smith's attacks on businessmen may be differently explicable at a personal level. A general distaste for the everyday reality of commercial society was likely to be manifest in a reclusive intellectual of modest means, however much weight one wishes to attach to Schumpeter's observation that 'no woman, excepting his mother, ever played a role in his existence', thereby ensuring that 'the glamours and passions of life were just literature to him'.[13] Yet the unspoken but implied suggestion that Smith was a mother-dominated homosexual who could not stand businessmen seems hardly adequate to deal with the logical paradox engendered by this ambivalence. Nor is it enough to note that just about the only attitude in life which he shared with Colbert was a disapproval of merchants.[14]

Whatever role may have been played by personal circumstances and social

---

[8]   He was made a Commissioner of Customs for Scotland in 1778; the *Wealth of Nations*, after the first edition of 1776, went into five editions in Smith's own lifetime (1723-90) and to nine editions by 1800.

[9]   See for example J.A. Schumpeter, *History of Economic Analysis* (1954), pp. 185-6; and A.W. Coats, 'Adam Smith and the Mercantile System', in A.S. Skinner and T. Wilson (eds.), *Essays on Adam Smith* (Oxford, 1975), p. 233.

[10]   See T.C. Smout, 'Where had the Scottish Economy got to by the Third Quarter of the Eighteenth Century?', in I. Hont and M. Ignatieff (eds.), *Wealth and Virtue: The Shaping of Political Economy in the Scottish Enlightenment* (Cambridge, 1983), pp. 45-72.

[11]   J. Cropsey, *Polity and Economy: An Interpretation of the Principles of Adam Smith* (The Hague, 1957), p. 94.

[12]   'Adam Smith as Civic Moralist', in Hont and Ignatieff (eds.), *Wealth and Virtue*, p. 194.

[13]   Schumpeter, *History of Economic Analysis*, p. 182.

[14]   'The aristocratic, intellectual, French paternity of the *Wealth of Nations* comes through strongly in the author's social attitudes; a contempt for the merchant ethos was at least one belief that Adam Smith shared with Colbert.' Charles Wilson in C.H. Wilson and E.E. Rich (eds.), *The Cambridge Economic History of Europe*, (Cambridge, 1977), v, pp. 18-19.

antipathy, an intellectual reason for these expressions of hostility to businessmen can be found in the relationships among certain constituent
elements of his theory of the path to greater wealth and liberty; his concept
of economic 'systems'; and his notion of continuous conspiracy.

It will be recalled that Smith's model of the progress of society, built up
partly from natural-law concepts and partly from 'philosophical' or 'conjectural' history, contained a four-stage theory of growth – hunting, pasturage,
farming and commerce. The desired goal was the last stage which would
combine liberty and commerce. The goal was to be reached by the operation
of what he saw as two basic human propensities. The division of labour
'from which so many advantages are derived' was the consequence of 'a
certain propensity in human nature . . . to truck, barter and exchange one
thing for another'.[15] With this first propensity went a second: 'the uniform,
constant, and uninterrupted effort of every man to better his own condition'.[16] This he regarded as a permanent and pervasive desire 'which,
though generally calm and dispassionate, comes with us from the womb,
and never leaves us till we go into the grave'.[17] Both the propensities were
'natural'. Linked to them was the doctrine of unintended consequences.
Nature ensured that men behaved in this way; the unintended consequences of their individual actions brought benefit to society. His best-
known statement to this end invoked the invisible hand. 'As every individual
. . . intends only his own gains . . . he is in this, as in many other cases, led by
an invisible hand to promote an end which was no part of his intentions'.[18]

Smith endowed his unintended consequences, it must be emphasized,
with the moral capacity of bringing benefit to society. They were thereby
given a different potential from other natural individual acts, such as
procreation. Here such unintended consequences for society as, for example, changes in the age-structure of the population, following upon variations in frequency of births, are in themselves morally indeterminate
whatever that society's views upon the proper limits to sexual behaviour. For
Smith, however, the unconscious result of his two propensities brought
benefit despite the conscious acts of foolish men. It worked via a natural
urge to use capital advantageously:

> Every individual is continually exerting himself to find out the most advantageous
> employment for whatever capital he can command. It is his own advantage,
> indeed, and not that of the society, which he has in view. But the study of his own

[15] *Wealth of Nations*, p. 13.
[16] Ibid., p. 326.
[17] Ibid., p. 324.
[18] Ibid., p. 423.

advantage naturally, or rather necessarily leads him to prefer that employment which is most advantageous to the society.[19]

And it also worked via the urge to self-betterment in overcoming government folly:

> The natural effort of every individual to better his own condition, when suffered to exert itself with freedom and security, is so powerful a principle, that it is alone, and without any assistance, not only capable of carrying on the society to wealth and prosperity, but of surmounting a hundred impertinent obstructions with which the folly of human laws too often incumbers its operations.[20]

The failure to reach the fourth stage, embodying both liberty and wealth, required an explanation. What had checked 'the natural progress of a nation towards wealth and prosperity'?[21] Smith laid much weight, in Book III, upon the relations between the towns and the countryside in European history as a force inverting the natural order of things. But the real enemy, presented to the reader in detail in Book IV, was the mercantile system. Invented by businessmen, it had been adopted by governments with the result that all those 'natural' individual efforts and propensities which would otherwise have led to greater wealth had been thwarted by those 'impertinent obstructions' built by foolish legislation. It was one of the two 'systems of political economy' which men had devised in the hope of enriching 'both the people and the sovereign'.[22] The other was 'the system of agriculture' under which head Smith briefly considered the ideas of François Quesnay, largely enshrined in the *tableau économique*, and the French Physiocrats. But the system had 'never been adopted by any nation';[23] so in Book IV it got but one short chapter as compared with the eight chapters devoted to the mercantile system. The latter was 'the modern system . . . best understood in our own country and in our own times'.[24]

Smith, as Professor Coats has emphasized, applied the term 'mercantile system' both to economic doctrines and to policy in practice, though he was primarily concerned with the latter.[25] He has, indeed, rather little to say of its theoretical content, confining himself largely to a few references to Mun and Locke. Moreover, what he does say is largely wrong. Despite his contention that it was a principle of the mercantile system that 'wealth consisted in gold and silver', mercantilist writers, as Schumpeter pointed

---

[19] Ibid., p. 421.
[20] Ibid., p. 508.
[21] Ibid., p. 638.
[22] Ibid., p. 397.
[23] Ibid., p. 627.
[24] Ibid., p. 397.
[25] Skinner and Wilson (eds.), *Essays on Adam Smith*, p. 220.

out, did not seriously confuse wealth with money.[26] Furthermore, although they did stress the balance of trade, they did not generally see it as the sole or vital channel by which wealth could be created. Likewise, although English governments did invoke the desirability of a favourable balance, usually in the commerce with a particular country, it was far from being a consistently operated instrument of economic doctrine. There are, indeed, serious shortcomings and inaccuracies in Smith's treatment of the way in which the miscellany of government devices, which he called the mercantile system, came into being. He is unequivocal in his belief that it was businessmen in pursuit of monopoly who invented this system: 'monopoly of one kind or another . . . seems to be the sole engine of the mercantile system'.[27] It was undoubtedly 'the spirit of monopoly which originally both invented and propagated this doctrine'.[28] And who wanted this monopoly, these restraints of imports, bounties, drawbacks and all the rest? The answer is clear: it was the merchants and the manufacturers, with their 'interested sophistry' who were 'by far the principal architects' of the whole mercantile system, at home and in the colonies.[29]

In designating this invention a 'system', he used exactly the same term as he did for the 'system of agriculture'. This is a total confusion. The one was a theoretical construct, conceived and planned by a group of French intellectuals, but never put into practice by any government. The other, in the reality of English history, was an unplanned miscellany of regulatory measures. On the continent of Europe, mercantilism, it has been said, 'was an essential concomitant of absolutism and developed in every state *pari passu* with the growth in the monarch's power'.[30] England, by contrast, witnessed a successful challenge to that power. What Smith dignified as a 'system' was a rag-bag of devices which emerged from Parliament and Crown by a uniquely English process. To present it as an equivalent of the Physiocrats' model is absurd. The confusion was worse confounded because Smith, having thus called the rag-bag a system, never asked why successive governments of England should have been persuaded to buy it – rather as a modern government might buy an early-warning air-defence system – by those scheming, sophistical businessmen. For example, despite his having devoted Book V to public finance, despite his awareness that such businessmen were a convenient source of loans to the Crown, and despite his condemnation of selective import duties as a method of revenue raising, he nowhere investigated the whole historical process by which the protective apparatus which came to surround English industry and trade from the

---

[26] Smith, *Wealth of Nations*, p. 418; Schumpeter, *History of Economic Analysis*, pp. 361-62.

[27] Smith, *Weallth of Nations*, p. 595.

[28] Ibid., p. 461.

[29] Ibid., pp. 461, 626.

[30] B. Behrens, Chap. 8, (Government and Society), in *Cambridge Economic History of Europe*, v, p. 573.

later seventeenth century onwards was very largely a product of war finance.[31] Nor, again, despite having much to say about the throttling of Anglo-French trade,[32] did he consider the particular circumstances of that politico-economic battle-ground which saw the balance-of-trade slogan used as an anti-French weapon though not thus deployed in other branches of trade.[33] He was content to invoke what he saw as the absurdities of the 'whole doctrine of the balance of trade' and of the 'modern maxims of foreign commerce'.[34]

As well as resting on dubious history – perhaps an unfortunate conflation of the orthodox and the conjectural – Smith's arguments also generated a logical dilemma. One system of political economy, that of agriculture, was presented as an act of intellectual creation. Quesnay was, reasonably enough, not depicted as having invented his system as a result of motivation by the propensities to truck and barter or by that for self-betterment, nor in pursuit of monopoly. It was done, according to Smith, and however misguidedly in his view, in pursuit of truth.[35] The other system of political economy, the mercantile system, was, said Smith, invented by businessmen. Now those same businessmen, as individuals, should presumably have been even better motivated than most other people by the propensity to truck and barter, and by that for self-betterment. Therefore, according to the rest of the Smith canon, their individual actions, thus motivated (and unrelated to any conscious search for truth) should have fallen within the doctrine of unintended consequences and, guided by the invisible hand, have led to increased wealth for the community, thus automatically furthering the 'natural progress of opulence'. Why did they not do so? Why were they apparently exempt from this particular process of natural law? Why should the work of the invisible hand have apparently been suspended for businessmen, so that their actions led to the creation, via an urge for monopoly, of that evil thing, 'the mercantile system'?

Smith resolved this dilemma within the *Wealth of Nations* by means of his notion of continuous business conspiracy. His expressions of hostility to businessmen were always cast in plural terms. He saw them as acting in concert to invent, maintain and exploit the mercantile system. In these matters no individual, propensity-motivated merchant or manufacturer ever appeared. Conversely, when mentioning businessmen in a wholly different context, the hostility vanished: merchants in the abstract were 'a

---

[31] R. Davis, 'The Rise of Protection in England, 1689-1786', *Econ. Hist. Rev.*, 2nd ser. xix (1966), 306-17.

[32] Smith, *Wealth of Nations*, chap 3 of Book IV, *passim*.

[33] D.C. Coleman, 'Politics and Economics in the Age of Anne: The Case of the Anglo-French Trade Treaty of 1713', in D.C. Coleman and A.H. John (eds.), *Trade, Government and Economy in Pre-industrial England* (1976), pp. 187-211.

[34] Smith, *Wealth of Nations*, pp. 456, 462.

[35] Ibid., p. 642.

profession no doubt extremely respectable';[36] they were commended as 'more spirited' improvers of land than country gentlemen.[37] What evidently obsessed Smith, in his hostility to businessmen, was their conspiracy as a group in pursuit of monopoly. He saw it as historically rooted in the corporate mercantile life of the towns:

> Country gentlemen and farmers, dispersed in different parts of the country, cannot so easily combine as merchants and manufacturers, who being collected into towns, and accustomed to that exclusive corporation spirit which prevails in them, naturally endeavour to obtain against all their countrymen, the same exclusive privilege which they generally possess against the inhabitants of their respective towns. They accordingly seem to have been the original inventors of those restraints upon the importation of foreign goods, which secure to them the monopoly of the home-market.[38]

Monopolistic trading companies did not merely excite his disapproval. More than that, he saw the opportunities which they offered to merchants to conspire against the public as *necessarily* tending to corrupt the morality of their members in the role of governors of a territory. Of the East India Company he observed that

> No other sovereigns ever were, or, from the nature of things, ever could be, so perfectly indifferent about the happiness or misery of their subjects, the improvement or waste of their dominions, the glory or disgrace of their administration; as, from irresistible moral causes, the greater part of the proprietors of such a mercantile company are, and necessarily must be.[39]

It was not only in such undesirable corporate entities that he saw mercantile plotting. All businessmen meeting together were likely to be conspiring against the public. And he regarded their actions in concert as so probably pernicious that he would clearly have liked to prohibit all meetings of businessmen – an exceedingly authoritarian notion which he had reluctantly to admit was impossible.

> People of the same trade seldom meet together, even for merriment and diversion, but the conversation ends in a conspiracy against the public, or in some contrivance to raise prices. It is impossible indeed to prevent such meetings, by any law which either could be executed, or would be consistent with liberty and justice. But though the law cannot hinder people of the same trade from sometimes assembling together, it ought to do nothing to facilitate such assemblies; much less to render them necessary.[40]

---

[36] Ibid., p. 603.
[37] Ibid., pp. 384-85.
[38] Ibid., p. 429.
[39] Ibid., p. 710.
[40] Ibid., p. 128.

This circumvention of a logical dilemma meant that what was in English historical reality a very unsystematic, piecemeal, contradictory muddle of tariffs, prohibitions, grants, bounties, drawbacks, navigation laws, charters and trade treaties – created as much for political and fiscal reasons as for economic, and certainly not in pursuance of a logically conceived economic theory – was presented as the mercantile system. It had allegedly been created by businessmen's conspiracy and foisted upon governments. It had to be thus presented because if the 'natural progress of opulence' had been perverted it must have been by something deliberately concocted by groups of persons with specific intents different from what would have been 'naturally' produced by individuals acting independently and guided by the invisible hand. If all systems of restraint were removed then, Smith claimed, 'the obvious and simple system of natural liberty establishes itself of its own accord'.[41] Yet another 'system': this one a product of those propensities plus the invisible hand; the agricultural 'system' a product of Quesnay's mind; and the mercantile 'system', a product of businessmen's conspiracy.

Smith's hostility towards businessmen as conspiratorial groups was thus an essential ingredient of his whole argument. This is not, of course, to contend that the hostility had no roots other than the demands of logic. It is highly probable that the sensitive intellectual, professor of moral philosophy and tutor to the Duke of Buccleuch, found the clamorous businessmen of eighteenth-century Glasgow socially uncongenial. A fertile soil would thus have existed for the growth in his model of economic change, of businessmen's dual paradoxical role as conscious demon kings but unconscious social benefactors. Similarly, the logic of his model demanded that what they created in that former role should have been an obstructive system. Here his conjectural history fitted poorly with his own knowledge of events; and he had to make a concession to reality. He admitted that English commerce had flourished since Elizabethan times,[42] during the reign of the mercantile system, and indeed especially since 1660, 'the happiest and most fortunate period'.[43] But, he said it had done so despite, and not because of, the mercantile system.

Smith's conception of the economy of the day embodied a view of a non-factory, pre-industrialized, trading and manufacturing community, without any significant fixed capital assets; and his picture of society likewise defined a hierarchical, though relatively mobile, community in which power rested, and should rest, in a 'natural aristocracy'.[44] In no way at all did he envisage, least of all approve of, a community in which the ownership of fixed

[41] Ibid., p. 651.
[42] Ibid., p. 393.
[43] Ibid., pp. 327-28.
[44] See Coats in Skinner and Wilson (eds.), *Essays in Adam Smith*, p. 227.

industrial capital and the exercise of political power might be coterminous. As already indicated, he regarded businessmen as unsuitable, and indeed morally blighted, rulers. In more mundane terms, he presented merchants as belonging to a profession which 'in no country in the world carries along with it that sort of authority which naturally over-awes the people, and without force commands their willing obedience'.[45] His view of the appropriate possessors of political authority was very different. 'Upon the power which the greater part of the leading men, the natural aristocracy of every country, have of preserving or defending their respective importance, depends the stability and duration of every system of free government.[46] However precisely defined, that 'natural aristocracy' certainly did not embrace businessmen of any sort. A merchant, indeed, was 'not necessarily the citizen of any particular country',[47] and his capital might 'wander about from place to place'.[48]

These various expressions of hostility towards, and contempt for, businessmen offer rich ironies when considered in the light of some modern attitudes. The name of Adam Smith is not infrequently invoked in Britain today by groups anxious to promote policies of economic *laissez-faire*, to stimulate 'the enterprise society', to advance the economic power of businessmen and correspondingly lessen that of the state; and by those who would find no difficulty in seeing businessmen as part of a modern 'natural aristocracy'. Smith's deep-rooted suspicion of conspiratorial tendencies has certainly been enshrined in various sorts of anti-monopoly legislation: in Britain in the short-lived combination laws, and then much later in the legislation passed since World War II; in the United States, in the more comprehensive anti-trust enactments from the Sherman Act onwards. But Smith's hostility, largely forgotten or ignored (or even unobserved) by the free-marketeers, has been appropriated by their opponents, the political far Left whose economic policy recommendations are otherwise in total contradiction to Smith's vision of commerce and liberty. So now the picture of businessmen as conspiratorial oppressors, humbugs and improper rulers goes along with a Left-wing dedication to an authoritarian economy with liberty circumscribed and commerce controlled.

If such divergent, not to say bizarre, legacies of the *Wealth of Nations* offer scope for irony, Smith's depiction of businessmen as quintessential conspirators seems today to be not so much untrue as unsurprising. Of course they have historically conspired and sought monopoly; they still do. But there is nothing strange about that. So have numerous other groups: religionists, dynasts, dictators, trade unionists, professional associations,

[45] Smith, *Wealth of Nations*, p. 603.
[46] Ibid., p. 586.
[47] Ibid., p. 395.
[48] Ibid., p. 345.

political bosses and parties, mafiosi and more besides. (In sixteenth- and seventeenth-century England, courtiers, rather than businessmen, were the chief successful pursuers of monopoly grants from the Crown.) Of course they have acted as pressure groups, and were particularly active in defence of those sheltering walls built by tariffs, treaties or agreements; they still are. But the representation of these doings as peculiarly productive of the mercantile system has not merely done an injustice to the course of English history but has fostered the illusion of a coherent set of economic policy recommendations or measures underpinned by specific doctrines. The illusion was given greater force by the popularising activities of such writers as J.R. McCulloch who attacked 'all regulations affecting the freedom of commerce or of any branch of industry'; tirelessly denounced 'the absurd notions relative to the balance of trade'; and deployed illustrations from the economic past solely to demonstrate the futility of pre-Smithian ideas and to parade the alleged universal wisdom of classical political economy.[49] Attack stimulated defence. Transmuted into 'mercantilism' and approved as *Staatsbildung* by the German historicists, half-heartedly reinstated in England by J.A. Hobson and by Keynes, Smith's mercantile system was ready for learned dissection by Eli Heckscher and for new-found enthusiasm by neo-Marxists. Almost inevitably, cries of neo-mercantilism' or 'the new mercantilism' greeted interventionist government actions, before and after World War II. Sundry pronouncements informed a credulous public that such actions were ultimately derived from attachment to the theory of the balance of trade and a doctrine which identified wealth with precious metals. Schumpeter's dismissal of 'that imaginary entity the "mercantilist system"' went unheeded.[50]

Smith's vision of commerce and liberty was a noble one. Even today it probably still offers the most promising route by which mankind may avoid the worse excesses of tyranny and channel its obsessive urge for self-destruction into the creation of wealth and the maintenance of freedom. Those hopes are not aided, however, by ignoring a paradox in Smith's argument and perpetuating confusions in his historical understanding.

---

[49] J.R. McCulloch; *A Dictionary . . . of Commerce and Commercial Navigation* (1832), pp. 55, 352. See also his various introductory comments in J.R McCulloch (ed.), *Early English Tracts on Commerce* (1856); reprd. Cambridge, 1952), pp. iii-xv.

[50] Schumpeter, *History of Economic Analysis*, p. 147, n.5 and p. 335. For some examples of the sundry re-incarnations of mercantilism, see D.C. Coleman, 'Mercantilism Revisited', *Historical Journal*, 23, (1980), 773-91; and for a specific instance, Joan Robinson, *The New Mercantilism* (Cambridge, 1966).

8

Historians and Businessmen*

In May 1960, Harold Nicolson, biographer, journalist, novelist, Member of Parliament and ex-diplomat, recorded in his diary that he had told his son Nigel that 'I must get a job as a hack-writer who wrote the history of City companies and that I should ask for a fee of £5,000; otherwise I should have to give up living in the Albany'.[1] In fact he was spared this ultimate descent into literary degradation because his publisher son fixed up a contract for him to write a book for the same fee on the much more socially acceptable topic of monarchy. But the diary entry nicely encapsulated a prevalent British attitude towards the history of business and businessmen: it was not a suitable subject either for the historian or for the literary man. Although Nicolson would not have been aware of it, by 1960 the historian's attitude was beginning to change. That it was so doing owed not a little to the publication in 1954 of the first two volumes of Charles Wilson's *History of Unilever*. Since then there have appeared a growing number of scholarly books which provide a view of the historical British businessman. What do they say? In particular, what do they say about the character of the big businessman?

---

* Adam Smith's observations about businessmen, as considered in the previous essay, were unique only in their temporal and philosophical context and in their acerbity. Comments by contemporaries can be found scattered through recorded history; and by historians in ever-growing numbers since the history of business became relatively respectable. This particular piece was a contribution to a *Festschrift* for Charles Wilson, who has done much to further the scholarly use of business records in Britain. The focus of the essay is the exceptionally successful, *not* the typical, businessman. Its aim being to emphasise the continuity of ambivalent attitudes towards such men, the selected examples stretch from the fourteenth to the twentieth centuries.

Both this essay and 'Gentlemen and Players' contain passing references to the representation of businessmen in literature. Since they were published a number of important books and articles have appeared on this very subject. Guides to them will be found in the publications by Neil McKendrick and by James Raven mentioned in the prefatory note to Chapter 6, above. See also J.R. Raven, 'English Popular Literature and the Image of Business, 1760-90'(unpublished Ph.D. thesis, Cambridge, 1985). The 'industrial novel' has apparently become embedded into literary studies; and it has achieved fictional fame in David Lodge's hilarious satire *Nice Work* (1988).

[1] Harold Nicolson, *Diaries and Letters*, ed. Nigel Nicolson, 3 vols. (1966-68), iii, 384.

Perhaps the most obvious and frequently made comment is that such men
were in various ways exceptionally energetic, vigorous, autocratic, dictatorial, dynamic figures who engendered awe, respect or fear rather than
affection. William Lever (1852-1925), founder of Lever Brothers and the
British end of Unilever, will serve as an initial exemplar. Wilson tells us that
he 'radiated force and energy', gave out an 'unending stream of commands,
prophecies and exhortations'; and 'by unremitting effort, boundless ambition and powerful imagination' he built up his business.[2] Anyone presumptuous enough to suggest a course of action was firmly put in his place –
which place was to carry out Lever's orders. His business was his life. 'My
happiness', he said, 'is my business . . . the possibilities are boundless . . . one
can organize, organize, organize . . . very big things indeed. But I don't
work at business only for the sake of money. I am not a lover of money as
money and never have been. I work at business because business is life. It
enables me to do things.'[3] In later life this particular god of happiness
could exact a toll even to the end. 'I ask myself', he wrote in 1923, two years
before his death, 'what has caused me to begin work at 4.30 in the morning
during the last two or three years . . . and I am bound to confess that it has
not been the attraction of dividends but "fear" . . . fear . . . that Lever
Brothers would have to pass their dividend. We have', he wrote ominously,
'been combing out inefficient men . . . and this has produced a state of
"fear" in the minds of the remainder.'[4]

Such characteristics have echoes in other histories of other businessmen.
'A smart, lively, energetic little man; born for action and full of eagerness
and enthusiasm to shine in his business': thus runs a contemporary comment in 1817 on the rising John Dickinson (1782-1869), the founder of the
paper-making firm of that name. He was hot-tempered, dictatorial, autocratic and highly successful.[5] John Gladstone (1764-1851), Liverpool 'merchant prince', owner of West Indian sugar plantations and slaves, father of
the famous statesman, was another 'man of driving energy' who sent out,
according to his biographer, 'a continuous stream of orders'.[6] Samuel
Courtauld (1793-1881), founder of the textile firm (*not* his twentieth-
century great-nephew of the same name), was, in a quite different line of
business, 'a man of prodigious energy', arrogant, domineering, autocratic,
ambitious; like Lever his business was his life.[7] Some reflections which he
made in the 1850s nicely anticipate those of the soap-maker of the next
century: 'it is not by any means to mere money gain so much as success in

[2] Charles Wilson, *The History of Unilever*, 3 vols. (1954 and 1968), i, 48, 49, 290.
[3] Ibid., p. 187.
[4] Ibid., pp. 291-92.
[5] Joan Evans, *The Endless Web: John Dickinson & Co. Ltd., 1804-1954* (1955), pp. 17, 21, 59.
[6] S.G. Checkland, *The Gladstones: A Family Biography, 1764-1851* (Cambridge, 1971), p. 228.
[7] D.C. Coleman, *Courtaulds: An Economic and Social History*, 3 vols. (Oxford, 1969 and 1980), i, 120-26.

well-contrived and well-conducted action that our interest and satisfaction in our business is found; the money gain is a legitimate result . . . but it is not the spirit and soul of it, infinitely less is it the measure of it'.[8]

Devotion to business and business achievement as the source of personal satisfaction rather than merely of money was more or less inevitably complemented by statements about the virtues of hard work, usually expressed retrospectively. Sam Courtauld worked very long hours and made sure that his partner knew it; in later life he preached a philosophy of the merits of work and energy and in 1880 accompanied a £1,000 birthday-gift to a nephew with a 2,500-word homily on the merits of work.[9] William Morris, Lord Nuffield (1877-1963), creator of the biggest and most success-ful business in the British motor industry, 'worked extremely long hours throughout his career' and maintained in later life that 'work is still the natural mission of every man'. Like Courtauld, he was driven by an urge to succeed, was individualistic, would tolerate neither interference from out-side nor rivals inside, and clung to power too long.[10] If Morris was difficult to work with and Lever's immediate subordinates were told where to get off, Sam Courtauld's own brother and partner, George, was finally driven to protest about Sam's carrying on a discussion about the renewal of their partnership in 1849 'in the character of a lord with his vassal'.[11]

Such complaints were not confined to Britain. Here is another junior partner complaining about his senior counterpart: 'It is now two years that I am your partner, and I tell you, since then I have known not one joyful day, and furthermore know not even now how much I earn'. In fact, however, that partnership lasted for fifteen years and the senior partner was another man who attracted all those familiar descriptions: ambitious, shrewd, tena-cious, possessed of great powers of organization, difficult, grasping, wilful, and once again, having a formidable temper. This was Francesco Datini, merchant of Prato, who died in 1410.[12] Jump the centuries again and the picture is much the same. David Colville (1860-1916), 'the driving force behind the growth' of what was to become the dominant firm in the Scottish steel industry and one of the biggest in the UK before nationalization, was the second generation of the family in the business. He 'possessed a magnetic personality'; he was '*the* master: everyone from the board to the office-boy knew it'. He had 'a violent temper', 'incredible energy', and it was his 'daemonic drive and energy' which built up the company.[13] Here is another man of the same generation in another business: 'more than one person described him as possessing boundless energy'; he was 'like a

---

[8] Ibid., p. 175.

[9] Ibid., pp. 121, 122.

[10] R.J. Overy, *William Morris, Viscount Nuffield* (1976), pp. 102-8.

[11] Coleman, *Courtaulds*, i, 125.

[12] Iris Origo, *The Merchant of Prato* (1957), pp. 15-16, 21, 65, 112, 172, 341.

[13] Peter L. Payne, *Colvilles and the Scottish Steel Industry* (Oxford, 1979), pp. 117, 131.

tornado who used to tear around the works and offices'. These were contemporary descriptions of Herbert Austin (1866-1941), founder of the Austin motor company and great rival to William Morris, Lord Nuffield.[14] And here is a tycoon of a similar generation: Harry McGowan, Lord McGowan (1874-1961), successor in 1931 to Alfred Mond, Lord Melchett, as Chairman and Managing Director of I.C.I. 'A natural autocrat', possessed of an excellent memory and a quick, probing mind, he dominated his Board, inspired respect rather than affection, bullied almost all his colleagues at one time or another, exercised such a complete dictatorship that I.C.I under McGowan was, it has been said, 'as near to being run by one man as any business of its size could be'.[15] And still later, in a different line of business, Sir Eric Bowater (1895-1962), creator of the modern paper-making giant, is said to have enjoyed unconcealed dominance over the firm and to have exercised 'naked autocracy'; to have possessed a temper which 'was very rarely lost, but terrifying if it was'; and whose behaviour towards the British and North American sides of the business was 'reminiscent of nothing so much as the style of government of earlier autocrats: the Norman and Angevin kings of England'.[16]

The majority of the samples so far considered have been nineteenth- and twentieth-century industrialists. Most of the big businessmen who date from before the Industrial Revolution and who have been caught in the historian's net were merchants and/or financiers. The seventeenth century offers some notable participants in the great business game. If a prize were to be given for unattractive historical businessmen, then two early-seventeenth-century operators would probably tie for first place. Sir Arthur Ingram and Lionel Cranfield, later Earl of Middlesex, were almost exact contemporaries, their lifespans both stretching from the 1560s and 1570s to the 1640s. Both were the sons of London merchants; both also started as merchants; both moved into the risky but lucrative half-world of government contracts and finance; and both finished up as landowners. Cranfield was a bigger merchant and made a fortune as such before entering politics and becoming Lord Treasurer in 1621-4; Ingram achieved his wealth and reputation as an intermediary between court and business, a 'fixer', a contact man, exploiter of court monopolies. Ingram's road to fortune has been described as 'littered with the wretched lives of those who had dealt with him as clients or partners'; and his character impressed his biographer as twisting, devious and unreliable, unreasonable and overbearing, excessively suspicious and always self-righteous.[17] His fortune is said to have represented 'the

[14] Roy Church, *Herbert Austin* (1979), pp. 161-62.
[15] W.J. Reader, *Imperial Chemical Industries: A History*, 2 vols. (Oxford, 1975), i, 380; ii, 135-36, 143, 235.
[16] W.J. Reader, *Bowater: A History* (Cambridge, 1981), pp. 89-90, 173.
[17] Anthony F. Upton, *Sir Arthur Ingram* (Oxford, 1961), pp. 259, 261.

parasitical wealth of a brilliant speculator who seized all the opportunities of a corrupt political system'.[18] Cranfield presented almost a mirror image: he was, it seems, arrogant and grasping, mean and suspicious, tactless and self-righteous, hard, ambitious and exacting, energetic and unscrupulous. He differed from Ingram apparently only in earning the epithets 'inflexible and intransigent' whilst Ingram's flexibility was so near slipperiness as makes no matter.[19] Cranfield's urge to make money was powerful and soon remarked upon; an early business partner told him in 1601 that 'the worm covetousness gnaws you, by stretching it to the uttermost as all the world takes notice you do'.[20] Cranfield and Ingram were partners themselves in sundry ventures, and in a letter of 1607 the former offered to the latter a classic invitation for the joint exploitation of opportunities for gain: 'one rule I desire be observed between you and me, which is that neither of us seek to advance our estates by the other's loss, but that we may join together faithfully to raise our fortunes, by such casualties as this stirring age shall afford'.[21] Not even this worked, for, treacherous to the end, Ingram managed in the 1630s to double-cross Cranfield when the latter was in difficulties.[22]

In contrast to this early-seventeenth-century pair stands a later-seventeenth-century counterpart whose character sounds like the exception to prove the rule in the shape of a man who made a great deal of money in public finance (he was described in his own day as 'the richest commoner in three kingdoms') and yet who was apparently popular, respected and honest.[23] Sir Stephen Fox (1627-1716) seems, according to his biographer, to have been 'one of the most likeable parvenus of any age'. He had a reputation for honesty and competence, great personal charm and considerable presence; nobody ever seems to have levelled any charge of malpractice against him; and he sent the diarist John Evelyn into raptures of praise: 'generous . . . of a sweet nature . . . never was man more fortunate than Sir Stephen: he is a handsome person, virtuous and very religious'; and as for his wealth, it was 'honestly gotten and unenvied, which is next to a miracle'.[24] It is almost a relief to find him possessed of a few resemblances to the emerging prototype of the big businessman: he was sometimes overbearing to dependents; he liked to get his own way; beneath the charm lurked a

---

[18] Menna Prestwich, *Cranfield: Politics and Profits under the Early Stuarts* (Oxford, 1966), pp. 64-65.

[19] Ibid., pp. 54-55, 65, 92, 508, 523-24.

[20] Ibid., p. 54.

[21] Ibid., p. 72.

[22] Ibid., p. 406.

[23] Christopher Clay, *Public Finance and Private Wealth: The Career of Sir Stephen Fox, 1627-1716* (Oxford, 1978), p. 302.

[24] Ibid., pp. 17, 232-3, 303; *The Diary of John Evelyn*, ed. E.S. de Beer, 6 vols. (Oxford, 1955), iv, 217-19.

sharp temper; he was intolerant of weakness or failure in others; and he became irritable in old age.[25] He begins to sound quite human.

Lest it should be supposed that I am suggesting that *all* leading business-men have been seen by historians as bad-tempered, over-energetic, innovating dynamos let me at this point introduce an associated historical character to modify the picture. Along with the vigorous innovator there has often gone a business associate of a different temperament. For the sake of a convenient label, he can be called the 'organization man', though that does not necessarily describe his function. He has characteristically appeared as the essential complement to the innovator. Sometimes he has been a finance expert, an accountant or a lawyer, a negotiator, a manipulator, a man concerned with structures of organization or tactics to be pursued, a man of careful judgement but not a visionary or a major innovator either in organization or in production techniques. He has been an important decision-taker in his own right, has sometimes been of crucial importance in a firm's development by preventing the daemon of innovation from taking decisions so radical and innovatory as to be crazy, and has sometimes succeeded him in command of the business, bringing in a necessary period of consolidation and stability. Francis D'Arcy Cooper, who succeeded Lever as Chairman of Lever Bros in 1925, provides a classic example of the man who had kept control over finance and who then ushered in a period of consolidation and rationalization.[26] In Colville's history, during the period of rapid growth under the aegis of the dynamic David, his brother Archibald was 'the only person who could withstand David's violent temper and harness his incredible energies to attain realistic objectives'. Archibald, in contrast to his flamboyant brother, was 'shrewd, calculating and cool'.[27] The history of Courtaulds provides more than one example of similar partnerships of different temperaments. The most striking was probably that of H.G. Tetley (1852-1921) and T.P. Latham (1855-1931) who between them, at the beginning of the twentieth century, transformed a family silk firm into a world leader in the first of the man-made fibres, rayon. Tetley seems to have had the standard ration of relentless energy, arrogant and domineering manner, furious temper, a single-minded devotion to business, and a ruthless impatience which sent out a stream of letters, plans, ideas, demands and orders. Latham, in contrast, was calm, close, calculating, shrewd, efficient, devoid of the imaginative vision of Tetley but possessed of a certain charm of manner and an ability to smooth the troubled waters left in Tetley's wake.[28] Similar examples of this duality could be provided from

[25] Clay, *Public Finance*, pp. 314-15.
[26] Wilson, *Unilever*, i, 297-303; ii, 309-14.
[27] Payne, *Colvilles*, p. 131.
[28] Coleman, *Courtaulds*, ii, 205-7.

the modern leaders of some well-known big corporations as well as from the merchants and financiers of an earlier age.

To these character-sketches of the businessman roughed out on the historian's pages should be added some recurrent motifs or highlights provided by the subjects themselves. One such motif is the observation of the separateness of the business world from other worlds. The former was consistently seen as a world inhabited by peculiarly malevolent men; it was full of traps; and it called in turn for special qualities for survival. 'You are young', wrote Datini in 1397 to one of his factors, 'but when you have lived as long as I and have traded with many folk you will know that man is a dangerous thing and that danger lies in dealing with him'[29] The worthy Fox three hundred years later had a wary eye for those with whom he dealt, and no doubt he needed it: 'as I am an honest man I don't know but I may want bread before I dye'.[30] John Gladstone warned his son Tom at Eton in 1820 about the hazards of the business life compared with public life. The latter was the 'road to honour and usefulness'. In the former, 'great respectability' was to be got by 'honourable, punctual, correct conduct', and the prime object of mercantile men was to accumulate or acquire property, but 'all their prudence and discretion is required to guard against measures that so often lead to ruin and loss of fortune'.[31] That the business world had its traps for the young is testified to in books of guidance and by the homilies addressed by older men to young merchants. 'God is a god of order among men', Sir John Banks (1627-99), East India Company merchant and financier, told a young protégé and apprentice: 'Keep your accounts punctual, be honest to all men. Be careful of your company, converse not with ill company. Many evils do follow thereon'.[32] Closely related to this theme was the frequently made distinction between private morality and business morality. The private lives even of Cranfield and Ingram seem to have been notably more attractive than their business counterparts; and both were apparently religious men.[33] The notion seems long-enduring and to stretch out through the centuries. Here is a modern version of it, written in a letter in 1965 by a leading businessman, Frank Kearton, just as he was about to become Chairman of Courtaulds: 'a positive and indeed a very baleful personality is needed to make a success of the tough businesses. One can still remain – I hope – sweetly considerate in private life, business is quite different.'[34] Eleven years later, as Lord Kearton, he became the head of the state-owned British National Oil Corporation. Presumably the same

---

[29] Origo, *Merchant of Prato*, p. 81.

[30] Clay, *Public Finance*, p. 315.

[31] Checkland, *The Gladstones*, p. 410.

[32] D.C. Coleman, *Sir John Banks: Baronet and Businessman* (Oxford, 1963), pp. 66, 145-46. The remarks were made in 1658 and 1662.

[33] Upton, *Sir Arthur Ingram*, p. 262; Prestwich, *Cranfield*, p. 537.

[34] Quoted Coleman, *Courtaulds*, iii, 319.

sentiments were deemed equally appropriate for a nationalized industry in 1976 as they had been for a private one in 1965 – or 1397.

Hunting down character has not of course been the only form taken by the pursuit of the historical businessman. Interest in the subject has been stimulated amongst economic historians by their central obsession with the Industrial Revolution. The question has inevitably been asked whether it was perhaps due in some measure to particular efficient and powerfully motivated businessmen. If so, what circumstances bred such beings? The search was on for the entrepreneur. That search – with all its exploration of psychology, social structure and religion – is not the subject of this essay. But a few features of motive and attitude are perhaps worthy of emphasis if only because, in this pursuit, they can be picked up in other contexts and at other times.

A feature which occurs in a number of accounts is the seeming importance of particular family circumstances in helping to provide the initial motivation which has set the future businessman *en route* for success. The young William Morris, the future Lord Nuffield, is said to have been spurred on to his vigorous early efforts by awareness of his having to be the main source of support for his mother, his father being in such poor health that by 1893, when Morris was only sixteen years of age, he could no longer work to support the family.[35] The ambitions of Sir Alfred Jones (1845-1909), future Liverpool shipping magnate and the only surviving son of an impoverished middle-class family in which the father's ill-health and early death left young Alfred's mother in a vulnerable position, were apparently much influenced by an urge to remedy this family decline.[36] Samuel Courtauld's driving energy was given impetus by his awareness – as the eldest son in a family of seven born of an idealistic father who was a singularly incompetent businessman – that he would sooner or later have to help to support the family and remedy its social position. He did.[37]

Whatever the initial motivation, it is clear that throughout Western history the businessman has very rarely come from high social strata; and if he has climbed the social ladder, the regard paid to him by the hierarchy in which he lived has often been both ambivalent and variable. Though Britain never had the formal penalty of derogation as in France during the *ancien régime*, sundry changing and far from logically consistent practices and prejudices combined to ensure a social pecking order of business activities. At the nether end were those involving manual labour and retail trade; at the top were overseas trade and international finance. Social attitudes to business and businessmen were long affected by two potent influences

[35] Overy, *William Morris*, p. 102.
[36] P.N. Davies, *Sir Alfred Jones* (1978), pp. 16-18, 25, 101.
[37] Coleman, *Courtaulds*, i, chap. 4, *passim*, and 125-26.

which had deep roots in Christian society: the moral suspicion of profits, embracing in particular the condemnation of usury; and the notion of social hierarchy. The former was commonly ill-enforced, the latter remarkably adaptable. In both, ambiguity in practice ensured a long-enduring detestation of the local money-lender, a continuing use of the term 'usurer' as a smear word; and first a tacit acceptance and then an honoured place for those who, in England at least, practised what came to be called 'merchant banking' and meant, mainly, arranging loans for foreign governments. So in twentieth-century Britain before the Second World War, to be a pawnbroker was mildly disreputable; to be a bank-clerk was respectable but petty bourgeois; to be a merchant banker was so prestigious as to require an acquaintanceship with (or better still membership of) one of a small group of dominant families who between them had a goodly sprinkling of peerages. When Datini went into banking at the end of the fourteenth century, however, some people commented that he would 'lose his repute' as a great merchant by becoming a money-changer, adding that 'there is not one of them who practices no usury in his contracts'.[38] And nearly three hundred years later, in late-seventeenth-century London, Evelyn wrote in his diary in August 1678 after dining with Sir John Banks that the latter was 'a merchant of small beginnings' who had amassed a large estate 'by usurie etc.';[39] and a half-century after that, Defoe, seen by some historians as a veritable spokesman for bourgeois mercantile ideology, was warning readers of his *Complete English Tradesman* against the wiles of 'usurers . . . [and] . . . money-lenders'.[40] What Evelyn did not note in his little smear about Banks' 'usurie' was that most of the money-lending had been made to Charles II's government. How, then, did Fox, who provided similar services, only on a larger scale, acquire such a splendid reputation for virtue, honesty, popularity and charm, in complete contrast to most of those who came to represent what eighteenth-century Tories so detested as 'the monied interest'?

The answer to this question provided by Sir Stephen Fox's biographer is interesting for the light which it sheds not simply on Fox, but on what impresses an English historian as having been important in determining attitudes to a businessman at that time. Fox, writes his biographer, 'made an immense fortune as a financier but he was a courtier who had learnt the ways of finance, *not a business man who was trying to pick up the rudiments of gentility*' (my italics).[41] He had indeed had a most unusual upbringing for a businessman. Coming from humble circumstances, he had secured employment as a boy in a more or less menial capacity in the royal household. As the latter went a-wandering during the Interregnum, he rose from page-boy to

---

[38] Origo, *Merchant of Prato*, p. 149.
[39] Evelyn, *Diary*, iv, 96.
[40] D. Defoe, *The Complete English Tradesman* (1727), suppl., p. 15.
[41] Clay, *Public Finance*, p. 304.

Clerk of the Stables and so on up the ladder of court appointments, eventually, on the restoration of Charles II, reaching those dangerous heights where money was borrowed, handled and disbursed on a large scale. By the time he had become both a royal financier and a financier in his own right he had 'no past of "trade" or petty moneylending to live down'.[42] So whilst Evelyn delivered his disapprobation of Banks or condemned Banks' fellow East India Company magnate Sir Josiah Child (1630-99) as 'this merchant most sordidly avaricious',[43] he could yet be enraptured of Fox and write a fulsome encomium on merchants in general as 'that most honourable and useful race of men (the pillars of all magnificence)'.[44] And when Pepys referred to Fox as a 'very fine gentleman'[45] he meant it in that literal sense which so appeals to the peculiarly English feeling for social order.

Money-lending and the regard for social hierarchy could thus be reconciled by the magic of gentility – which had ultimately to be in the eye of the beholder and might have to wait a generation. And 'trade' became respectable, though not proof against charges of avarice, the more it was concerned with exports and imports and could thus be seen, as to some extent it was at that time, as almost a series of acts of state. Indeed, the very age of Evelyn and Fox was one which, briefly, saw a remarkable enthusiasm for the alleged glories of commerce. The merchant, in the abstract, was lauded by writers of varying political hue. Without the merchant, asserted one writer in 1686, 'the world would still be a kind of wilderness'.[46] In 1711 Addison can be heard eulogizing merchants as the most useful members of the commonwealth because they 'knit mankind together in a mutual intercourse of good offices, distribute the gifts of nature, find work for the poor, add wealth to the rich and magnificence to the great'.[47] And in George Lillo's play *The London Merchant*, a moral tale which ran to packed houses in Drury Lane after its first performance in 1731, the very virtuous and very boring merchant Thorowgood tells his apprentice Trueman that 'the method of merchandize' has promoted 'arts, industry, peace and plenty; by mutual benefits diffusing mutual love from pole to pole'.[48] Such attitudes towards business stood in total contrast to the anti-merchant sentiments typical of a group of mid sixteenth-century writers to whom most traders were rogues:

[42] Ibid.

[43] Evelyn, *Diary*, iv, 305-6.

[44] Evelyn, *Navigation and Commerce* (1674).

[45] Quoted Clay, *Public Finance*, p. 17.

[46] *The Character and Qualifications of an Honest Loyal Merchant* (1686).

[47] Joseph Addison, *The Spectator*, no. 69 (19 May 1711), quoted H.R. Fox Bourne, *English Merchants* (London, 1886), pp. 205-6.

[48] George Lillo, *The London Merchant* (1731; ed. and with introd. by Bonamy Dobrée, 1948), p. 41.

'next to sham priests, no class of men is more pestilential to the common-wealth'.[49] Or, more explicitly:

> All merchants, buyers and sellers in London or elsewhere are commonly poor men's sons natural born to labour for their living, which after they be bound apprentices to be merchants, all their labour, study and policy is by buying and selling to get singular riches from the communalty, and never worketh to get their living neither by works of husbandry nor artificiality, but liveth by other men's works, and of naught riseth to great riches, intending nothing else but only to get riches, which knoweth no common weal.[50]

By the second half of the eighteenth century not dissimilar sentiments had reasserted themselves. Writers as diverse as Samuel Johnson, Oliver Goldsmith and, in a quite different way, Adam Smith, were all showing notably less ardour for the abstract merchant than that of their immediate predecessors. Smith's indictment of the 'mean rapacity' of merchants and manufacturers which had caused commerce, 'which ought naturally to be . . . a bond of union and friendship', to become 'the most fertile source of discord and animosity'[51] provided at least a partial echo of the anti-merchant attitude of the sixteenth century.

The coming of industrialization did not bring radical change to contemporary comments on the businessman. They retained their variable and ambivalent nature. Their targets came inevitably to include more manufacturers than merchants. In so far as the businessman figured in contemporary novels or drama the balance of comment shifted decisively towards hostility. Romantic admiration in the manner of Samuel Smiles proved less potent than that 'literary Luddism' of English fiction in the nineteenth and twentieth centuries which has been examined in detail by Neil McKendrick.[52] My concern with it here is simply to emphasize that ambivalent attitudes preceded as well as followed the Industrial Revolution. Sympathetic portraits of the businessman do exist in English fiction, but when he does appear – and there are large areas of the literary scene from which he is entirely absent – his character tends to range from the unpleasant to the comic, from the sinister to the absurd. A suitable butt for satire in Jacobean and Restoration drama, he pops up in sundry places and guises to illustrate the long-running English fascination with class and with social climbing by

---

[49] Martin Bucer, quoted R.H. Tawney, *Religion and the Rise of Capitalism* (1929), p. 142.

[50] 'How to Reform the Realm in Setting them to Work and to Restore Tillage'. *c.* 1535-36. quoted in R.H. Tawney and E. Power (eds.), *Tudor Economic Documents*, 3 vols. (1924), ii, 126 (spelling modernized).

[51] Adam Smith, *The Wealth of Nations*, Modern Library edition (New York, 1937), p. 460.

[52] See his valuable editorial introductions to four volumes (and especially the last two) in the Europa Library of Business Biography series (now seemingly terminated), viz: Overy, *William Morris*, pp. vii-xliv; Clive Trebilcock, *The Vickers Brothers* (1977), pp. ix-xxxiv; P.N. Davies, *Sir Alfred Jones* (1978), pp. ix-lvi; Church, *Herbert Austin*, pp. ix-l.

the self-made; from Dickens to Lawrence he struts and snarls as an unloved figure in an unloved industrial landscape; and in more modern manifestations he is sometimes presented as embodying ambiguous fantasies of sex and power, as in Anthony Powell's creation, Sir Magnus Donners. And for an updated version of the sixteenth-century anti-merchant sentiments one could hardly better those expressed by Canon L.J.C. Collins in 1962 concerning the 'economic gangsterism of capitalism'.[53]

So when modern professional historians have looked at the historical big businessman and sketched not wholly endearing personalities, they have doubly reflected long-enduring attitudes in British society. In one sense they may well have themselves been influenced consciously or unconsciously by the ambivalence or hostility of the literary tradition. Many will have been through educational processes similar to those which have helped to sustain that tradition. Yet the very fact that they have tackled so unpopular, indeed unfashionable, a topic suggests a substantial commitment to objectivity, even to sympathy, which should have minimized this influence. More important is the refraction of these social attitudes though the historical businessmen themselves as they made their way to power and wealth, leaving their marks as evidence for the historian to use. If the latter has seemed to create stereotypes – the impatient entrepreneurial dynamo or the patient organization man – it is largely because these are the immediate equivalents in business history of the ambitious politicians, the scheming prelates, the astute lawyers, and all the other more familiar climbing plants in the historical garden. In time, more varieties will doubtless be discovered. Nature may come to imitate art. So far, the likely extent of this must be small. When Lever said 'my happiness is my business; he is unlikely to have known that he was almost precisely echoing the words which, some 250 years earlier, William Wycherley had put into the mouth of his pompous, fictional businessman, Sir Jaspar Fidget, when the latter told his wife and her companions to go to their 'business, I say, pleasure' whilst he went to his 'pleasure, business'.[54]

The longevity of ambivalent attitudes towards the businessman is worthy of emphasis. They are much older than is popularly supposed by those who look only at modern industrialization and its problems. A recent (and grossly overpraised) book has, for example, declared that something called 'the decline of the industrial spirit' in England is attributable to anti-business sentiments in English culture *since* 1850.[55] By starting only in 1850 the author neatly evades the task of having to explain why that 'industrial spirit'

[53] *Guardian*, 19 March 1962, quoted Coleman, *Courtaulds*, iii, 230 and n.
[54] William Wycherley, *The Country Wife* (1675).
[55] Martin J. Wiener, *English Culture and the Decline of the Industrial Spirit, 1850-1980* (Cambridge, 1981).

presumably succeeded earlier in rising so vigorously despite the prior existence of similar anti-business sentiments. The attitudes are old but they still survive; they continue to coexist with the enjoyment of the fruits of business. The very facilities which permit our historical studies are amongst those fruits. Yet our society has retained the suspicion of profits, looked disapprovingly at acquisitiveness, found the businessmen unappealing, and gazed unenthusiastically at the self-made unless or until they have conformed to our notions of social ordering. Until very recently, we have even looked upon the very study of business history as a sort of intellectual derogation.

Those who have attracted this opprobrium, and indeed those who have been examined by the historian, have in the main been untypical businessmen in the sense that they were tycoons, made large fortunes, rose to the top of the tree, created new enterprises or the like. The average businessman, whether a provincial trader of the fifteenth century or a garage proprietor of the twentieth, has performed at a less spectacular level of achievement. He has not been a major innovator in any sense; he has typically run a small to middle-sized firm and made moderate profits, or, in recent times, has been a salaried director. If he has moved up the scale of prosperity and the social hierarchy he has become a solid citizen of the middle class. Unlike the tycoon, he has not sought to live in some remote baronial fantasy, like Citizen Kane or, as John Evelyn said of Josiah Child's new seat, 'in a cursed and barren spot, as commonly these overgrown and suddenly monied men do for the most part seat themselves'.[56] He is more likely to have lived in an Elizabethan house in the middle of a sixteenth-century town or a mock-Elizabethan house in the suburbs of a twentieth-century town. Unfortunately the average businessman rarely figures individually on the professional historian's pages. He remains hidden as a number in a total, an anonymous bit of an aggregate, subsumed within calculations of output or of firms within industries. Of course, in this he is no different from average historical lawyers or average historical politicians. When history was assumed to be 'past politics', it was the political leaders who figured in it, not back-bench Members of Parliament. So it is not inherently unreasonable that business history as it progresses should want to know about business leaders: their functions within the firm or industry, their origins, achievements, motivation, methods, personalities and relations with the wider

---

[56] Evelyn, *Diary*, iv, 305-6. He had commented similarly on the habits of the new rich when, in 1677, he had visited Sir Robert Clayton, scrivener and banker, whose house in Surrey, from being a mere farm, had been 'erected into a seat with extraordinary expence. 'Tis in such solitude among hills as, being not above 16 miles from London, seems incredible, the ways up to it are so winding and intricate.' (Ibid., ii, 331.) His ambivalence is also evident in his comments in 1679 on the 'excessively rich' Clayton: 'some believe him guilty of hard dealing, especially with the Duke of Buckingham whose estate he had swallowed, but I never saw any ill by him, *considering the trade he was of*' (my italics; ibid., ii, 357).

world. But the historian of business, like other sorts of historian, will have to be prepared also to look more closely at a wider range of businessmen at varying levels of society. The creation of employment, the building of wealth, the use of resources: all have depended and still depend upon the decisions of businessmen, whether they are private capitalists, salaried directors, or the bosses of nationalized industry. Their historical doings are part of the totality of history. And until historians are willing and, indeed, actively encouraged to look at the businessman in history in much the same way as we try to look at other actors in the historical drama we shall be missing a good part of the play.

9

War Demand and Industrial Supply: The 'Dope Scandal', 1915-19[*]

According to one's viewpoint or disposition the episode here examined may be variously regarded: as the war-time consequence of the shortage of a component in the aircraft industry; as an incident in the widespread manufacturing processes built upon discoveries in the chemistry of cellulose; as an example of what is fashionably known as 'spin-off'; or as an instance of the typical war-time relationships between governments and business, compounded of patriotism and profits, of opportunism and muddle.

It is with the requirements of early aircraft production that the story must begin. Until the use of aluminium the normal material for the outer skin of aircraft was a heavy linen fabric treated with a substance commonly called 'dope' in order to make it taut, wind-resistant and weather-proof. It was also used for airships and balloons. So dope and its ingredients soon acquired industrial and military consequence. Precisely when and how the need presented itself as capable of being met by one of the many products of the newly emerging cellulose chemistry is not clear. Around 1900 nitro-cellulose came into use as a base for making varnishes and lacquers as well as cinematograph film and that unattractive commodity called celluloid. So experiments were made, successfully, with nitro-cellulose as a base for

---

[*] All the other essays in this book which are concerned with businessmen consider them generically, with illustrations drawn from various periods and places as thought necessary. This piece, however, is concerned with a particular group engaged in one specific venture. Some, though not necessarily all, of those involved might well be seen as exemplifying many of those unattractive characteristics of the businessman as set out by Adam Smith. This was certainly not my intention in writing the essay which, like chapter 8 above, was a contribution to a *Festschrift*. Its primary aim was not dissimilar to that of chapter 3, that is to illustrate the industrial impact of the state in pursuit of war. In this case that impact came well after the Industrial Revolution had left its mark though before Britain had made much headway in industries based upon organic chemistry. The combination of muddled policy and commercial opportunism which characterised this episode undoubtedly produced some unintended consequences, though they were not quite of the sort Adam Smith earlier had in mind.

aeroplane dopes in place of the sundry pastes, glues, oil-based varnishes, and rubber compositions which were never of much use. It was discovered that by adding certain chemicals the extreme inflammability of nitro-cellulose dope could be reduced. Nevertheless, its dangers provided a strong stimulus, here as in other fields, to find an alternative base. It was found in the shape of cellulose acetate as a result of experiments proceeding between, approximately, 1900 and 1909 – the year in which Louis Blériot made his famous flight across the English Channel. Even so, the then state of powered flight was unlikely to have induced visions of soaring demand from an aircraft industry. Within the next decade, however, thousands of tons of dope, mainly cellulose-acetate based, were used in hundreds of thousands of aircraft, as the warring powers discovered alike their destructive value and their destructibility.[1]

Since its initial discovery in 1865, cellulose acetate – obtained by treating cellulose with acetic acid and acetic anhydride – had been the subject of various patents and the repository of many hopes. This was especially true after the important patent of the English chemists C.F. Cross and E.J. Bevan of 1894; and thereafter much work was done, with a view to various industrial uses, in England, Germany, France, and the USA. The primacy for the development of a soluble form of cellulose acetate is usually given to the German chemist Arthur Eichengrün, working with the Bayer Company. It was made at that company's Elberfeld works, and in about 1905 was being marketed under the trade name of 'Cellit'. In 1909 he patented another process of dissolving cellulose acetate; and the resulting substance, primarily intended for use in the manufacture of non-inflammable cinematograph film, was marketed under the name of 'Cellon'. The other possibilities of 'Cellit' and 'Cellon' – for both of which names Eichengrün was the registered trade mark holder in Britain and elsewhere – were soon evident, notably as a base for lacquers and varnishes. Sundry companies were set up, including the British Cellon Company, which was registered as a private company in 1913. Its origins lay partly in the enterprise of an Englishman, A.J.W. Barr, in 1911, and partly in the acquisition of Eichengrün's patent rights in 'Cellon'. It planned to make sundry commodities including aeroplane dope, importing its cellulose acetate from Bayer. A company prospectus of June 1912 printed a testimonial from the pioneer aviator S.F. Cody; its wording nicely illustrates this particular aspect of the early days of flying: 'Now that I have tested my machine by flying to Hendon yesterday, reaching an altitude of 4,850 feet, encountering 3 rain-showers or traversing 3 heavy rain-

---

[1] *History of the Ministry of Munitions* (12 vols. 1922), 12, pt. 1, pp. 136-43; L.F. Haber, *The Chemical Industry, 1900-1930* (Oxford, 1971) pp. 213-14, and 214 n. 1, quoting French estimates that on average 120kg. of dope were used per plane. From figures given in H.A. Jones (and Sir W. Raleigh), *The War in the Air* (Oxford, 1922-37), Appendices volume, pp. 154-55, it would seem that Britain, France, USA, Italy and Germany together built well over 200,000 airframes during the war, thus using around 24,000 tons of dope on new aeroplanes alone.

clouds, after landing I examined the fabric to find that it was in perfect condition . . . I have decided to varnish my next new machine with "Cellon".'[2]

By the outbreak of war in 1914 no soluble cellulose acetate had been made in Britain on a commercial scale, as distinct from laboratory work. Makers of paints and lacquers who were interested in its use, such as the paint firm, Pinchin Johnson & Company, had to import it; so did a number of firms that had gone in for the manufacture of aeroplane dope; and so too, did the Royal Aircraft Factory at Farnborough which made its own dope. But enemy Germany was not the sole source. In France, the chemical enterprise, Usines du Rhône, had succeeded in developing a form of soluble cellulose acetate and in 1913 had a factory capable of turning it out at the rate of one ton per day. There was another source open to the British: the enterprise developed by the brothers Henri and Camille Dreyfus at Basle in Switzerland. They had established a factory to make cellulose acetate in 1912. The new demand for aeroplane dope, which military aviation created, now offered to these men a range of remarkable opportunities and produced some equally remarkable consequences.

Henri Dreyfus, born in 1882, was a Swiss of French-Alsatian origins. A chemist, he took out numerous patents and, in 1912, in conjunction with his elder brother Camille, and another Swiss, Alexander Clavel, a silk dyer, set up a company for the manufacture of cellulose acetate and other chemicals. It was called the 'Société de Cellonit Dreyfus et Cie'. To use the word 'Cellonit' in a company's title when 'Cellit' and 'Cellon' were already someone else's registered trade marks for forms of soluble cellulose acetate was perhaps asking for trouble. The validity and originality of the Dreyfus patents and process have been called into question, both then and later, by various chemists.[3] Nevertheless, whatever his claims to originality as an inventor, his firm had apparently made a process work and, in 1914, was the only one to have done so outside France and Germany.

At the beginning of the war the Basle company was developing its business in Britain, as elsewhere, and in September 1914 offered supplies to

[2] A facsimile prospectus of Cellon Ltd. is one of a collection of records relating to the 'Dope Scandal' in Courtaulds archives [hereafter: CA] consulted by kind permission of Courtaulds Ltd. Much of the above paragraph is derived from various papers in these files; see also Haber, *The Chemical Industry, passim*; and my *Courtaulds. An Economic and Social History* (Oxford, 1969), ii, pp. 178-84.
[3] None of the pre-war Dreyfus patents for cellulose acetate was accepted in Germany. Several documents in the files of Courtaulds' own adviser on international patent matters during and after the First World War, Dr. E. Lunge, are highly critical of many of the Dreyfus claims. As Lunge was of German-Swiss origin and had worked with German companies before the war, this is not perhaps surprising. But certainly Lunge's, and other people's, scepticism about Dreyfus's later British patents for making artificial silk by the cellulose acetate process proved well-founded.

the War Office.[4] During a commercial visit, in about March 1915, and specifically in relation to the requirements of the Royal Aircraft Factory, Camille Dreyfus met the head of the contracts branch of the aeronautical department of the War Office. According to evidence later given by this official, it was in pursuit of a policy of independence of foreign sources for important war stores, that he then asked Dreyfus whether he would consider manufacturing cellulose acetate in Britain.[5] Dreyfus agreed, provided that there should be a contract for not less than 100 tons. The War Office, after negotiations with firms of dope makers, in July 1915 invited tenders from three firms for 100 tons of cellulose acetate, to be manufactured in Britain. The Dreyfus company alone tendered, but in its tender reserved the right to deliver 50 per cent of the total from its works in Switzerland. The tender was accepted. It should be emphasised that at this date 100 tons undoubtedly seemed an immense amount; in the summer of 1915 it was thought that twenty tons would meet the whole requirements of the army and navy for twelve months;[6] the official estimate for the war department's needs was later increased though only to forty-three tons for the year ending September 1916.[7] There still seemed plenty to spare in the contract, even though a shortage of dope was beginning to be apparent.

The Basle company first tried to take over a small factory in London run by a firm called the Safety Celluloid Company, who were customers of the Dreyfus'. On the strength of these expectations, Camille is alleged to have told the War Office (though subsequently denying making any such statement) that manufacture could begin in a fortnight. That was in November 1915. In fact that particular venture fell through; and the company continued until 1917 to meet the contract from its Basle factory, a factory which was only three miles from the German frontier. Meanwhile, however, the establishment of a company to start operations in Britain had been brought about by a curious amalgam of capitalism and militarism. The catalyst appeared, improbably enough, in the person of a Canadian businessman, Lieutenant Colonel W. Grant Morden, who was also an officer in a Canadian cavalry regiment and a member of the Canadian Expeditionary force. In

---

[4]   This was the first move in the whole episode described here. My account of it is largely derived from the following sources: the *Report of the British Cellulose Enquiry Committee* (Parliamentary Papers 1919, xi) [hereafter: *Report*] and, in CA, transcripts of its verbatim evidence (which was never published), together with statements of facts, and drafts thereof, briefs to Counsel, copies of correspondence with government departments, contractors and others, as well as sundry supporting documents and a book of press cuttings for 1918-19; the *Fifth Report from the Select Committee on National Expenditure* (Parliamentary Papers 1918, iv) [hereafter *Select Committee*] and, also in CA, a typescript of part of the verbatim evidence before that committee (also never published); and the *History of the Ministry of Munitions* loc. cit.

[5]   CA transcripts: evidence of A.E. Turner, p. 6 and of Camille Dreyfus, pp. 5-6; both stressed that the initiative came from the British end not the Swiss.

[6]   CA transcripts: evidence of A.E. Turner, p. 10.

[7]   *History of the Ministry of Munitions*, 12, pt. 1, p. 138 n. 1.

August 1915, at the age of thirty-five, he was appointed to the post of 'Personal Staff Officer to the Minister of Militia and Defence for Canada, Overseas', the minister in question being Sir Samuel Hughes.

Grant Morden was a financier and a director of various Canadian companies, in shipping and other activities. On his own evidence he had not, before August 1915, ever heard of cellulose acetate, had no official connection with aeroplanes or the air service, and no prior acquaintance with the Dreyfus brothers. But he evidently had a big net of business contacts, into which all sorts of interesting fish swam from time to time. In exactly the same month as his appointment took effect he was visited in London by a M. Magnier, a Frenchman who had been given his name by one of Morden's acquaintances who happened to be head of the British Chamber of Commerce in Paris. Morden had obviously been represented as a company promoter, likely to be interested in speculative ventures. For Magnier promptly set about trying to interest this Canadian officer and shipping director in a new way of making cellulose acetate for aeroplane dope. This was the proposition, helped along with the contention that the British War Office was dependent on supplies from a firm in Switzerland, close to the German frontier and indeed represented as being German.

Morden took it up with gusto. Within a short time he had met the War Office official mentioned above, who told him all about the cellulose acetate position and the desirability of manufacturing in Britain;[8] and had set the ball rolling at the feet of two other businessmen with rather closer interests in the commodity in question. One, already known to Morden but apparently brought in at the suggestion of his chief, Sir Samuel Hughes, was Sir Trevor Dawson, a director of Vickers Ltd.; the other was Edward Robson, chairman of Pinchin Johnson Ltd. Neither had any direct chemical knowledge of cellulose acetate or dope but both saw possibilities, for different reasons, in stimulating its manufacture in this country: Robson, because Pinchin Johnson already used it in making paints and varnishes; Dawson, not only because Vickers made aeroplanes and airships – of which department Dawson was in charge – but because, as armaments manufacturers, they were interested in acetone which was used both as a solvent for cellulose acetate and in the making of explosives. In September 1915 they jointly formed a private company called The Actose Manufacturing Company, purchased a factory near London, and tried to make the Frenchman's scheme work.

It was a complete failure: Magnier made no worthwhile quantity of cellulose acetate and by January 1916 the venture was abandoned. But this setback did not deter Morden. He went to Paris; through intermediaries he learnt more about, and got in touch with, the Dreyfus firm; in February 1916 he and Robson went to Basle, and entered into an agreement with the

[8] He also disabused Morden about the Dreyfus's alleged German origin.

Swiss manufacturers to set up a British company to make cellulose acetate *and other chemicals* (my italics). The agreement named two groups: Morden, Dawson and Robson (called the English Group) and the Dreyfus brothers and Clavel (called the Swiss Group). It provided for the setting up of an English company with a share capital of £300,000–£400,000, to cover an estimated £85,000 thought adequate to erect a factory; the English Group were to raise £115,000 in cash by an issue of 6 per cent bonds; the Swiss Group were to have half the share capital to cover the value which the Dreyfus brothers put on the patents and 'secret processes'; and, out of the £115,000 they were to have £30,000 in bonds as well as a cash payment of £10,000. The agreement also effectively liquidated the Actose venture by providing that the English Group (who *were* the Actose Company) should take over that company's plant at cost; and, finally, it envisaged the creation of separate American, Russian and Canadian companies. Perhaps more than any other clause it was the last which gave the clearest indication of one at least of Morden's real hopes. In his evidence to the British Cellulose Enquiry Committee of 1919 he stressed no more than one occasion that his motives were wholly patriotic and that he 'did not want to make any money out of the war'. When questioned on the contemplated creation of overseas companies, however, and of 'a very big enterprise to work these patents', he answered simply: 'We did that very deliberately. We wanted to get the control of this for all the various countries.'[9]

As a direct consequence of this agreement the British Cellulose and Chemical Manufacturing Company Ltd. was registered as a private company in March 1916. One important change, however, was made in the arrangements. The Swiss Group were reluctantly persuaded by the English Group to agree to a much smaller initial capitalisation. So the company was floated with a nominal share capital of £4,000; and at the same time it was agreed that it should be reconstructed within two years with a capital of £400,000 or more. The debenture capital was increased to £120,000. The £4,000 was divided into 160,000 6*d* shares. The choice of thus unusually low denomination of share was subsequently explained by spokesmen for the company as having been made for the purpose of 'defining interests'. But from Morden's examination by the Cellulose Enquiry Committee, it is evident that, apart from hopes of capital gains, his reasons for adopting this procedure were two-fold. First, to attract as little public attention as possible: as all the capital was placed privately, without any prospectus, no application was made to the Capital Issues Committee of the Treasury. Second, to have a supply of nominal, low-denomination shares either to sell or give away as bonuses to brokers, clients of friends who could be persuaded to purchase the highly speculative debentures. Asked by the Cellulose Enquiry Committee

---

[9] CA transcripts: evidence of Grant Morden, first day, p. 14.

what were the terms on which his friends came in, Morden said simply that
they were given 400 shares for each £1,000 of debentures subscribed for.[10]
The possible results of the whole operation were neatly summarised during
his examination by that committee:[11]

Q. So if . . . (the Company) . . . was highly successful the investment of 6d would
be an enormously profitable investment?
A. Yes, undoubtedly.
Q. In point of fact, this was a means of securing all the profits of the concern, over
the 6 per cent, to the group to whom your 160,000 shares would be issued.
A. Yes.
Q. Without their risking a great deal in taking up the shares?
A. Exactly.

The immediate outcome of this exercise in war-time share-pushing is
shown in the following distribution of major shareholders and debenture
subscribers (Table 9.1).[12] The Prudential Trust Company of Canada of
which, not surprisingly, Grant Morden was a director, was introduced partly
to get round the statutory limitation to fifty of the numbers of shareholders
in a private company, and partly to assist in keeping voting control together
for the English Group. It also acted as trustee for the debenture holders.

One other financial arrangement – which was later to arouse particular
suspicion – was negotiated at this time. During the first, abortive scheme for
taking over a works in England, consequent upon the War Officer's proposal to Camille Dreyfus in 1915, one of the directors of the Safety Celluloid
Company suggested that an application should be made to the government
for some sort of tax relief.[13] Camille Dreyfus had some discussion with the
financial authorities about an exemption such as, it was claimed, 'was very
common in Latin America and other countries in order to encourage the
establishment of new industries'.[14] The British authorities remained unim-
pressed; the request was refused. However, when the 1916 agreement was
made the English Group undertook to try to secure relief from taxation for
a period of five years. Much heavier guns were then brought to bear upon
the financial powers. Dawson wrote to Reginald McKenna, the then Chancellor of the Exchequer; Morden wrote to Walter Long, then president of
the Local Government Board and later Colonial Secretary (whose son
worked in the London office of one of Morden's companies and subscribed
for £1,000 of debentures in the company); Long, senior, in turn wrote to
McKenna. After some negotiations it was finally agreed, in November 1916,

[10] Ibid., p. 30.
[11] Ibid., pp. 18 and 19.
[12] The full list is published in *Report*, appendix A.
[13] CA transcripts: evidence of Camille Dreyfus, eighteenth day, p. 6.
[14] CA draft 'preliminary statement', dated 16 September 1918; in the final version, submitted to the committee, the reference to Latin America was discreetly removed.

Table 9.1

NAME	NUMBER OF SHARES ALLOTTED	DEBENTURES SUBSCRIBED (£)
Vickers Ltd	19,800	25,000
Albert Vickers	1	10,000
Douglas Vickers	—	3,000
Edward Robson	1,620	—
Sir A. Trevor Dawson	2,104	1,000
Lt. Col. Grant Morden	1,705	—
Sir Samuel Hughes	1,000	—
George Holt Thomas	1,600	4,000
Berthold Kitzinger	4,300	10,250
Henry Michael Isaacs	2,000	5,000
Camille & Henri Dreyfus and Alexander Clavel	79,998	30,000
The Prudential Trust Co. of Canada	40,470	—

Main beneficial owners of these shares:

E. Robson	10,250	—
T. Dawson	12,250	
G. Morden	12,900	
	35,650	

	154,597	88,250
Others	5,403	31,750
TOTAL	160,000	120,000

that the War Office would refund to the company a sum equal to the excess profits duty actually charged, during a period of five years from the formation of the company, subject to certain conditions.[15]

With all the financial arrangements, public and private, completed or in train; with a board consisting of Morden as chairman and Dawson as his deputy; Henri and Camille Dreyfus, Clavel, and three others; with the Dreyfus brothers installed in England as managing directors: with all this done, a start was made in finding sites for a factory. Eventually in June 1916 land was bought from the Derby Corporation at Spondon and sundry offers for plant were placed. There then started a long tale of delays and unfulfilled promises. Difficulties with labour; unfamiliar machinery and consequent late delivery by manufacturers; too low a war-time priority for securing supplies: problems such as these soon combined to make nonsense of an optimistic statement by Camille Dreyfus when he told the War Office that he hoped to begin manufacturing by the end of August. The Basle factory continued to supply cellulose acetate under the 100-ton contract of 1915, and negotiations for a formal contract with the British company were started. It was not, however, until January 1917 that the company got its first contract: for forty tons, the balance still due under the 1915 contract.[16] And it was not until the relevant authorities called for a special report on the situation at Spondon, and the services of yet another Canadian Army officer had been secured specifically to expedite supplies, that finally deliveries started on a very small scale in April 1917, in gradually increasing quantities thereafter (see below, p. 192).

Meanwhile, an ominous rumble of troubles to come could be heard. It is difficult precisely to pinpoint their origins. They were unlikely at this stage to have had much to do with the circumstances attending the company's financial birth for this was little known. Some arose from criticisms of the quality of the product supplied from Basle under the 1915 contract. Certain of the officials in the aeronautical inspection department of the War Office, in the Royal Aircraft Factory and of the Admiralty, said that it was inferior to that of the Usines du Rhône which was also being imported by such dope makers as the British Cellon Company. Others said it was better. It seems, at least, to have been variable.[17] Some troubles may have arisen from the familiar xenophobia of the times. The government had, after all, given its support to foreign entrepreneurs whose optimistic claims were not matched by punctual performance – for whatever reasons. And some may have been helped into being after rival tenders were turned down. United Alkali, the

---

[15] CA transcripts: evidence of Morden, first day, p. 27; evidence of Sir Trevor Dawson, sixth day, pp. 1-2; correspondence as to remission of Excess Profits Duty. *Report*, p. 10.

[16] There was some dispute about whether this was a contract for a further forty tons, but the evidence of A.E. Turner (pp. 15-16) shows that it was intended to be simply the balance of the original 100 tons.

[17] Much conflicting evidence was given on this subject. See *Report*, p. 11.

large but technically old-fashioned and economically decaying amalgamation of alkali producers,[18] had made a tentative offer to the Admiralty in about May 1916. Their suggestion was that they should start manufacture using the process favoured by Usines du Rhône; it was referred to the War Office and declined. So too was a further proposition made in October 1916.[19]

These troubles would probably not have mattered very much had it not been for the rapid expansion of the aircraft programme in 1917. (1914, 200; 1915, 2,342; 1916, 6,633; 1917, 14,832; 1918, 30,782; total, 54,799 – of which 52,027 were built at home.) Although, as the above figures show, the rate of increase was faster before then, the absolute numbers of aeroplanes being built became such as to put much heavier pressure on component supplies.[20] The general extension of the air war meant that Allied demands rose accordingly, yet at the same time the intensification of the German submarine campaign was threatening supplies of acetic acid, mainly obtained from America. Moreover, the demand for it was increasing not only from the expanding aircraft programme but because the trench warfare department wanted it for the manufacture of tear gas; acetone, too, was in short supply as demands for it likewise increased. By July 1917 the cellulose acetate position was getting very serious.[21] The output of the Spondon factory, though rising, was still well below expectations:[22] April, 900lb; May, 1,900lb; June, 5,500lb; July, 12,700lb; August, 17,300lb; September, 27,200lb. Moreover, this was now the sole British source for cellulose acetate dope as the French had commandeered the whole output of the Usines du Rhône. So temporary recourse was again had to nitro-cellulose dope. It was used on training machines and others for service at home which were thus spared the dangers of being only too readily set on fire by incendiary bullets. Experiments were made with aluminium wings but there was not enough aluminium. In September 1917 the shortage of acetic acid became so acute that it came under government control. To economise on raw materials, a 'standard' dope with agreed specifications was determined.[23]

As indicated earlier the Dreyfus brothers, from the beginning of their

---

[18] On the position of United Alkali, see W.J. Reader, *Imperial Chemical Industries. A History*, (Oxford, 1970), i, *passim*, and especially pp. 229 and 289.

[19] This approach has been supported by an Admiralty suggestion that there should be an alternative source of supply – *Select Committee*, p. 8. Nothing came of a direct approach to Dreyfus made in 1916 by Max Muspratt, chairman of United Alkali, suggesting that the latter should take a small interest in the company.

[20] *The War in the Air*, iii, appendix vii.

[21] *History of the Ministry of Munitions*, 12, pt. 1, pp. 139-40.

[22] Figures from CA preliminary statement, p. 20.

[23] *History of the Ministry of Munitions*, 12, pt. 1, pp. 139-43. On the experiments with aluminium see CA transcripts: evidence of A.E. Turner, p. 19.

involvement in Britain, had had it in mind to manufacture chemicals other than cellulose acetate.[24] The shortages of 1916-17, however, created favourable circumstances for moving in this direction. Already in 1916 they were discussing with Vickers Ltd. the possibility of making not only acetone but also methyl acetate, an alternative solvent in dope manufacture; synthetic acetic acid; non-inflammable celluloid; and, *inter alia*, artificial silk. Such ambitions would be costly; and the existing capital would be quite inadequate. In November 1916 a scheme was devised by which further capital up to £300,000 was to be provided by a syndicate ('The Explosives Syndicate') consisting of Vickers, Nobels Explosives Company Ltd., and the Chilworth Gunpowder Company. This was to cover the extension of the factory primarily to manufacture synthetic acetic acid. Experimental work was started with the help of an immediate loan of £10,000 from the syndicate.

The main cellulose acetate factory had, however, still to be completed and money was fast running out. In January 1917 a loan of £60,000 was arranged by Morden from the Union Bank of Canada. When the production at last began in April, Camille Dreyfus celebrated the achievement by suggesting to the Ministry of Munitions – which, since February 1917, had taken over responsibility for aircraft supplies – that the company be given a contract for the alternative solvent, methyl acetate; and also by proposing the installation of a plant to make acetic acid, acetone, carbide and ethyl alcohol. In the cause of national self-sufficiency, it was agreed. In June, along with a new contract for twenty-five tons of cellulose acetate per month, came an order for 2,500 tons of methyl acetate or acetone. Work on the new acetic acid and carbide plant was put in hand on a further 190 acres at Spondon acquired with Ministry help, and with the aid of the £300,000 from the Explosives Syndicate; the latter also provided a further £15,000 on account of the scheme for artificial silk and other such items – though little or nothing seems in fact to have been carried out in this direction at that time. Sir Henry McGowan of Nobels Explosives had become a director of the company in April 1917.

Income and expenditure were rising substantially. A further contract, for 700 tons of cellulose acetate, was placed in August 1917. At the agreed price of 9*s*.per lb this was worth over £705,000. But to effect the requisite increases in capacity and to erect the acetic acid and carbide factory (involving an electric power plant) more money than that initially provided by the Explosives Syndicate proved necessary. A further £200,000 was borrowed from the Union Bank of Canada; and the government itself provided money, in the form of a loan of £200,000 from the Ministry of Munitions. But rising prices and the growing scale of the undertaking not

[24] There was indeed a temporary and small-scale manufacture of the chemically related drug, aspirin, at Spondon.

only made even these sums inadequate but also served to emphasize the bizarre financial structure of the company. The reconstruction, promised in 1916, became imperative. In September 1917 Morden started negotiations with the Beecham Trust with a view to forming a public company. The scheme was thus dependent on the company obtaining permission from the Treasury Issues Committee, but this was refused. Morden pressed the committee further, even, in the course of correspondence, to the extent of making the incautious claim of the monopolist: 'We are the sole source of supply for the Government and no aeroplane can fly without our product'.[25] Despite the committee conceding, in December, that it might reconsider its refusal, this scheme was abandoned. Instead, a complex series of negotiations was put in train, resulting in the registration, in March 1918, of another private company. This time it had a nominal capital of £3,500,000 and bore the curious title of The British Cellulose and Chemical Manufacturing (Parent) Company Ltd. – thus providing the rare spectacle of a parent, albeit a financial one, coming to life two years later than its effective offspring.

In the course of 1917 as the company's operations grew bigger and better known, and as at least some people got to know of the involvement of the Explosives Syndicate, those 6*d.* shares began to change hands privately at larger and larger sums. Around March and April 1917 a few began to change hands between £1 and £2.10.0; then they began to rise so that by the summer £3.10.0 was normal; after October the rise continued to £10. The total number of shares changing hands at £1 and upwards was small, less than 5,000 out of 160,000 and the circle of buyers and sellers very narrow. But a few speculators did very well indeed. Berthold Kitzinger sold 3,290 shares between 13 April 1917 and 1 February 1918 at prices ranging from £2.5.0 to £8.2.6, thereby making a gross profit of over £12,500. Charles W. Small sold 500 shares in march 1918 at £10 per share – a gross return of £4,987.10.0 on an initial outlay of £12.10.0.[26] The implications were obvious. The Cellulose Enquiry Committee, having in 1919 extracted from Morden the information about the sales (though not the calculations about the profits) made its views clear enough:[27]

> Q. . . . I can appreciate you were not a seller. It was far too good a thing to sell at that time was it not?
> A. I did not go into it as a share speculation.

---

[25] CA correspondence with Treasury (Capital Issues Committee), 6 November 1917.

[26] Assuming that Kitzinger paid 6*d* for each of 3,290 shares (his original holding was 4,300) they cost him £82.5.0; the proceeds of his sales were £12,616.3.4. Both Kitzinger and Small had subscribed to debentures. CA transcripts: evidence of Morden, first day, pp. 103-7; preliminary statement, pp. 30-32.

[27] CA transcripts: evidence of Morden, first day, pp. 107-8.

Q. I know, so you told us, but having got into it for other reasons did you not appreciate you had got into a gold mine?

A. No, I believed after the War there was a good future for this business. It was going to be a key industry.

It was on the future and some 'bullish' buying that hopes rested. The negotiations with the Beecham Trust had assumed a share value of £10. When the 'parent' company was formed, the valuation of those 6d. shares was £14.10.0 and the allotted capital of £3,100,000 in £1 shares divided as follows:

	£
To existing shareholders at the rate of £14.10.0 per 6d share	2,320,000
To the Explosives Syndicate in respect of £335,000 cash and of £100,000 additional cash from Nobels	780,000
	3,100,000

The 'Parent' company then became entitled to the shares of the 'operating' company, and indeed began to finance it. As a part of this deal further finance was provided by the Central Mining and Investment Corporation Ltd. to the extent of a loan of £190,000. The capitalisation of the new money from the Explosives Syndicate and Nobels posed a problem of the proportion of the equity to be maintained in the hands of the Swiss Group. As Morden put it in evidence, 'the Dreyfus people refused to reduce their holding under 33½ per cent'.[28] They then held 45 per cent; so on the basis of what the Explosives Syndicate wanted, 33½ per cent meant £14.10.0 per 6d. share. It may have been a convenient calculation but it was soon to have lively repercussions.

The distant rumble of troubles ahead became much louder in the course of 1917-18 as the company's monopolistic position and government support, even before the financial reconstruction, attracted increasingly adverse comment. Another attempt to breach the monopoly – this time by the rapidly expanding and extremely successful artificial silk firm Courtaulds Ltd. – illustrates clearly how it all seemed to the outsider.[29] In October 1917 a meeting took place at the instigation of an official of the technical department of the Air Board who thought little of the Spondon product. It was attended by a representative of Courtaulds; and it discussed the supply of aircraft dope in Britain which was said to be 'seriously inadequate both as to quality and output'. The upshot was an invitation to

[28] Ibid., evidence of Morden, second day, pp. 5-6.

[29] The account of the episode which follows is derived from CA: letters E. L(unge) to Air Board 29 October, E.L. to J.D. Kiley, M.P., 13 November, Air Board to Kiley, 29 November, E.L. to Air Board 11 December 1917; E.L. reports to chairman and deputy chairman of Courtaulds, 13 and 24 November 1917; also correspondence between E.L. and Munitions Inventions Department, May-August 1918. Although Lunge's attitude to Dreyfus and his associates was decidedly hostile (it was reciprocated) the outline of the episode in *Report*, p. 13 substantiates this account.

Courtaulds to consider the possibility of going in for cellulose acetate manufacture on a large scale. Courtaulds, like all other firms apart from the Dreyfus enterprise, had not extended their laboratory experience of it to the stage of commercial production, even on a pilot scale. Nevertheless, they signified their interest, saying that they would be willing to put up all the capital involved. Once the idea was conveyed to the supply department of the Ministry of Munitions, however, it was firmly suppressed. Courtaulds were informed that it was not considered advisable to start any new plant to make cellulose acetate, and that the present and prospective output was adequate. Certain M.P.s were consulted and requested to investigate the evident discrepancies between the views of the two departments. To no avail. Of course, Courtaulds were no more wholly disinterested patriots than were the businessmen who had promoted the British Cellulose and Chemical Manufacturing Company. They had already investigated the possibilities of cellulose acetate in the manufacture of artificial silk; and they strongly suspected, and rightly, that the Dreyfus brothers were getting, with government assistance, a well-equipped chemical works ready for use in artificial silk manufacture after the war was over. Meanwhile, it was all ammunition for a much bigger attack soon to be launched.

Trouble for the company also arose from a different source. The rate of twenty-five tons per month, specified in the June 1917 contract, was not reached until after January 1918. Thereafter the Spondon factory's output rose satisfactorily as the following figures show:[30]

1917	(lb.)	1918	(lb.)
October	46,000	January	51,900
November	30,700	February	95,700
December	47,200	March	127,200
		April	12,000
		May	172,200
		June	144,900
		July	182,900

But whilst output rose so did prices of raw materials and labour – and by March there were over 5,500 men working at Spondon, of whom 2,334 were employed by the company and 3,206 by the contractors building the massive extensions required by the acetic acid and carbide plants.[31] The company sought a revision in the terms of their contracts. After protracted negotiations with the Ministry of Munitions, entirely new arrangements were made. The most important features of these were: the cancellation of the tax concessions; the drawing up of new contracts worth nearly £3m and, most

[30] CA preliminary statement, p. 20.
[31] Ibid., p. 16.

significantly, more money from the government. These new advances had reached £485,000 by August, had risen to £900,000 in October 1918 and reached £1,450,000 in June 1919. The new arrangements had been embodied in an agreement dated 27 June 1918. By that time deliveries of methyl acetate under the contract of June 1917 had only just started; and no deliveries of acetic acid ever had been made by the time the war ended in November 1918.[32] But within a month of the June 1918 agreement the balloon had gone up in the shape of the Fifth Report of the Select Committee on National Expenditure.[33]

The Select Committee on National Expenditure had earlier appointed a sub-committee to enquire into the doings of the Ministry of Munitions; and in October 1917 this body had started to investigate the curious case of cellulose acetate supply. Its pryings soon began to reveal all manner of interesting information supplemented by evidence cheerfully offered by disgruntled potential competitors such as Courtaulds,[34] by officials who disapproved of the Dreyfus product, and by others who felt themselves excluded from the delights of 6d shares which in two years became £14.10.0 shares. The result was a vigorously critical, partly inaccurate, and far from impartial report. It disliked what it saw as lack of adequate consultation between the supply, contracts and finance branches of the Ministry; berated the supply department for its refusal to sanction alternative sources and its support of a monopoly; commented adversely on the delays in output and variability of quality of the Spondon product; revealed, in general terms, the nature of the company's financial history; and was very critical of the lack of supervision over the substantial programme of capital expenditure consequent upon the extensions sanctioned in the summer of 1917. Its recommendations were threefold and far-reaching: that the works of the British Cellulose Company should be taken over by the government; that a technical committee should be appointed to advise on the completion and management of the factory; and that the Ministry should, without delay, consider the advisability of securing an alternative source of supply.

Signed on 23 July, the report came out on the 26th on which day the chairman of the sub-committee, Godfrey Collins,[35] took the unusual step of promptly sending a copy to the press, underlining in blue pencil various

[32] *History of the Ministry of Munitions*, 12, pt. 1, p. 140; also 7, pt. iv, chap. 4, p. 70. The great shortage of acetic acid and of dope solvents, which had appeared to jeopardise the whole Allied air programme in 1917, was relieved partly as a result of changes in the poison gas requirements and partly from new sources of supply (ibid., 12, p. 140).

[33] Parliamentary papers, 1918, iv.

[34] CA Secretary of Select Committee to Secretary of Courtaulds, 5 April 1918, and E.L. to ditto. 11 April 1918.

[35] Liberal, Greenock.

passages relating to the company.[36] It was an obvious invitation to the press to make a meal of it, and in due time they did. Immediate reactions, however, were comparatively subdued. The criticisms in the report were repeated, in some detail, and the *Morning Post* had a leader which accused the Ministry of Munitions of having created 'at vast and still incalculable expense, a monopoly which has hitherto failed to supply the needs of the country'.[37] But an incentive to do better than this was soon provided in the House of Commons on 1 August. Sir Frederick Banbury,[38] launched himself on a speech which opened with the claim that the report laid bare, 'financial methods which had been practised in the old days by a well-known man in the City called Baron Grant, and afterwards by Whittaker Wright and Ernest Terah Hooley.' And it ended by saying roundly that 'a more discreditable transaction has never been brought to the knowledge of this House'.[39] Aside from attacks on the remission of excess profits duty and on delays and monopoly, it was the financial methods which were his chief target. This Tory spokesman of the City was followed by a Liberal, R.D.Holt,[40] who contended in sweeping terms that he had 'seldom read an account of a more gross scandal than this question of the Cellulose Acetate Company'. Dawson and Morden were presented as sinister company promoters; and Morden's appointment on the staff of the Canadian Minister of Militia evoked the observation that that minister, Sir Samuel Hughes, was 'a person of the worst reputation in Canada and who happens to be one of the shareholders in the £14.10s. for 6d. transactions'. He claimed to have seen a list of those shareholders: 'When the House sees that list it will be horrified'.[41] The press took up the theme, led by the *Daily Chronicle* which on 5 August published a list of the shareholders and, soon followed by other papers, started to relish what it called the 'Dope Scandal' and the *Evening News*, not to be outdone, called the 'Great Dope Scandal'.

On the same day as the *Daily Chronicle* began its attack the House of Commons took up the debate again. Sir William Bull,[42] defending the company, criticised the Select Committee's report as full of misrepresentations, and asked for an independent tribunal to look into the case. F. Kellaway, parliamentary secretary to the Ministry of Munitions, made some very defensive statements and announced that a departmental committee

---

[36] *Hansard*, 109, 5 August 1918, pp. 1035, 1039-41.
[37] *Morning Post*, 29 July 1918.
[38] Unionist, City of London.
[39] *Hansard*, 109, 1 August 1918, pp. 746-51.
[40] Liberal, Hexham.
[41] *Hansard*, ibid., pp. 751-53.
[42] Unionist, Hammersmith. Bull was an interested party. A lawyer and a friend of Morden and Dawson, he had been consulted over the financial reconstruction of the company. He was also parliamentary private secretary to the Colonial Secretary, now Walter Long whose son, as noted above, was a debenture holder.

would be set up to enquire into the matter. But Holt persisted, not only making much of the 6*d*. to £14.10.0 share rise but also, following the *Daily Chronicle*'s lead, commenting on the fact that Morden's fellow London director of the Prudential Trust Company of Canada turned out to be connected with another government department.[43] Several other members, including Herbert Samuel (later Viscount Samuel)[44] and J.B. Dillon,[45] pressed for something more than a departmental committee. Finally, the Chancellor of the Exchequer, now Bonar Law, noting allegations of improper influence in high places, intervened to state his belief that something more than a departmental enquiry was needed and to say that he would later announce the form that a tribunal would take.[46]

Whilst waiting for this body to be constituted the press kept up the hue and cry, especially the *Daily Chronicle* which made the running. It continued its revelations about the company by publishing more details of the financial reconstruction and a full list of the shareholders in the 'Parent' company complete with the holdings, addresses, and in some cases, occupations, other business interests, and government connections.[47] Just as frustrated would-be participants in the dope business had helped to feed the Select Committee, it was soon obvious that a disgruntled employee (almost certainly the former secretary[48]) with access to the company's office files, was feeding the *Daily Chronicle*. For the next instalment contained facsimile copies of 1915 trade advertisements by the Société de Cellonit Dreyfus et Cie, one in an English journal and the other in the German *Chemiker Zeitung*. Heavy with xenophobic innuendo, the article also provided the names and holdings of the shareholders in the Basle company; gave details of the agreement between the 'Parent' Company and the Prudential Trust Company of Canada; and claimed comprehensively that 'the more we probe the matter the uglier the sordid story becomes'.[49] The *Westminster Gazette*, which was currently conducting a campaign against the businessmen chosen by Lord Beaverbrook to run the new Ministry of Information, weighed in with the contention that 'on the story as told by the Committee we are in face of the greatest financial scandal of the war'.[50] The suggestion of improper

---

[43] *Hansard*, 109, pp. 1041-46. The director in question was C.G. Bryan, appointed to deal with propaganda in America in the then recently created Ministry of Information.

[44] Liberal, Cleveland; chairman of the Select Committee.

[45] Irish Independent, East Mayo.

[46] *Hansard*, 109, p. 1054.

[47] *Daily Chronicle*, 6 August 1918. Amongst the shareholders in the reconstructed company was Professor Sir John Cadman who held various technical advisory posts to the Ministry of Munitions.

[48] One Boris Berliand, a Russian, who was sacked by the company in July 1918. CA preliminary statement p. 39; transcripts, sixth day, evidence of M. Greenhill, pp. 47-50; photographic copy of letter Berliand to Camille Dreyfus, 12 May 1918.

[49] *Daily Chronicle*, 7 August 1918.

[50] *Westminster Gazette*, 6 August 1918.

influence was enabling hostile sections of the press to blow up a fairly small scandal into a potentially very large scandal. The *Manchester Guardian* spoke gravely of the need for the enquiry to be 'as deep and as wide as possible unless the scandal is to shake public confidence in the capacity and even in the integrity of the nation's administration';[51] and the *Spectator* observed of 'what is popularly called "The Dope Scandal" . . . (that) no worse instance has yet been revealed of the laxity of financial control'.[52]

Sooner or later the name of Dreyfus was bound to evoke a response in the layers of national anti-Semitism. A very literary one came in the unmistakable prose of G.K. Chesterton in the *New Witness* which he then edited. Supporting the *Daily Chronicle* for, as he said, 'turning the Great Dope Scandal into a formidable feature of the daily press', he picked up a sentence which had occurred in that paper – 'The Dreyfuses . . . were a thoroughly patriotic Swiss firm' – and proceeded to make unpleasant fun of it. Two brief excerpts may serve to catch the flavour:

> Camille Dreyfus and Henri Dreyfus are not Switzers violating their own neutrality, they are not Englishmen betraying their own country or serving their own country, they are not Germans betraying Germany or serving Germany. They are ordinary Jews who need have no sort of patriotism for any of these countries . . .
>
> International Israel is not always positively 'Pro-German' but it is for our purposes always negatively Pro-German.

and

> When a Jew has done certain disputed things, or formed certain doubtful connections, it may or may not be just to call that Jew a traitor or to call that Jew a swindler. But if, at the very beginning, we have not even the courage to call that Jew a Jew, we shall certainly do nothing and get nowhere.[53]

On 8 August, Bonar Law announced the composition of the tribunal. It comprised three peers: a judge, Lord Sumner, a Lord of Appeal; and two senior and suitably respectable businessmen, Lord Inchcape, shipowner, and Lord Colwyn (formerly Sir Frederick Smith), cotton manufacturer and colliery owner. Their terms of reference were brief and general.[54] The company promptly engaged leading counsel, including Sir Edward Carson and Douglas Hogg (later Lord Hailsham) to represent them, and at the same time issued writs for libel against the *Daily Chronicle* and the *Saturday*

---

[51] *Manchester Guardian*, 9 August 1918.

[52] *Spectator*, 10 August 1918.

[53] *New Witness*, xii, 302 (16 August 1918).

[54] They were to enquire into and report upon 'the formation and financial arrangements of the British Cellulose and Chemical Manufacturing Co. Ltd. and associated companies, and upon their relations with Departments of the Government'. Despite expressed views that the tribunal should have the power to take evidence on oath this power was not granted.

Review.[55] The press continued for some time to keep the pot boiling, displaying much critical interest especially in Morden's activities, not least because he had become Unionist candidate for Brentford and Chiswick. *John Bull* and the *Daily Express* found cause to champion his doings: the latter, already owned by Morden's friend and fellow-Canadian, Lord Beaverbrook, referred to him in glowing terms as one of Canada's 'leading businessmen'. But much of the comment was hostile, especially from the *Daily Chronicle* and even *The Times* viewed his selection as a candidate while the tribunal was sitting as 'most unsatisfactory'.[56] The months passed and the newspaper campaign abated, an abatement aided by the silencing of the *Daily Chronicle*. It had become critical of other and bigger aspects of Lloyd George's administration, so in October 1918 it was bought by one of the prime minister's henchmen, and the offending editor departed rapidly.[57] In November the war was over; in December Morden became M.P. for Brentford and Chiswick. The 'Dope Scandal' was still far from dead, however, for questions continued to be asked in Press and Parliament alike, about the non-appearance of the tribunal's report.[58] In the summer of 1919, when its publication was known to be imminent, the subject was revived, to herald the report itself which finally appeared in August 1919.

Within the limits of its powers and in the time available, the tribunal had done its job fairly thoroughly, receiving, as the report said 'a very voluminous mass of documents' from the relevant departments; examining thirty-two witnesses, some at considerable length; and having commissioned from a leading firm of accountants a full analysis of the company's finances. The report provided a careful and much more detailed history of the whole episode than did that of the Select Committee. In language and in findings its tone was sober and wholly unsensational. To the vociferous critics it was a whitewash; to the company's supporters, a vindication; to those in the middle, an anti-climax. The tone was bland and the chosen path offered information rather than condemnation. Having, for example, given the details of the tax concession the report went on to use such soporifics as: 'We apprehend that it does not fall within our province to interpret the true meaning of this concession, the terms of which seem to have been variously

[55] The *Saturday Review* had published, on 3 August 1918, an attack on similar lines to that of the *Daily Chronicle*, under the title of 'Dopers and Doped'.

[56] *Daily Express*, 11 December; *Daily Chronicle*, 10 August, 21 September, 4 October; *Times*, 6 December 1918.

[57] The much bigger aspect was the affair of General Maurice, although the editor, Robert Donald, had also exhibited others signs of hostility to Government policies. On the whole matter, see H.A. Taylor, *Robert Donald* (1934), pp. 165-93; A.J.P. Taylor, *English History, 1914-45* (Oxford, 1965), pp. 117-18 and his *Beaverbrook* (1972), pp. 154-58.

[58] E.g. 17 and 22 October, 12 November 1918 (*Hansard*, 110, pp. 305, 593-94, 2497-98); 7 April, 3 and 17 July, 13 August 1919 (*Hansard*, 114, pp. 1054-55; 117, pp. 1194-95; 119, pp. 594-95, 1309). *Daily Telegraph*, 23 October 1918; *Times*, 14 March 1918; *New Statesman*, 26 April and 9 August 1919; *Truth*, 19 March 1919.

construed, nor are we called upon to discuss whether it was politic or impolitic'.[59] They were, however, on firm ground in pointing out that in any event it never operated because no profits had been made.

This indeed was crucial. From the unpublished minutes of evidence it is obvious that the committee found neither the conduct of the financial arrangements nor the running of the organisation at all to their liking; though they sensed chaos rather than crime, they patently mistrusted Morden; they had great difficulty in making Henri Dreyfus stick to the point and in detecting his meaning through a fog of words and technicalities; and Camille Dreyfus, who in February 1918 had left to run the associated company set up in America, incurred their explicit displeasure by failing to turn up to give evidence, despite many promises, until July 1919. But whatever pickings were made by a few people in share deals or whatever may or may not have stuck to the fingers of various persons in the company, there was no evidence here of massive profits directly made by the exploitation of wartime scarcity. The report did at least go so far as to observe that the contrast between the nominal capital of the original company and that of the 'Parent' company was 'so glaring that, for much of the criticism to which they have been exposed, we think that the promoters and others connected with the company's financial arrangements have only themselves to blame.'[60] On the question of improper influence, the committee concluded that there had been neither 'favouritism nor corruption'. In examining the position of monopoly which government support had given the company they were, again, on strong grounds in stressing the big difference between 'a general, and even a practical, knowledge of the manufacture of such a chemical product' and the special knowledge and skills needed to provide, regularly, large and reasonably uniform quantities of it.[61] No British manufacturers had such knowledge; and, the report decided, there were good reasons for the government to continue in its support of the company, rather than sanction an alternative factory especially as shortages of men and materials increased in 1917. Finally, this gentle rebuke was given to the company's critics: 'If all the facts, which we have sifted with so negative a result, had been available last year to the critics of the Company and its proceedings we think that their conclusions would, to say the least, have undergone large modifications.'[62] The 'Dope Scandal' was dead.

Its longer-term consequences, however, were only just becoming apparent. In 1920 the British Cellulose and Chemical Manufacturing Company became a public company with the stated intention of making artificial silk.

[59] *Report*, p. 10.
[60] Ibid., p. 14.
[61] Ibid., p. 12.
[62] Ibid., p. 14.

It marketed the latter under the brand name of 'Celanese', and in 1923 became British Celanese Ltd. Across the Atlantic, from similar war-time roots, there sprouted the Celanese Corporation of America and Canadian Celanese. The Spondon plant, equipped as a war-time measure and with the aid of government money, grew into a substantial chemical-textile works. Indeed, largely under Henri Dreyfus's direction, it became in time a remarkable pioneer example of a vertically integrated plant, its activities ranging from the production of basic chemicals, through the spinning of cellulose acetate yarn, to include the weaving of fabrics and the making of garments, mainly women's underwear. A vigorous selling and advertising campaign ensured that by the 1930s, Celanese had become a household name.[63] This was the real pay-off for the Dreyfuses from aircraft dope. The experiments with making artificial silk from cellulose acetate which had been carried out before the First World War in various countries had not resulted in commercial production partly because of technical difficulties and partly because of the striking success of the rival viscose method pioneered by Courtaulds. No doubt if war demand for dope had not been answered in the particular way that it was, someone else would still have developed this branch of artificial fibre manufacture. But the historical path actually followed was a product of those war needs.

Spin-off or pay-off: the coin had another side too. The circumstances of the company's birth and the legacy of its promoters, together with the personalities of the Dreyfus brothers, particularly Henri, helped to give British Celanese a stormy, not to say disastrous financial history. The investment of government money, transmuted into the form of a holding of £1,450,000 preference shares issued when the company went public in 1920, helped to keep it in the public eye; and questions about it were asked in the House of Commons at intervals throughout 1920-22.[64] By 1927 there was no longer any government money in the company but nor had there been any profits. Instead, there had been, as there were to be in the 1930s, warring groups of shareholders battling with the directors over the control and capitalisation of the company. Year after year there were the all too familiar accusations about over-optimistic forecasts. In 1929 the *Economist* observed that the 'disturbing fact about this company has always been, and continues to be, its inability to turn into cash receipts the enormous potential values of which so much has been repeatedly heard'; and in 1936 it was still commenting, wryly, on 'the bumper earnings which remain so persistently round the next corner'.[65] By 1938 the preference dividends were eight years in arrears. And it was not until 1944, the year in which Henri Dreyfus died, during the Second World War and twenty-eight years

---

[63] For some details of these developments, see my *Courtaulds*, ii, pp. 183-84, 270-72.
[64] See, e.g. *Hansard*, 126, 127, 143, 153.
[65] *Economist*, 27 July 1929, 14 November 1936.

after its original parent company had been born during the First World War, that British Celanese Ltd ever paid a dividend on its ordinary shares. Meanwhile, during the 1920s and 1930s, not only had the company been the object of sundry rumours, speculations and conflicts, but it engaged in expensive litigation. Once again there were accusations about the dubious validity of Dreyfus patents. Between 1931 and 1937, at Henri Dreyfus's instigation, a series of extremely expensive lawsuits were waged in defence of his artificial silk patents: they were all lost, at every stage right up to the House of Lords.[66] By 1960, British Celanese Ltd., Cellon Ltd, and Pinchin Johnson Ltd. had all been absorbed by Courtaulds.

Finally, the Dope Scandal can be seen as providing an example, in microcosm, of the moral dilemma of the capitalist economy in war. For behind the rhetoric of political combat and popular journalism there clearly lay unresolved doubts about that uneasy mixture of patriotism and profits which had already spawned the very word 'profiteer' and the very act of profiteering. It may be that Morden was, as he claimed both in public speeches and in evidence to the Cellulose Enquiry Committee, out of pocket to the extent of some £20-25,000 and that he had arranged it all in the name of patriotism.[67] But it was also obvious, whatever the evidence, or lack of it, that all sorts of people found it hard to reconcile such claims with the distribution of 6*d*. shares to well-placed persons and to businessmen of sometimes dubious reputation. The logic of capitalism demanded the inducement of profit. But was this the right way to go about it?

From the evidence given to the Cellulose Enquiry Committee it is clear that Morden was the prime mover in using the tricks of the questionable financier. If the subsequent career of Henri Dreyfus may perhaps have confirmed the view of those who had earlier expressed scepticism about him, that of Grant Morden seems to have amply justified the 1918 critics of this ambitious and too plausible Canadian. Apparently seeking to emulate his friend Beaverbrook, he added newspapers to business and politics. In 1920 he bought the *People* and, shortly afterwards, on playing a major part in arranging the finance for Odhams Press Ltd., when it absorbed *John Bull*, became chairman of Odhams.[68] Never a man to let a chance go by, he celebrated his position by writing to Lloyd George in March 1922 in order to offer the Prime Minister, should he decide to relinquish office, the job of editor of *John Bull* at a salary of £35,000 per annum.[69] But Morden's massive extravagance, in setting himself up as a country gentleman and host to politicians, combined with an over-developed urge for speculation, led to

[66] *Courtaulds*, ii, pp. 351-57.
[67] CA transcripts: evidence of Morden, third day, p. 17.
[68] R.J. Minney, *Viscount Southwood*, (1954), pp. 163-64, 178-85.
[69] Beaverbrook Library, Lloyd George Papers, Grant Morden to Lloyd George, 21 March 1922.

so large a pile of debts that in 1925 he was forced to dispose of *The People*, by then declining in circulation. He relinquished the chairmanship of Odhams; but he still had fingers in all sorts of business pies, including a syndicate interested in cellulose acetate for films and artificial silk.[70] The slump, however, was soon to leave its mark. His assets tumbled in value; despite generosity from Beaverbrook, to whose Empire Preference campaign he gave active support, his liabilities grew; and in 1930 he was bankrupt. Bankruptcy proceedings dragged on over the whole of 1931. In the early months of 1932, nearly penniless and with failing eyesight, his wife and four children were being maintained by the generosity of a few friends who raised a fund to help the family – but ensured that the money was not paid directly to Morden himself, for, as one of them wrote, 'I cannot imagine Grant with a few hundred pounds without "trying a spec".' In June 1932, after a collapse, both mental and physical, he died.

So maybe it was at least one benefit for the British Cellulose and Chemical Manufacturing Company that, after its founders had to relinquish some of their shares on the 1920 reconstruction,[71] Morden transferred his interests and his gambling instincts elsewhere.

Nevertheless, the company had been saddled with a legacy which helped to blight its subsequent financial history and might have been avoided if less brash financial methods had been used in the original flotation and subsequent development. But to the problem of how to finance and organize the supply of aircraft dope, the British government of 1916 had no prepared answer. For its officials and executives were faced with a product about which they knew virtually nothing, save that it was not made in Britain, and with urgent needs for an utterly new arm of war. In the assorted names of patriotism and profits, of self-sufficiency and private enterprise, they yielded to the sales-talk of the company promoter and thereby generated, albeit on a small scale, one of those characteristic bits of economic policy, the results of which turn out in the end to be so different from what anyone expected.

---

[70] Minney, *Viscount Southwood*, p. 185; Beaverbrook Library: Hannon Papers, Box 16. The brief account which follows of Morden's end is largely derived from these papers. I am grateful to Mr. A.J.P. Taylor for drawing my attention to them. For reports on Morden's bankruptcy and death see the *Times*, 2 and 6 April, 23 May, 18 July, 1 August, 31 October, 5 December 1931, 30 January, 11 February, 27 and 29 June 1932.

[71] CA transcripts: evidence of Morden, third day, pp. 17-20; evidence of Dawson, sixth day, pp. 3-6.

10

*The Uses and Abuses of Business History**

A promotional document for the Business History Unit, dated May 1977 contained this nicely balanced sentence: 'Company history is to business history as personal biography and individual monographs are to political history'.[1] It went on to announce that the time had arrived to move on from company history to 'wider conceptual studies'.

Two years later, by which time the Unit had been set up and its Director appointed, its first annual report, of August 1979, echoed this message by stating that the Unit emphasized 'the wider aspects of the subject, building on the history of individual companies and encompassing business as a whole'.[2] This statement was repeated as a sort of *leitmotiv* in all the Unit's

---

* The establishment of business history as an academic subject is hardly imaginable without the Industrial Revolution and its historiography, whatever the antiquity of the genus business-man. In Britain, its relationship to economic history, to economics, and to business studies is still in a confused and shifting state. Some professional historians had some initial success in wresting the writing of commissioned company histories from the hands of the hacks but then they were confronted with a special case of the gulf between professional and lay. This was that the resulting works were largely regarded as not for reading but simply for existing: they were seen as public relations objects. The myth-consuming public wanted heroes or villains, not analysis of past costs and profits; the former doings of particular companies were not seen by economists as appropriate theory-fodder; orthodox historians looked upon such commissioned works with lofty disapproval; neither the advocates of business studies nor most businessmen saw such company histories, however scholarly, as aids in tackling the problems of today and tomorrow. A readership had to be built up. It was; and it still consists very largely of a growing body of other business historians.

The present essay is an only slightly amended version of a public lecture given at the London School of Economics in November 1986. It addressed some of the questions raised by the emergence of this sort of historical work and made some tentative suggestions for its future development. Since that time the study of business history in Britain has continued to advance. Some progress has been made in moving on from the limited horizons of company histories; and some useful collections of essays have been published. More posts have been established and filled, for example at Reading as well as existing ones at London and Glasgow; and an increasing interest has been shown at some polytechnics. An Association of Business Historians has been founded.

[1] Printed document circulated as part of the appeal for donations to set up the Business History Unit, may 1977, p. 2.

[2] Business History Unit, *First Annual Report*, p. 3.

subsequent annual reports. In 1983, however, the unit's Director, writing in the *Business History Review*, lamented that in Britain 'progress in systematic integrative work, going beyond company history towards comparative business history dealing with wider themes, has been halting'. Most business historians, he said, clung 'to a tradition which, at its best, is a triumph of narrative skill . . . but at its worst is narrow, insular, and antiquarian'.[3] In his inaugural lecture of the same year he castigated British business historians as 'inveterate empiricists', obsessed with simply getting the story right; their works were said rarely to go beyond 'the narrative method applied to the single case'. A few names of such erring authors were thoughtfully provided, stretching back over some thirty-odd years of British business history writing. For good measure, he added that 'the signs of progress in allying theory and applied research in this field are not encouraging'.[4]

At this point I should make it clear that I have no quarrel with the stated intentions and that I very largely agree with Professor Hannah's sentiments, even if his all-embracing condemnation seems a trifle severe. How has this situation come about? What can be done to change it?

Business history has its own built-in Catch-22 or something rather like it. It will be recalled that Joseph Heller's novel was set in an American Air Force bomber unit operating in Italy during the Second World War. If pilots went on flying more and more bombing raids (or 'combat missions' in U.S.A.F. terminology) they were crazy and could be grounded. But if they applied to be grounded they were not crazy but sane, and therefore could be required to go on flying more missions. That was Catch-22. Or, as the *O.E.D.* puts it, 'a dilemma in which the victim always loses'. Business history's very own Catch-22 works like this. Business history, by definition, must use the records of business companies. The only way that business historians can normally get access to those records, however, is to be commissioned to write company histories. But if they go on writing company histories they are failing to write business history in the wider sense. So they are stuck with their 'single cases' and 'inveterate empiricism'.

The analogy with the original Catch-22 must not be pressed too hard. Writing a company history is not quite like a 'combat mission' – though I can think of some episodes in which the analogy has been uncomfortably close. But the fact remains that however scholarly, accurate, fair, objective and serious that company history is, its content is necessarily shaped by the need for the author to give his client something approaching what he wants. And what he normally wants is a narrative history of Snooks & Co., warts and all

---

    [3] Leslie Hannah, 'New Issues in British Business History', *Business History Review*, lvii (1983), p. 166.
    [4] Idem., *Entrepreneurs and the Social Sciences: An Inaugural Lecture* (London School of Economics, 1983), p. 4.

maybe, but still recognisably Snooks, *not* a comparison of Snooks with other companies, *not* an analysis of how Snooks' business behaviour supports or refutes the theories of X, Y or Z. The historian may, if he is so minded, slip in a few of these other ingredients; and the client may accept them as the price to be paid for hiring an academic. But the constraints are real. So business history remains identified with company history which is seen as having limited use, alike to universities, business schools, or, indeed, businessmen. The multiplication of such histories thus inhibits wider business history; but access to those vital records can only be got by writing those company histories. And so Catch-22 rules. Before asking how to escape from it let us consider how it came to exist.

Thirty or forty years ago the great majority of such business histories as had been written here, or indeed elsewhere, were house-histories. They were largely devoid of any scholarly value and consisted primarily of reminiscences and anecdotes. In Britain, from about 1920 onwards, a tiny handful of serious work had appeared in which scholars had used some business records. Those records had found their way into museums or county record offices; or they were in the private possession of collectors, antiquarians, or the descendants of long-dead merchants or manufacturers. They had come to the notice of scholars by sundry routes and casual discoveries.[5] But they all had one quality in common: they were records of *defunct* firms. The real change came when the idea emerged of *live* business firms commissioning academics to write their histories.

The creation of a climate congenial to such a change may have been helped in the early 1930s as a result of the activities of two newly created professors of economic history: Eileen Power, here at the London School of Economics, and G.N. (later Sir George) Clark at Oxford. The latter, in his inaugural lecture of January 1932, remarked that it had 'become the fashion lately to talk about "business history".' The term was based simply on the type of records used, those of private business firms; and Clark saw it, fairly enough, as a reaction against the hitherto dominant use of public records which were only indirectly economic in the sense that they told merely of the intervention of governments in economic life.[6] So economic historians were acting as prime movers in setting up a pressure group to lobby against the destruction of business records. After a couple of years of preliminary negotiations, the pressure group emerged in 1934 as the Council for the Preservation of Business Archives. It was launched with the customary aids: a public meeting, a letter to *The Times* signed by worthies (including eminent

---

[5] Typical examples of such records and their provenance can be found in H. Heaton, *The Yorkshire Woollen and Worsted Industries* (Oxford, 1920), pp. 438-39; and G. Unwin, A. Hulme and G. Taylor, *Samuel Oldknow and the Arkwrights* (Manchester, 1924), pp. v-iv.

[6] G.N. Clark, 'The Study of Economic History', reprinted in N.B. Harte (ed.), *The Study of Economic History* (1971), pp. 77-79.

bankers, distinguished academics, and the Master of the Rolls); and an article in the *Observer* featuring the then Director of the London School of Economics, Sir William Beveridge. G.N. Clark was its chairman; and its secretary was A.V. Judges, a lecturer in economic history at the London School of Economics. It survives and prospers today as the Business Archives Council.[7]

The whole purpose of this exercise was the preservation and listing of records. There was no mention of the analysis of business behaviour historically or in modern times; nor was there any suggestion that historical work on these records might be of the slightest use to business itself. Representatives of manufacturing industry seemed to have played little or no part in the proceedings. None of the three leading academics had ever worked on anything approaching modern business history: Eileen Power was a medievalist, Judges' concern was with Tudor and early Stuart England, and Clark's historical interests lay in the seventeenth and early eighteenth centuries and in Anglo-Dutch relations at that time. A dozen or so years later, Clark's concern with Dutch history was certainly to provide an important link to the new pattern of commissioning. Meanwhile, in 1938, the Bank of England commissioned a 250-year anniversary history from the then professor of economic history at Cambridge, J.H. (later Sir John) Clapham. This, however, was very much an official commemoration of a venerable British institution, seen as distantly related to God.

Of greater moment for the future of business history in Britain was the approach, in 1947, to Clark by the then chairman of Unilever, Geoffrey Heyworth (later Lord Heyworth), with a request for advice on the writing of a history of this big Anglo-Dutch multinational manufacturing enterprise. Clark, who had by this time moved to the chair of modern history at Cambridge, declined to write it himself and passed the enquiry on to a younger colleague, who had also written on Anglo-Dutch history, Charles Wilson.[8] The resulting multi-volumed *History of Unilever* was to set a trend which is still with us. Since 1954, when the first two volumes of *Unilever* appeared, commissioning has resulted in academic company histories in numerous industries: chemicals, textiles, glass, brewing, steel, metal manufacturing, tobacco, shipping, insurance, banking, and oil. Nationalised industries have joined the queue, in the shape of electricity supply, railways, and coal. The scale of production has sometimes been lavish, with some big multinationals getting big multi-volume histories. In all these, and more, business histories of high scholarly quality have appeared.

The motivation behind this commissioning boom was, I suspect, rather more complex than might appear at first sight. It seems very unlikely that any board of directors *collectively* believed that the resulting book would

---

[7] See the account of its origins by Peter Mathias in *Business Archives*, 50 (Nov. 1984).
[8] *Geoffrey Heyworth: A Memoir* (Unilever, n.d. ?1985), pp. 7-13.

serve any purpose in influencing its own decision-making. The most probable reason for the acceptance of such projects by boards of directors is that they saw them as fairly inexpensive public relations exercises, sitting somewhere between prestige advertizing and patronage of the arts. After a time, even imitation may have crept in as companies, famous and less famous, followed one another in hiring scholars to write their histories. The revelation of past mistakes may even have been thought to redound well to the image of a prospering company, in the happy delusion that prosperity would endure.

But all this is only the final stage of the commissioning process. It normally begins earlier, and almost always with the whims, fancies or convictions of a particular director or of someone in the higher reaches of management and who has the ear of an influential and persuadable member of the main board. Informing those whims or convictions, there have been a variety of hopes. Sometimes, in a family firm, an urge has been felt to reveal the doings of past generations, not always necessarily to their glory, sometimes indeed to destroy the myth of great-uncle William's percipience in juggling the stock market or buying raw cotton. Sometimes the motivation has come from such specific impulses as the wish to help change the image of business which has so often persuaded university graduates in Britain to shy away from careers in business; and to demonstrate to future generations that the serious history of companies is as vital and compelling as the history of politics.[9] Or again, some special set of historical circumstances affecting a business may have seemed of such consequence as to demand revelation to the public: unhappy experience of government intervention is an obvious and potent example. More generally, however, it is likely that those who originally initiated the commissioning process have possessed an especial regard for history, genuinely believing that the managers of today would gain from a knowledge of the comparable process in the past. Such persons tend to believe that truth pays better than concealment; that there exists a better way of doing things than that currently employed; and that learning is aided by an understanding of how the present grew out of the past. It seems fairly clear that Heyworth was such a man. It was his thinking on these lines – including a belief, in which he was undoubtedly right, that British management lagged behind American practice – that led to his commissioning of the Unilever history.[10]

What has been the result in Britain of this commissioning activity thus motivated? The end products, in the form of numerous handsomely produced volumes from prestigious publishing houses sit impressively on sundry bookshelves. They are very largely unread by anyone except other

[9] See the article by Sir Arthur Knight, 'A Need for Business Chronicles', *Guardian*, 18 Feb. 1981.
[10] *Geoffrey Heyworth: A Memoir*, p. 10.

business historians. Apart from that originating inspirer of a history, who will read it, members of the commissioning company will merely dip into it out of curiosity about past leaders of the firm; those to whom complimentary copies have been distributed will glance at the illustrations. In those very rare cases of histories dealing with very recent times former members of the firm who have left in less than harmonious circumstances will look to see if there any possible grounds for a libel action. Few businessmen from companies other than the commissioning company will be in the least interested. Few professional economists, inside or outside of the university world, will pay any heed to them because the history of individual firms is not seen as helping the theory of the firm. Business schools will very largely ignore them in the teaching of the nation's future management.

The normal reviewing fate of such books, outside specialist periodicals, is either to be passed by in silence or to be given patronising appraisals by reviewers with no obvious qualifications who can be guaranteed to complain that the presence of statistical tables spoils the story. In a recent publication, bearing the imprint of the *Economist* and claiming to list '600 essential books for the international manager', company history written by academics scored a really big hit: *one* such book was mentioned. The editors of this compilation listed instead the easily readable and confident prose of other sorts of authors. And they went out of their way to complain that commissioned histories were 'usually paralysingly narrow and dull'; and that academics were 'so constrained by the supposed requirements of scholarly respectability that they often tend to be cautious, jargon-ridden and out of date'. Such strictures, let it be said, are by no means always wide of the mark. But those responsible for them hardly demonstrated their own regard for accuracy by misspelling the name of the one academic author of the one company history of which they approved.[11]

At the other end of the spectrum, most orthodox political historians will not only deem such histories irrelevant but will doubt if such remunerated historical writing is quite proper as a form of scholarship. A distinguished historian from the London School of Economics once described business history to me as a sort of 'applied history', thereby placing it below the salt and indcating a distinction akin to that, so uniquely beloved by the British, between pure and applied science. This view from the heights of orthodoxy is not made any the less jaundiced by the fact that business history has had to seek academic status against a prior background in which the writing of company histories was seen as a form of inferior journalistic hack-work. It was something done to supplement income otherwise got from more reputable literary activities. Furthermore, business history evidently hovers on the dangerous brink of being thought 'useful' in a direct vocational sense.

This is not the occasion to detail the results of these various circumstances

---

[11] *The Good Book Guide for Business* (1984), p. 250. They got the spelling right on p. 268.

which have attended the birth and growth of the subject. But it is perhaps worth emphasising some of their combined effects in strengthening the grip of Catch-22.

Even in the USA – where academic business history dates from the 1920s – troubles arising from them were being aired at conferences sponsored by the Harvard Business History Group a quarter of a century or more ago. It was already being questioned whether company history had not reached 'the point of diminishing returns'.[12] In Britain in 1958, when the journal *Business History* started up thirty-two years after its counterpart in the USA, there was much discussion about the nature and purpose of business history. From some quarters a note almost of apology was to be heard. The Historical Association, for example, produced a pamphlet on the subject. It was concerned to explain how company histories should be written; and to say that historians were the appropriate people for businessmen to commission. It presented 'serious business history' as appealing to the businessman 'not only as something which can satisfy his curiosity about the past but also an important public relations activity'.[13] Curiosity and public relations. But not a word about usefulness in analyzing the functioning of business or informing decision-making. In the light of the separation between historians and economists in Britain, such an attitude is hardly surprising. Those with experience of the American scene were stressing some rather different matters: the use of economic theory in business history; the possible contribution of business history to a better understanding of how economic systems work; the differences of attitude towards the subject in Britain and the U.S.A. because in the former business history was nowhere taught 'as an integral part of vocational training'; and the need for company histories to be organized around a set of clearly stated dominant themes.[14]

A dozen or more years on, at a conference on business history at the Cranfield Institute of Technology in 1973, designed to put together business historians and those engaged in management studies, similar worries got similar airings. But a note of disillusionment can already be heard. From the management side came the hope that business historians here would go beyond the 'case-studies' approach but also the regret that 'performance has not yet caught up with precept'.[15] For the business historians Professor Peter Mathias, rehearsing the dislike of historians for 'any direct utility for the present' as a justification for their work, saw the current pattern of business history as set in its ways. 'Historians', he observed, 'are used to

---

[12] See the discussions in *Business History Review*, xxxiii (1959) and xxxvi (1962).

[13] T.C.Barker, R.H. Campbell and P. Mathias, *Business History* (Historical Association, 1960), p. 4.

[14] For example, Barry Supple in *Business History Review*, xxxiii (1959), pp. 575-57; and in *Business History*, iv (1962); and Peter Payne in *Business History*, v (1962), pp. 11-21.

[15] A.M. Bourn, 'Business History and Management Education', *Business History*, xvii (1975), p.21.

tackling change in the institution as a whole, and in the longer term. This is what most firms want when a history is commissioned – and most of the studies using primary documents from business firms will be commissioned books'. Events seem to have proved him right. He thought, moreover, that it would be mainly from management studies and applied economics that would emerge 'the business history suitable in focus to their needs . . . rather than from business history as economic historians have been writing it'.[16] By that time the new business schools had been founded, at London and Manchester; and other management and business studies centres were developing. Yet in 1981 when Professor Hannah wrote his report for the S.S.R.C. on *New Horizons for Business History*, there were still very few welcoming signs visible in those quarters. Neither London nor Manchester business schools offered business history courses in any form. Rigid divisions persisted between the bulk of professional economic historians (the main source of authors of academic company histories) and teachers in business schools. Neither group much read each other's writings; bridge-building was minimal.[17] Catch-22 was simply being reinforced.

So much for the business history past, for the tightening grip of Catch-22. What can be done about it?

I will consider the general question – what is the use of business history? – in the combined context of three assumptions. They should be reasonably acceptable and uncontroversial statements. Here they are. First, the performance of the British economy has been declining relative to that of its major competitors over the last hundred years; and it is desirable to reverse that decline. Second, the business company is now, and has been over the past hundred years, the single most important organizational unit in the British economy. (I include within the term 'business company', nationalized industries which, despite government financial support, have to operate according to profit-making criteria and whose managements have therefore to make decisions similar to those of private firms.) Third, all business decisions, like other decisions, taken in the present are necessarily made with some awareness of the past. This assumption operates whether the awareness is right or wrong, and whether that past is distant or very recent. It includes decisions made in the proud belief that history is bunk.

These assumptions obviously have varying degrees of generality. They are, however, interdependent. Let us take the first and most general. Although cast in aggregate terms it is ultimately a statement about the consequences of a large number of individual decisions, some obviously

---

[16] Peter Mathias, ibid., pp. 3-16.
[17] *New Horizons for Business History* (S.S.R.C., 1981), p. 18.

more important than others, taken by businessmen. The standard economists' enunciation of it is in terms of levels of national income per head, output, exports, productivity, and other familiar indicators. The business historian's view of that process is, or should be, in terms of how and why businessmen reacted to, or helped to create, changes in market demand; and how and why they managed and shaped their units of production in order to meet the demands generated in those markets. The businessmen necessarily worked within a variety of constraints – economic and technical, social and political. And they were necessarily influenced by the past, or to be more precise, by sundry notions of the past.

Some such notions have been, and still are, of a highly general nature. Today two interrelated general notions about our economic past are in wide circulation, having recently gained much popularity. The first, in very broad terms, goes like this. Because Britain pioneered the industrial revolution and in Victorian times became economic top nation, therefore, what the country needs today is a return to Victorian values; and the recreation of something called 'the enterprise culture' or 'enterprise society'. The second notion says that the great British rot set in after about 1850 and is attributable to something called 'the decline of the industrial spirit'; and this happened, it is said, because our educational and cultural values became profoundly anti-business.[18]

Taken by themselves, these notions are largely dangerous nonsense. Significant symptoms of anti-industrial attitudes can, of course, be found; but they existed before, during and after the industrial revolution. To propagate the belief that relative economic failure is the result, not of wrong business decisions, but of some amorphous spirit is to disseminate a perilous delusion. People will believe such things because they offer comforting excuses. In reality, it was not so much that any 'industrial spirit' declined after the high noon of Victorian Britain but, on the contrary, that too many of the attitudes of mind associated with the industrial revolution persisted too long. Enduring habits of thought and action about such matters as the organization of the firm, capital-labour relations, marketing, or technical innovation continued well into the twentieth century long after they had ceased to be appropriate. It was such attitudes as these which strongly influenced the decisions of business management (and, for that matter,

---

[18] The *locus classicus* of this notion is Martin Wiener, *English Culture and the Decline of the Industrial Spirit, 1850-1980*. It has enjoyed an extraordinary burst of popular influence, apparently fitting in well with opinions expressed by some members of the present British government. For an admirable survey of the contradictions between this notion and the ideas to be found in the currently well-regarded literature on management techniques, see John Turner, 'In the Time of the Entrepreneurs', *Times Literary Supplement*, 11 July 1986.

trade unions). They were derived from the very different circumstances of the industrial revolution. That was indeed a triumph of individual enterprise; and to be applauded as such. Moreover, it had taken place in a society whose elite was no more enthusiastic then about manufacturing business than it was to be a century later. It was, however, a triumph of individual enterprise in *practical know-how*. It owed little to scientific discovery and still less to organized research. It was effected in a labour market untrammelled by powerful trade unions and a product market little troubled by competition. Not surprisingly, the values which were carried forward included an aggressive and often pig-headed individualism; a deep suspicion of science; a complacent belief that tried methods were the right methods; an affection for machines primarily as labour-displacing devices; and a marketing philosophy which enshrined a faith that the customer would come to you, rather than vice-versa. Despite all the worries about American and German competition around 1900 it has taken a very long time for effective change to become apparent. To wax nostalgic about values bred in Victorian Britain by the industrial revolution will do no good whatever. Enterprise, like patriotism, is not enough. Its quality and nature are all-important.

Let me provide just one illustration of these points. In 1784 Joseph Black, the celebrated chemist, in the course of a letter to James Watt, remarked apropos the inventor of the puddling process of making wrought iron, Henry Cort: 'He is a plain Englishman without Science but by the dint of natural ingenuity and a turn for experiment has made such a Discovery in the Art of making tough Iron as will undoubtedly give to this Island the monopoly of that Business'.[19] Just about the whole of the technical side of the industrial revolution is summed up in that comment. Its wider implications remained pertinent long after 1784. Its spectre can be seen, for example, lurking behind a remark of 1922 about the 'comparative intellectual ease with which the fabric of British capitalism has been built up'.[20] That remark was made by J.A. Hobson, the heretic economist whom Keynes tried briefly to rehabilitate but who has remained outside the pale of economic orthodoxy. Hobson was right just as Black had been earlier. And the correctness of his vision is testified to by the numerous and much publicized complaints which can be heard from the 1880s to the 1980s about the British business community's inadequate regard for scientific research, about the poverty of British technical and scientific education, and about the social disregard in Britain for engineering and technology. The obsessive

[19] Joseph Black to James Watt, 28 May 1784, quoted in E. Robinson and D. McKie (eds.), *Partners in Science* (Cambridge, MA, 1970), p. 140.

[20] J.A. Hobson, *Incentives in the New Industrial Order* (1922), p. 63.

mystique of the 'practical man' lingered far too long as an inheritance of Victorian values. There is no point in replacing it now by a nostalgia for the industrial revolution.

Alongside all this misplaced nostalgia there exists, of course, an alternative version of the British business past. This one presents the process of industrialization as a battle won by bourgeois capitalists over the downtrodden working class. It still thrives in some quarters but it is hardly a version which appeals to businessmen; and I do not propose to spend any time on it. Suffice to emphasize that the dissemination of *neither* version will serve any useful purpose in helping to reverse that relative decline in the British economy.

What can help, however, is the examination of the behaviour, past and present, of that most important organizational unit of the economy, the business company. Business schools and departments of management studies concentrate on the rational and the quantifiable, on the immediate present and the likely future. How can a better understanding of the business past contribute? There are, I suggest, four main roads to be followed.

First, business historians themselves should set about filling in some notable gaps in their own labours. One of these is to start to draw conclusions from their existing work on company histories. Thirty or so years ago, such an advocacy would have been meaningless – for Britain at least – simply because the great commissioning boom had not begun. But now there is material to work on; and a general introductory text on British business history has yet to be written. The material is not, of course, in an ideal form for the necessary analysis and comparison, partly because of the narrative shape of the company histories; and partly because of the absence of a consistent set of questions addressed by the authors to their varied source material. This inconsistency stems, in turn, from the absence, or at any rate inadequacy, of any appropriate theoretical structure. More of that anon. Meanwhile, it is good to note that there are some signs of an increasing use of these histories; particularly in conjunction with the second sort of assault which needs to be mounted by business historians.

This second road of advance is the gaining of access to the records of companies for the purpose of tackling specific questions, analyzing the results and making comparisons. Research of this nature is likely to yield much more valuable results for our historical understanding of how British business has functioned, both successfully and unsuccessfully, than will the mere compilation of narrative company history. The viability of this approach depends, of course, on the willingness of firms to open their records to bona fide scholars who are not otherwise committed to writing a commissioned history of a company. Sometimes comparative or analytical work can be a by-product of such a commission. And there are some valuable examples of this in various volumes which are currently emerging from the Business History Unit.[21] But the problem of access to private business records, and especially to recent records, has to be faced. It demands a brief digression.

Over a quarter of a century ago, Professor Payne, in the course of a review of a number of American business histories, made this comment:

> Anyone having had the experience of trying to persuade British businessmen to open their recent archives to historical and economic research must applaud the liberality and far-sightedness of the American companies to whose records these authors have had access.[22]

That was in 1962. Since then there have been some heartening examples of real change from the situation when it was rare for any serious work on such records in Britain to extend beyond 1914 and still rarer for it to go beyond 1939. A new willingness has emerged in a few cases to permit meaningful enquiry into the experience of British companies after the Second World War. Even so, an informal thirty-year rule has only too often confined comment on recent managements and their decisions to bland generalities excused by resort to that familiar metaphor of inaction or concealment: the time is not yet ripe . . . There are still some firms who refuse all access to records. For such cases, all that remains is hope that suitable pressure will some day bring suitable enlightenment.

But the problems posed by the very recent past, even for happily co-operative businesses, are genuine and not to be brushed aside. They range from the proper confidentiality of bank accounts to sensitivity about hurt feelings and the constraints imposed by the British libel laws. There are also quite other sorts of problems: historical judgment on very recent matters is inherently difficult; and there is a danger that the latest may present itself as the best. Legitimate and sensible methods do exist for tackling these difficulties; and resourceful business historians may well find that companies are more willing than is generally supposed to assist serious research. And they may even find the E.S.R.C. willing to help finance such research.

Which brings me to the third road of advance. This is the hope that some companies will themselves support or even commission research into the

[21] See especially Professor Hannah's *Inventing Retirement* (Cambridge, 1986), a work originally commissioned by the Legal and General Group but which also draws upon the archives of several other insurance companies, as well as other organizations, in its investigation of the development of occupational pensions in Britain. Also R. Davenport-Hines (ed.), *Markets and Bagmen: Studies in the History of Marketing and British Industrial Performance* (Aldershot, 1986) and Geoffrey Jones (ed.), *British Multinationals: Origins, Management and Performance* (Aldershot, 1986). Apart from work emanating from the Unit, an interesting example of a comparative discussion drawing extensively on recent company histories is B.W.E. Alford, 'Lost Opportunities: British Business and Businessmen during the First World War', in N. McKendrick and R.B. Outhwaite (eds.) *Business Life and Public Policy* (Cambridge, 1986).

[22] *Business History*, v (1962), p. 13.

recent history of specific issues. Let me make it quite clear at this point that I am *not* proposing an end to the commissioning of scholarly company histories. I am suggesting rather that such commissioning should be supplemented or in part replaced by supported historical research into issues seen as relevant to current problems. This is, of course, the most speculative and optimistic of the possible roads to the past. It is so because it implies that some businessmen at least will come to see business history in a light very different from that which has hitherto prevailed. It means seeing it as potentially useful in the sense of revealing something about a firm's past decisions which can have value in influencing present and future decisions. This is a long way from viewing it simply as a public relations exercise embodied in those handsomely produced volumes of unread company histories. Movement along this road depends, of course, on a willingness to accept the third of my assumptions, that is, that present decisions are necessarily made in an awareness of the past, and to accept it moreover not just as a formal truth but as something of practical value.

Whether the initiative comes from outside or inside the firm matters less than the mere fact of properly conducted research into the history of specific issues in the development of business enterprises in the recent past. Examples of such issues might include price determination and policy (an old chestnut); the criteria for judging investment decisions or plant location; the responses to market signals or the adaptability of the management structure to expansion; the approach to labour productivity and wage determination; or the attitude towards technical research and development. The list is readily extensible. If such work is dependent upon the willingness of firms to open their recent records so it also makes certain demands upon business historians. Some, such as the maintenance of proper standards of scholarship or the need to respect appropriate criteria of responsible confidentiality, are obvious. To adjure business historians to write up the results of their research in a readable and lively manner is also obvious but, alas, also necessary. That task is not made any easier, however, by a further demand. This is to provide appropriate criteria of analytical consistency in asking questions of the historical evidence and drawing conclusions therefrom. The issue of theory must now be faced.

The absence of any strong backbone of theory has been a criticism levelled at British business history on more than one occasion. It is a justifiable criticism, and there are justifiable retorts. One, as already noted, is that the pattern of commissioning narrative company histories has precluded or inhibited concern with theory. Equally important, however, is the simple response: what theory? Orthodox British economic theory, built up from the Marshallian neo-classical synthesis and then from Keynesian and post-Keynesian macroeconomics, is simply of very little use to business historians. It can help to provide a very broad framework of enquiry, but not much more. A number of economists – Edith Penrose, Philip Andrews, and Robin Marris for example – have attempted to tackle the issues involved;[23] but such works have had only a limited impact alike on the writing of business history and the formulation of economic theory. The fact remains that the neo-classical theory of the firm, even when modified to take account of varying sorts of market imperfection, is not about firms, as entities. It is about price-adjustment, for products and factors, in various assumed conditions of competition.

By far the most important flow of new ideas in this whole field has come from America. It has come in the shape of A.D. Chandler's justly celebrated works on 'strategy and structure' in the evolution of U.S. business; and in such contributions as those of Herbert Simon and Oliver Williamson.[24] Chandler's writings have formulated generalizations based upon extensive historical research into American business behaviour; the essentially theoretical orientation of Williamson's best known book, *Markets and Hierarchies*, has, nevertheless, a distinct flavour of that institutionalist school which has had a much greater influence on American economic thinking than on British. But all such work has an historical dimension in that it seeks to relate the firm's decison-making process over time to the framework of markets and institutions in which it takes place. As the author of a recent British foray in this direction, Scott Moss, has put it: 'the theory of business strategy . . . is more in the nature of a theory of economic history, since it is concerned with issues of institutional development as well as with the factors influencing the taking of individual decisions.'[25]

One particular field of business activity which has offered scope for some limited co-operation between theory and history is that occupied by multinational companies. Just as the break-up of European empires and the emergence of new economically underdeveloped nations brought a great efflorescence of 'development economics' in the 1950s, so in the 1960s awareness of massive direct investment overseas by U.S. firms brought the coining of the term 'multinational' and a still-running flood of books and articles about them. The political implications and the European destination of much of this investment provoked British and continental European economists and historians into print. Recent conferences and publications have seen theories put to the test of historical research into company records. Some very useful findings have emerged. The 'transaction-cost' approach, currently the darling of some theorists in an effort to explain investment patterns, has proved in practice difficult to use because not

[23] Edith Penrose, *The Theory of the Growth of the Firm* (Oxford, 1959); P.W.S. Andrews, *Manufacturing Business* (1949); Robin Marris, *The Economic Theory of Managerial Capitalism* (1967).

[24] Alfred D. Chandler Jr., *Strategy and Structure* (Cambridge, MA, 1962) and *The Visible Hand* (Cambridge, MA, 1977); Herbert Simon, *Administrative Behaviour* (3rd Edn., New York, 1976); Oliver Williamson, *Markets and Hierarchies* (New York, 1975).

[25] Scott Moss, *An Economic Theory of Business Strategy* (Oxford, 1981), p. 206.

readily quantifiable.[26] Indeed, it may even begin to look a little like one of those 'empty boxes' of economic abstractions which Clapham attacked in a celebrated article almost seventy years ago.[27] The multinational entity itself has been demonstrated to be both older and more diverse than theory supposed, so much so that the value of the very concept of a multinational has been doubted.[28]

These are not the only examples of attempts to carry out comparative work, using theory to frame questions to put to historical business records. Jonathan Boswell's comparison of the varying responses of three big steel companies to the need for change and adaptation in the inter-war years provides a quite different example.[29] Though relating to the experiences of half a century ago, it is very far from irrelevant to much more recent times. Or again, light on such highly pertinent issues as the 1970 collapse of Rolls-Royce is shed in Hague and Wilkinson's history of the Industrial Reorganization Corporation.[30] A very different example of recent business history is provided by Andrew Pettigrew's examination of a particular aspect of I.C.I's experience. His book, *The Awakening Giant* demands a special word because it travels some part, at least, of the road along which business history may need to go.[31]

It is research into one major issue in a company's very recent history, 1960-83; it was sanctioned and supported by the board – though obviously owing its existence to the enthusiasm of one director, the then chairman; it was not a commissioned history of the company. It is built upon a basis of both documentary sources and a wide range of interviews; and it also draws upon the findings of an existing commissioned history, Dr. Reader's well-known study which covers the years of I.C.I's history up to 1952.[32] Its prime concern is very specialized – the experience of using American O.D (organisation development) techniques in four of I.C.I's divisions; it is emphatically not a book for bedtime reading. But it does demonstrate the powerful influence upon current experience of inherited attitudes and traditional practices, not simply in the company as a whole but varyingly in particular divisions, even in particular plants: in short, of their historically dominant 'cultures'. The history of the business mattered, not only the

---

[26] See Mark Casson, 'General Theories of the Multinational Enterprise', in Peter Hertner and Geoffrey Jones (eds.), *Multinationals: Theory and History* (Aldershot, 1986).

[27] J.H. Clapham, 'Of Empty Boxes', *Economic Journal*, xxxii (1922), pp. 305-14.

[28] See D.K. Fieldhouse, 'The Multinational: A Critique of a Concept', in A. Teichova, M. Lévy-Leboyer and H. Nussbaum (eds.), *Multinational Enterprise in Historical Perspective* (Cambridge, 1986).

[29] J.S. Boswell, *Business Policies in the Making* (1983).

[30] D. Hague and G. Wilkinson, *The I.R.C.: An Experiment in Industrial Intervention* (London, 1983), pp. 184-205.

[31] Andrew Pettigrew, *The Awakening Giant: Continuity and Change in I.C.I.* (Oxford, 1985).

[32] W.J. Reader, *Imperial Chemical Industries: A History* (2 vols. Oxford, 1970 and 1975).

twenty-three years covered in Pettigrew's study but also the earlier shaping of I.C.I. The past affected the present when, under the stimulus of change in the external economic environment, attempts were made to bring about internal change in organization and management, so as to achieve greater competitiveness.

Professor Pettigrew's book comes from the school of Industrial and Business Studies at Warwick University. So it will serve to introduce the fourth and final road along which I suggest business history might sensibly travel. This is the one leading to penetration into the curricula of business schools and management studies. To a very real extent this is dependent on a successful passage along the other three roads. But it should be given some welcome impetus by this study of I.C.I.'s recent history. For it carries the message that business studies have something to learn from business history, provided that the latter is properly focused. Efforts to build change into British business organizations will be aided by a fuller and more analytical understanding of the history of those organizations.

I.C.I.'s experience is just one example of the more general problem of how to adapt, or sometimes even revolutionize, that abiding culture of a firm which is the product of history. Over the last few decades the need to do this has hit many large organizations in the older industrialized countries, in the U.S.A as well as in Britain. The reasons are various: new techniques, new sources of competition, government attacks on state-supported monopolies, to name but some. In the U.S.A. the break-up of A.T. & T. (American Telephone & Telegraph) and the regulated monopoly of its Bell telephone system provides a classic example of government-inspired attack. This firm, then the largest in the world, was pervaded by an historical culture which had evolved since early in the century. Professor Temin's history of the events leading up to the A.T. & T. divestiture in 1982 demonstrates the value of truly recent business history.[33] It concentrates on a specific issue; and it was made possible by a freedom of access to very recent public archives and company records which puts a shaming spotlight on the British obsession with secrecy, embodied in thirty-year rules, official and unofficial. Temin's history, like Chandler's work, will be read and used by businessmen as well as by those concerned with the teaching of business studies.

Back to Britain. Take the example of our nationalized British railways. Here again, the historically fashioned culture of the railways, generated long before nationalization but continued thereafter, provides a similar instance of the deep-seated tension between long-entrenched procedures and the need to establish new patterns of organization, new strategies and structures, in the face of market decline, rising costs, and new techniques. Dr. Gourvish's history, *British Railways 1948-73*, illuminates this particular instance of a pervasive fact of economic life for only too much of British

---

[33] Peter Temin, *The Fall of the Bell System* (Cambridge, 1987).

industry.[34] (It would, incidentally, have been able to provide still more illumination if the official 30-year rule had not precluded access to some relevant public records.)

The very existence of this pervasive problem of building change into British industry suggests to me that those responsible for education in business management will be failing the needs of their subject if they continue to ignore the lessons of the business past. Business historians, in turn, will have to mend their ways. For if the subject is to make its due impact on the curricula of business education, it will, in part at least, have to abandon a merely narrative focus. This is not to advocate throwing narrative out of the window. Narrative remains essential to any account of change over time; but in business history it must be combined with the analysis of economic issues pertinent to management and organization. Business historians may even have to look upon their sort of history as possessing direct utility. And that, of course, is to risk lowering it in the traditional pecking order of prestige dear to 'straight' historians. Too bad. This is not a resort to the parrot cry of 'relevance'; it is simply to emphasise that business history has sometimes to follow different paths to different ends. Yet at the same time it must continue to insist of its practitioners that they abide by the standards of historical scholarship. A tall order, perhaps, but surely not out of reach.

These, then, are some routes by which business history's own Catch-22 may be circumvented.

The title of this essay refers to uses and abuses. So here is a quick concluding summary of both. Take the abuses first: anecdotal, soap-opera history; unreadable academic company histories which are all narrative and without analysis of issues; a mere public relations purpose in commissioning company histories; and all unread histories. And the uses of a better sort of business history? A deepened understanding of the most important unit of organization in our economy; a recognition that the business past matters as much as the political past; and an aid towards effecting change in an economy which badly needs it.

---

[34] T.R. Gourvish, *British Railways 1948-73* (Cambridge, 1987).

Index